DESIGNED
TO BE
LIKE
HIM

Discovery
House
PUBLISHERS

BOX 3566 • GRAND RAPIDS, MI 49501

*PUBLISHING BOOKS THAT FEED
THE SOUL WITH THE WORD OF GOD.*

DESIGNED

New Testament
Insight for
Becoming
Christlike

TO BE

LIKE

HIM

**J. Dwight
Pentecost**

with Notes and Questions by Ken Durham

Library of Congress Cataloging-in-Publication Data

Pentecost, J. Dwight.
  Designed to be like him : New Testament insight for
becoming Christlike / J. Dwight Pentecost.
      p.   cm.
  ISBN 0-929239-88-1
  1. Christian life—Biblical teaching. 2. Jesus Christ—Example—Biblical
teaching. I. Title.
BS2545.C48P46   1994
248.4—dc20   94–11513
                                                                    CIP

Discovery House Publishers is affiliated with Radio Bible Class, Grand Rapids, Michigan 49512

Discovery House books are distributed to the trade by Thomas Nelson Publishers, Nashville, Tennessee 37214

Printed in the United States of America

94 95 96 97 98 99 / CHG / 10 9 8 7 6 5 4 3 2 1

CONTENTS

INTRODUCTION

"Christ lives in me." What a great affirmation by Paul, but how little understood and how much less appropriated by the average Christian today.

The Word of God has much to say about the "things that pertain to life and godliness" (2 Peter 1:3). It presents "doctrine which accords with godliness" (1 Timothy 6:3) and exhorts us to "pursue righteousness, godliness, . . ." (1 Timothy 6:11). It challenges us to "exercise [ourselves] toward godliness" (1 Timothy 4:7). Godliness is God's standard for His child.

The natural human being is a complex individual. How much more complex is the child of God, to whom God has imparted a new divine nature (2 Peter 1:4). Many believers fall short of God's standard in daily life because they have not been instructed in the principles of the Word of God. They do not understand themselves. They have no concept of the enormity of the conflict in which they are engaged. They have not learned the value of the death of Christ in its relation to deliverance from dominion by sin. They have never discovered the principles of the Word of God which govern Christian conduct. They have not seen the steps to maturity in Christian experience.

The truths in this book, prepared for the average reader, are gleaned from study of the Word of God and are designed to be truths which accord with godliness (Titus 1:1). They were first prepared for my students at Dallas Theological Seminary and for the congregation at Grace Bible Church in Dallas. The response was so gratifying that I felt encouraged to prepare them for a wider audience.

May the Lord Jesus Christ, who lives in believers, be pleased to speak through these pages to bring many to a knowledge of His indwelling presence and power, so that they might "wage the good warfare" (1 Timothy 1:18) and "put on the new man which was created according to God, in true righteousness and holiness" (Ephesians 4:24).

J. DWIGHT PENTECOST

Thou art calling me, Lord Jesus,
  As Thy living witness here.
Only by Thy life within me
  Can I any witness bear.

Thou art calling me, Lord Jesus,
  To be working one with Thee.
Only by Thy life within me
  Can there any service be.

Thou art calling me, Lord Jesus,
  To prevailing power in prayer.
Only by Thy life within me
  Can I intercession share.

Thou art calling me, Lord Jesus,
  To a victor's holy life.
Only by Thy life within me
  Is there conquest in the strife.

Fill me, Holy Spirit, fill me,
  All Thy filling would I know.
I am smallest of Thy vessels,
  Yet I much can overflow.
            —*Lewis Sperry Chafer*

CHAPTER 1

GOD'S PURPOSE FOR EACH ONE OF US

1 Corinthians 6:19–20

The greatest theme that can occupy a Christian's heart and mind is the glory of God. God, who has shared Himself and revealed Himself in His Son, Jesus Christ, has shown Himself to be a God of glory. From the Bible we know God's glory commands heaven's undivided attention, and that the earth was created to express and reveal God's glory. All created intelligent beings who recognize His perfection, His attributes, and His character give glory to God when they serve, honor, worship, adore, and praise Him.

As every schoolchild once knew by rote, it is indeed true that "the chief end of man is to glorify God, and to enjoy Him forever."

The theme of God's glory runs throughout the Bible. To reveal His glory, God takes lowly things, things that have no glory in and of themselves, and transforms them and uses them as His instruments—so that we in turn might glorify Him. And because He is sovereign, right, and free, God may use material things, created beings, supernatural events, or His own Son for the purpose of bringing glory to Himself.

Creation

The Bible tells us that the creation was designed to bring honor and glory to God. Psalm 19:1 praises God and proclaims that "the heavens declare the glory of God; and the firmament shows His handiwork." And the apostle Paul, writing to the Colossians, reminds us in 1:16, "By Him all things were created that are in heaven and that are on earth, visible and invisible, whether thrones or dominions or principalities or powers. All things were created through Him and for Him."

Note the last words of that verse: "All things were created *for Him*" (italics added). The purpose of creation was not just to benefit earth's creatures, but to glorify God. In short, the universe was created to reflect the glory of an all-glorious God. From creation, then, we can learn much concerning God's power, wisdom, and nature.

In the Garden

As we look back at the opening chapters of Genesis, we find that God not only made Himself known through creation, He also *personally* walked with Adam in the Garden of Eden. Genesis 3:8 reads, "They heard the sound of the LORD God walking in the garden in the cool of the day, and Adam and his wife hid themselves from the presence of the LORD God among the trees of the garden." Adam and Eve knew of God's presence not only by the sound of His voice, but also by the sight of His glory. Throughout the Bible, God demonstrates His presence by His visible, brilliant Shekinah glory, the awesome shining of the glory of His Person. In Genesis 1–3, then, it appears that God's purpose in coming into the garden was to reveal His physical glory to Adam and Eve, that they might respond by adoring and glorifying Him. This was not only satisfying to the perfect heart of God, it was the fulfillment of God's purpose for man and woman.

But this relationship between mankind and God's glory did not last long. Adam and Eve rebelled against God and were expelled from the garden. They were no longer fit for the presence of God, and they were unfit even for the place where God's glory had been revealed. Therefore, "The LORD God sent him out of the Garden of Eden to till the ground from which he was taken. So He drove out the man; and He placed cherubim at the east of the Garden of Eden, and a flaming sword which turned every way, to guard the way to the tree of life" (Genesis 3:23–24).

It appears that after mankind's fall, God established a temporary place of sacrifice outside the garden. And just as cherubim later would watch over the mercy seat in the tabernacle, so cherubim watched over this first meeting place between God and man. Most important, this place of sacrifice included the "flaming sword," a manifestation of God's glory. This was the same glory in which Adam and Eve had walked before they sinned; but now they were separated from that glory by an instrument of death and judgment.

Moses

In Exodus 33 we find that God took a humble man, Moses, and so transformed him by revealing His glory that Moses himself became an instrument to reveal the glory of God. After receiving the greatest revelation of God's glory since the Fall, Moses asked God, "Please, show me Your glory" (Exodus 33:18). God replied, "I will make all My goodness pass before you" (33:19). This revelation of God's perfect goodness would be a manifestation of His glory and bring glory to Him. God further said to Moses, "I will proclaim the name of the LORD before you. I will be gracious to whom I will be gracious, and I will have compassion on whom I will have compassion." In other words, as God revealed His grace and mercy to Moses, and to the people of Israel who were guilty of sin, this also would bring glory to Him.

Then God said, " 'You cannot see My face; for no man shall see Me, and live.' And the LORD said, 'Here is a place by Me, and you shall stand on the rock. So it shall be, while My glory passes by, that I will put you in the cleft of the rock, and will cover you with My hand while I pass by. Then I will take away My hand, and you shall see My back; but My face shall not be seen' " (33:20–23).

To understand what God said, the last verse might be translated, "I will take away My hand, and you will see My afterglow, My radiance; but My face shall not be seen."

When Moses asked God to reveal His glory, God said He would hide His servant in a cleft, or crack, in a rock. Then God would cover Moses so that he could not see His face, but would open His fingers, so to speak, so that the light of the glory of God could shine through. In Exodus 34:5 the episode continues: "Then the LORD descended in the cloud and stood with him there, and proclaimed the name of the LORD."

The result of this revelation was that Moses' life was transformed, as we read in Exodus 34:29–30: "Now it was so, when Moses came down from Mount Sinai (and the two tablets of the Testimony were in Moses' hand when he came down from the mountain), that Moses did not know that the skin of his face shone while he talked with Him. So when Aaron and all the children of Israel saw Moses, behold, the skin of his face shone, and they were afraid to come near him." This was not a glory that inherently belonged to Moses. Rather, Moses reflected the glory of God which he had seen when God opened His fingers and revealed His afterglow.

Yet when Moses finished speaking to the people of Israel for the first time afterward, "he put a veil on his face. But whenever Moses went in before the LORD to speak with Him, he would take the veil off until he came out; and he would come out and speak to the children of Israel whatever he had been commanded. And whenever the children of Israel saw the face of Moses, that the skin of Moses' face shone, then Moses would put the veil on his face again, until he went in to speak with Him" (Exodus 34:33–35). There was open-faced communion between God and Moses, but Moses put the veil between himself and the people of Israel.

In 2 Corinthians 3:13, Paul explained why Moses veiled his face. "Unlike Moses," wrote Paul, "who put a veil over his face so that the children of Israel could not look steadily at the end of what was passing away." It was not that Israel could not look on the glory of God reflected in Moses' face. Rather, the glory given to the face of Moses was a passing, transitory, temporary manifestation of God's glory. Moses realized that the glory would diminish and pass away, so He veiled his face to prevent Israel from seeing the passing of that glory.

The Tabernacle

After a time, Moses' face no longer reflected the glory of God. God no longer used this transformed person as a vehicle for revealing His glory. Next He used the tabernacle as the instrument to reveal His glory to His people. Once it was completed according to His directions, "The cloud covered the tabernacle of meeting, and the glory of the LORD filled the tabernacle. And Moses was not able to enter the tabernacle of meeting, because . . . the glory of the LORD filled the tabernacle" (Exodus 40:34–35).

Remember, the tabernacle had no external beauty of its own. It was covered on the outside by animal skins which soon became weather-beaten, dull, and unattractive. But God used that which was unattractive and which had no glory of its own as the instrument through which He revealed His glory to Israel.

When God revealed His glory, it was a radiance that could not be hidden. When the ministering priest walked into the Holy Place and passed beyond the veil into the Holy of Holies, his attention was not drawn to the blood-encrusted mercy seat, which was far from attractive to the natural eye. What attracted his attention was the presence of God's Shekinah glory abiding between the cherubim. Because he stood in the place where the glory of God was revealed, everything else became insignificant as he went about the ritual of offering the blood.

When the children of Israel, God's redeemed nation, looked at the tabernacle, they looked past its humble exterior to the Shekinah glory that dwelt within it. Its beauty and attractiveness were not in its animal skin coverings, but in the abiding glory of God.

The Temple

After God's people became settled inhabitants in the land of promise, when the tabernacle no longer served their needs, David wanted to build a temple for the Lord. But God did not permit him to construct the temple, because David had been a man of war. However, the Lord did tell David that a temple would be built by a son named Solomon, who would be a man of peace. Therefore David collected materials for building the temple and gave instructions concerning its construction. He said it must be "exceedingly magnificent, famous and glorious throughout all countries" (1 Chronicles 22:5).

The account of the temple's dedication is found in 1 Kings 8:10–11: "It came to pass, when the priests came out of the holy place, that the cloud filled the house of the LORD, so that the priests could not continue ministering because of the cloud; for the glory of the LORD filled the house of the LORD." In His condescending grace, God had moved into this building made with human hands, that He might use it as the place where He manifested His glory.

Without a doubt, the temple must have been one of the most spectacular buildings ever built. Solomon had used millions of dollars' worth of gold, silver, and precious gems to adorn it. Yet it was not the architecture nor the rich adornments that brought glory to God, but rather the abiding presence of God in His Shekinah glory.

Unfortunately, the temple, which had been built as a place where God's glory would abide, eventually degenerated into a place that glorified only Solomon's wisdom and honor. In 2 Chronicles 9:3–6, we read the queen of Sheba's reaction to the beauty of the temple: "When the queen of Sheba had seen the wisdom of Solomon, the house that he had built . . . and his entryway by which he went up to the house of the LORD, there was no more spirit in her. Then she said to the king, 'It was a true report which I heard in my own land about your words and your wisdom. However I did not believe their words until I came and saw with my own eyes; and indeed the half of the greatness of your wisdom was not told me. You exceed the fame of which I heard.' " Rather than revealing the glory of God, the temple promoted the glory of Solomon. Though it had been designed for His use, the temple now was prostituted to bring glory to the builder rather than to God whose glory had dwelt there. Therefore it became necessary for God to judge it.

Ezekiel's prophetic writings record the departure of God's glory from the nation of Israel. In Ezekiel 8–9, the prophet was taken into the temple where, in the place that should have held the altar of sacrifice—the meeting place between God and man—there had been erected what the prophet calls an "image of jealousy" (Ezekiel 8:3). Next, Ezekiel was told to look into the sanctuary of the temple, where he found the walls decorated with all the heathen idols of the nations surrounding Israel. As the prophet listened, he heard women weeping for Tammuz, an abominable Mesopotamian goddess of fertility. And the temple, which had been set apart to bring glory to God, now was set apart to the glory of all the Babylonian, Assyrian, Phoenician, and Egyptian false gods.

In Ezekiel 10:3–4 we read, "The cherubim were standing on the south side of the temple when the man went in, and the cloud filled the inner court. Then the glory of the LORD went up from the cherub, and paused over the threshold of the temple; and the house was filled with the cloud, and the court was full of the brightness of the LORD's glory." The Shekinah glory of the Lord, which previously had come to occupy the temple, had departed from the sanctuary and was next seen over the threshold of the temple entrance. The glory of God then left the threshold and hesitated over the east gate: "Then the glory of the LORD departed from the threshold of the temple and stood over the cherubim. And the cherubim lifted their wings and mounted up from the earth in my sight. When they went out, the wheels were beside them; and they stood at the door of the east gate of the LORD's house, and the glory of the God of Israel was above them" (10:18–19).

A further step in the departure of God's glory is seen in Ezekiel 11:22–23, where Ezekiel saw that "the cherubim lifted up their wings, with the wheels beside them, and the glory of the God of Israel was high above them. And the glory of the LORD went up from the midst of the city and stood on the mountain, which is on the east side of the city." Now the Shekinah glory had gone to the Mount of Olives, outside the city and away from the temple area entirely.

The prophet next saw the glory leave the land entirely and depart into Chaldea, or Babylon (11:24). Over the city and the sanctuary could now be written *Ichabod,* which means, "The glory has departed."

After God's people went into exile in Babylon, a remnant returned to their land and built another temple—a humble little place compared to the temple Solomon had built. But God spoke to His people through the prophet Haggai and said, " 'Once more [it is a little while] I will shake heaven and earth, the sea and dry land; and I will shake all nations, and they shall come to the Desire of All Nations, and I will fill this temple with glory,' says the LORD of hosts. 'The silver is Mine, and the gold is Mine,' says the Lord of hosts. 'The glory of this latter temple shall be greater than the former,' says the LORD of hosts. 'And in this place I will give peace,' says the LORD of hosts" (Haggai 2:6–9).

Thus God promised that His glory, which had left Solomon's temple, would come to the temple built after the exile in Babylon, and that Israel would see His Shekinah glory revealed again in their midst.

The Person of Christ

In the New Testament we read about the coming of this glory to God's people. John testified that "the Word became flesh and dwelt among us, and we beheld His glory, the glory as of the only begotten of the Father, full of grace and truth" (John 1:14). What did John mean when he said, "We beheld His glory?" The answer is found in Luke 9:28–36, where Peter, James, and John went up onto a mountain with the Lord to pray. "As He prayed, the appearance of His face was altered, and His robe became white and glistening. And behold, two men talked with Him, who were Moses and Elijah, who appeared in glory and spoke of His decease which He was about to accomplish at Jerusalem. But Peter and those with him were heavy with sleep; and when they were fully awake, they saw His glory and the two men who stood with Him" (9:29–32). Peter, too, recounted in his writings that he saw the glory of God as it was revealed in Jesus Christ (2 Peter 1:16–18).

The glory, then, that the Old Testament spoke of and that the prophets foretold would be seen again was made evident in the Person of Jesus Christ.

But even this would be a temporary means of manifesting God's glory. In Luke 9:31 Moses and Elijah spoke of Christ's "decease," the death Jesus would accomplish in Jerusalem when He became God's sacrifice for the sins of the world. Isn't it amazing that Elijah did not speak with Jesus about the glories of prophecy? Nor did Moses talk with Him about the triumphs or failures of the Law. Rather, they talked with the Lord about "His decease which He was about to accomplish at Jerusalem."

Just as creation and Eden were temporary in manifesting God's glory, just as Moses was a temporary instrument to reveal God's glory, and just as the tabernacle and the temple were temporary places God chose for His glory to abide, so Jesus Christ's life on earth was a temporary manifestation of the glory of God among humanity.

The Church

After the death, resurrection, and ascension of Jesus Christ, God did not leave Himself without a means of revealing His glory. Ephesians 2:21–22 reminds us that it is the fellowship of believers, which has become the household of God, "in whom the whole building, being joined together, grows into a holy temple in the Lord, in whom you also are being built together for a habitation of God in the Spirit."

The function the tabernacle and the temple once performed in manifesting the glory of God has now been assigned to believers who are incorporated into the church when they are saved by faith. God's purpose in bringing the church into existence was to manifest through the church His wisdom, grace, and power; that all believers should be instruments who bring praise, honor, and glory to Him.

This is what the apostle Paul had in mind when he penned 2 Corinthians 4:6–7: "It is the God who commanded light to shine out of darkness who has shone in our hearts to give the light of the knowledge of the glory of God in the face of Jesus Christ. But we have this treasure in earthen vessels, that the excellence of the power may be of God and not of us."

God has chosen those who had nothing in themselves to bring glory to Him, and through them—by the transforming work of the Holy Spirit—He will bring glory to His own name and to the name of His Son, Jesus Christ.

Paul brings this out again in Ephesians 1:6 when he speaks of the Father's work in our redemption and points out that all that the Father has done He has done "to the praise of the glory of His grace." In verses 7–12 Paul writes further about the work of the Father through the Son in our redemption. Why has He redeemed us? "That we . . . should be to the praise of His glory" (1:12). In verses 13–14 the apostle again speaks of the work of the Father through the Spirit in our redemption. To what end? "To the praise of His glory" (1:14).

This is why Paul writes in Colossians 1:27 that "Christ in you" is the "hope of glory." Please notice that it is *not* the individual who will manifest the glory of God; it is the transforming presence of God the Father, God the Son, and God the Holy Spirit who take up residence within the child of God!

Yet even this wonderful form of revealing God's glory is temporary. For our Lord will call to Himself every believer in Christ, and the church will no longer be on the earth as a living temple to manifest the glory of God (see John 14:3; 1 Thessalonians 4:13–17).

The Personal Presence of Christ

After all believers have been transported into heaven, those people who are still on earth will see the fulfillment of our Lord's words in Matthew 24:30: "Then the sign of the Son of Man will appear in heaven . . . they will see the Son of Man coming on the clouds of heaven with power and great glory."

This display of Christ's glory will be a sign of such magnitude and significance that the nations of the earth amassed at the campaign of Armageddon will forget their natural hatred for each other and will unite in a great federation to oppose the return of the Son of God to reign on earth. This human opposition to Christ's return will fail, and Christ will physically return to earth to subdue and subjugate all His enemies. The Son of God will reign as King of kings and Lord of lords, sitting upon a throne of glory, as foretold in Matthew 25:31: "When the Son of Man comes in His glory, and all the holy angels with Him, then He will sit on the throne of His glory."

God ultimately will reveal His glory to this earth when the Son of God, who is also the Son of Man, receives the scepter entitling Him to David's throne, and reigns in power and great glory. God will be glorified in the personal presence of His Son on this earth.

In Colossians 3:4 Paul wrote, "When Christ who is our life appears, then you also will appear with Him in glory." Many people mistakenly interpret the phrase *in glory* as synonymous with "in heaven," as though Paul meant "you also shall appear with Him in heaven." But that is not what Paul intended to say. The words *in glory* describe the condition of the child of God when Jesus Christ returns. Literally it means, "When Christ who is our life appears, then you also will appear with Him as glorified beings." In other words, we shall be so transformed by the Son of God that we will be instruments of praise bringing glory to God; and the Son of God will continue manifesting the glory of God throughout his thousand-year reign on the earth, as well as throughout the unending ages of eternity.

Revelation 7:9–12 provides us with a picture of the praise and glory that will be given the Son of God once He has put down every enemy and subjected the entire earth to His authority. "After these things I looked, and behold, a great multitude which no one could number, of all nations, tribes, peoples, and tongues, standing before the throne and before the Lamb, clothed with white robes, with palm branches in their hands, and crying out with a loud voice, saying, 'Salvation belongs to our God who sits on the throne, and to the Lamb!' And all the angels stood around the throne and the elders and the four living creatures, and fell on their faces before the throne and worshiped God, saying:

'Amen! Blessing and glory and wisdom, thanksgiving and honor and power and might, be to our God forever and ever. Amen.' "

And why will the white-robed multitudes give glory to God and to the Lamb? Because they have "washed their robes and made them white in the blood of the Lamb" (7:14).

Revelation 21:10–11, 23–24 describes the place the redeemed will live when they return to the earth with Christ to reign with Him. It is the place they will occupy from then on throughout eternity. John wrote, "He carried me away in the Spirit to a great and high mountain, and showed me the great city, the holy Jerusalem, descending out of heaven from God, having the glory of God. And her light was like a most precious stone, like a jasper stone, clear as crystal. . . . The city had no need of the sun or of the moon to shine in it, for the glory of God illuminated it, and the Lamb is its light. And the nations of those who are saved shall walk in its light, and the kings of the earth bring their glory and honor into it."

This habitation which will be prepared by the Bridegroom for His bride is a place which will be characterized by God's glory. There, all those redeemed by the blood of the Lamb will manifest the glory of God. The habitation as well as the inhabitants will become vehicles for God's glory throughout the ages of our Lord's reign and the unending ages of eternity.

As much as Scripture has to say concerning our glorification in Christ, the Bible places greatest emphasis on that glory which will come to Him when we are translated into His presence. The hymn writer has worded it this way:

> The Bride eyes not her garment,
> But her dear Bridegroom's face;
> I will not gaze at glory,
> But on my King of grace;
> Not at the crown He giveth,
> But on His pierced hand,
> The Lamb is all the glory
> Of Immanuel's land.

God has chosen today to accomplish that for which the earth was created, for which Moses was transformed, for which the tabernacle was erected and for which the temple was built, and for which Jesus Christ came into the world the first time. He has chosen each of us that we might be instruments to bring glory to God. That is why Paul could write that he wanted Christ to "be magnified in my body, whether by life, or by death" (Philippians 1:20). The compelling motive in the life of every Christian must be to glorify God.

Notes

1. While we might think that "glorifying" or "giving glory" is a concept foreign to our modern minds, that's really not the case. In the business world, articles and books give honor and recognition to men and women who have succeeded in that realm. In sports, stadiums and arenas are filled to overflowing with cheering fans who give "glory" to their favorite teams and athletes based on their performance. The entertainment world, too, is filled with those who receive praise and "glory" because of who they are. We all possess the capacity to give glory to those we consider worthy of our respect and honor.

   Therefore, if we do not—in our words and actions as well as our thoughts—give glory to God, it is not because we are not capable of giving glory. It may be we do not consciously consider Him worthy of our attention. Perhaps we do not know enough about Him to realize how worthy He is of all glory. Or we may not know or understand our responsibility to give Him glory. But as we will see in this study, glorifying God with our lives is far more important than bringing glory to any other person or thing.

2. Because the biblical account of creation often is ridiculed or questioned, even in some Christian circles, we can miss the significance of Adam and Eve's place in the actual history of the human race. In Mark 10:6–8, the Lord Jesus clearly considered the Genesis account of Adam and Eve to be historical, which should put an end to any doubts we might have about its reliability. Most important, what took place in the garden when Adam and Eve sinned has left us in dire need of fellowship with God and some means of giving glory to Him. Recognizing this need—a need we cannot meet ourselves—is the first step toward becoming vehicles of His glory.

3. Notice how removed Moses was from the direct glory of God during his encounter, yet even that left him changed. Although we will not encounter the physical glory of God until we meet Him face-to-face, we can get a glimpse of His glory through the pages of Scripture—and that, too, should leave us changed. The shining of Moses' face faded because he could not repeat that encounter with God; yet we can go to His Word as often as we wish to get a glimpse of Him.

4. Israel's eventual failure to recognize that it was the abiding glory of God that was important, not the external appearance of the tabernacle and the temple, eventually led to their spiritual, moral, and political downfall. What should this tell us about the condition of the church today? Do we emphasize the importance of God's glory reflected through personal righteousness and obedience to Him; or are we preoccupied with external appearances and our acceptability in the world's eyes? Do we bring glory to the Father by bearing much fruit (leading others to Christ) of which Christ spoke in John 15:8; or do we spend most of our energy and resources simply adorning the temple?

5. Because it is now the body of Christ on earth, the church has become God's instrument for revealing His glory to the world. That not only means that every believer has a responsibility to fulfill that function; it also means that the world will respond to us in the same way that they would respond to Jesus Christ if He were here in the flesh. This should help us understand why some unsaved people will *accept* our representation of God's glory, while others will violently *reject* it. If we are truly reflecting His glory, we will encounter both types of responses.

6. A generation ago, it was inconceivable that a human government might actually oppose the Son of God Himself; yet in our day we are witnessing a growing open hostility toward the Name and Person of Jesus Christ. The events foretold in biblical prophecy, culminating in physical opposition to Christ's return, should motivate us more than ever before to live for Him and tell others about Him.

7. There are many things in our day-to-day lives that can draw us away from God's purpose for us: to give Him glory. Moral temptations, financial pressure, physical hardships, difficult relationships, and a host of other distractions may seem to us more important than learning about Him and His purpose for us. Yet the Bible shows us where we will spend eternity, and that the focus of that eternal existence will be God and His glory. What, then, can be more important to us *right now* than knowing Him more intimately, obeying Him more faithfully, glorifying Him more consistently?

Questions

1. Read Psalm 19:1. How do the "heavens declare the glory of God"? Can we see this even among the unsaved (whether or not they realize it)? Compare this verse to Romans 1:20, and see if you can explain why the world system seeks to explain the existence of the universe apart from a Creator God. How is this done (Romans 1:22–23)?

2. What do you think it meant for Adam and Eve to "walk with God" in the garden? What effect did Adam and Eve's sin have on their perception of God and His glory (Genesis 3:8–13, 24)? What effect will sin in our lives have on our understanding of Him and His glory?

3. In the tabernacle and the temple, what had to be placed on the mercy seat between sinful human beings and God's glory behind the veil (Leviticus 16:14–15)? What does this tell us about the only way we can have access to God's glory, or glorify Him? What now takes the place of the blood on the mercy seat (see 1 John 2:2)?

4. When Christ was on earth, why didn't He shine with the Shekinah glory of God (compare Leviticus 16:2 with Hebrews 10:20; notice the word *veil*)? What will be His appearance when He returns to earth (see Revelation 1:14; 19:11–12)? What will our appearance be with Him (Colossians 3:4)? What, then, should be the goal of our lives from now until we go to be with Him?

5. Based on this chapter, explain the effect the following verses should have on your life:
     – Matthew 5:16
     – John 15:8
     – Romans 15:6
     – 1 Corinthians 6:18, 20
     – 1 Peter 2:12
     – 1 Peter 4:16

CHAPTER 2

WHAT IS FELLOWSHIP?

1 John 1:1–10

In the opening chapter we learned that man's chief end is to glorify God and to enjoy Him forever. God has revealed His glory to humanity, and we should respond to that revelation by ascribing to Him glory, majesty, dominion, and power. Colossians 1:16 tells us that "by Him all things were created that are in heaven and that are on earth, visible and invisible, whether thrones or dominions or principalities or powers. All things were created through Him and for Him." This assures us that creation was no accident—just as it confirms that all created things were brought into existence in order to glorify God.

Next, however, the question arises: "How can we glorify God?" The answer is, by fellowship with Him. We were created to have fellowship with God; and we were made a new creation in Jesus Christ in order to have fellowship with Him, that through our fellowship we might bring glory to God. This was John's thought when he explained why he wrote his first letter: "that you also may have fellowship with us; and truly our fellowship is with the Father and with His Son Jesus Christ" (1 John 1:3).

The problem today is that the term *fellowship* is used by many people to mean many different things. Therefore we need to consider what the Bible has to say about it so we can understand what God's idea of fellowship is.

Man Made in God's Image

In Genesis 1:26–27, God states His purpose in creating man and woman: "Then God said, 'Let Us make man in Our image, according to Our likeness; let them have dominion over the fish of the sea, over the birds of the air, and over the cattle, over all the earth and over every creeping thing that creeps on the earth.' So God created man in His own image; in the image of God He created him; male and female He created them."

Four times in these two verses we read that God's purpose was to make man in His image. Therefore, in order to understand the spiritual concept of fellowship, we must look more closely at these statements and understand what constitutes the image of God reflected in Adam.

Tracing the words translated *image* and *likeness* throughout the Bible, we find that they are used first and foremost to show the essential relationship that exists between God the Father and God the Son. Second Corinthians 4:3–4 explains that the gospel "is veiled to those who are perishing, whose minds the god of this age has blinded, who do not believe, lest the light of the gospel of the glory of Christ, who is the image of God, should shine on them." This confirms that Jesus Christ in His essential being is *the image of God*. This same truth is affirmed in Colossians 1:15, which tells us that Jesus Christ is *the image of the invisible God*.

This same word, then, used to explain the relationship between the Father and the Son, is used of the relationship that existed between God and unfallen man in Genesis 1:26–27. In the New Testament, this same idea is the basis for Paul's argument that a man should not cover his head, "since he is the image and glory of God" (1 Corinthians 11:7).

But what does it mean that humanity bears the image of God? The word *image* or *likeness* emphasizes resemblance, the correspondence between one thing and another. The word translated "likeness" literally conveys the idea of a coin that has been stamped in a die, so that what is on the die reappears on the coin. Anyone who examines a coin can tell what was engraved on the die, because the coin bears the image of the die that stamped it.

It is important to remember that when Scripture teaches that man is made in the likeness of God, it is *not* teaching that man is a "little god." Rather, the Bible teaches that by representation and manifestation, there is within man that which also exists within God; and that which exists within God was manifested both in Adam as he was created, and in Jesus Christ in His humanity.

How does man bear the image or likeness of God? Before we answer that question, we need to consider two common misconceptions. The first misconception is that Adam's body was fashioned in the likeness of God so that Adam, in his physical structure and makeup, resembled God. This is hardly an adequate explanation in light of Scripture. In 1 Corinthians 15, for example, Paul contrasts the physical body we now have with the body we will have following resurrection and glorification. He also teaches that the image man bears in his physical body is not an image of the heavenly, but of the earthly. Because there is a marked difference between a body suited to heavenly existence and a body suited to an earthly existence, we cannot know what God looks like by looking at ourselves, or by imagining what Adam looked like in his unfallen state.

The second misconception is that Adam was made in the moral, or ethical, likeness of God. This would mean that the image of God in Adam was a spiritual likeness of God rather than a physical likeness, that Adam in his inner being bore a likeness to the God who created him. While this sounds like a vast improvement on the first misconception, it is really no improvement at all. The Bible makes it clear that Adam was not created holy. Holiness is an unchangeable, inviolable, unalterable, incorruptible quality of God's being. God cannot sin. God, who is holy, cannot become unholy. If Adam had been created holy, it would have been impossible for him to sin. But that was not the case. Adam was created with an untried innocence. He was given the capacity of choice, and he could choose to sin or choose to obey God.

But to say that Adam's likeness to God was a moral likeness is to say that God has been kept from sin only by a choice, and that He could just as easily choose to sin. Because our God is a holy God, that is an impossible notion.

Man Given Personality

How, then, can we explain the likeness or image of God in man, without violating the full revelation of God in Scripture? When we look closely at the creation record in the opening chapters of Genesis, we discover that God did something for Adam that He did not do for any other created thing. God "breathed into his nostrils the breath of life; and man became a living being" (Genesis 2:7). God did not breathe spirit into any animal He created. By contrast, Adam was endowed with capacities that set him apart from all the animal creation. God gave Adam a personality, so that Adam, as a person, could have personal fellowship with God, who is a Person.

God created all matter, but material substance does not possess personality, thus God cannot communicate Himself to material substance. God created the plant kingdom, but the plant kingdom simply does not possess the capacity for fellowship with God. God created the animal kingdom, but (contrary to what some groups claim today) animals cannot glorify God by entering into fellowship with Him, because they do not possess God-breathed personality. But when God created Adam, He made Adam in the image and likeness of Himself, a person with all the essential elements of personality. Thus Adam could enter into fellowship with God and glorify Him as a result.

What were these capacities, then, that God gave to Adam and the human race, so that humanity might enjoy fellowship with the Creator?

First, we know that God has a mind, and part of the personality of God is His intellectual capacity. He knows! God, in fact, possesses all knowledge and infinite wisdom. In terms of Christian doctrine, we call this God's *omniscience*.

Second, God possesses the capacity of emotion. God loves. Throughout Scripture, in fact, the emotion of God is one of the essential elements of His character.

Third, God possesses the capacity of will. God can choose, and God can act upon the exercise of His will. The perfect will of God, expressed and exercised in perfect harmony with all other aspects of His personality, permeates the Scriptures.

Scripture, then, shows us that God is a person in the richest and fullest sense of the word because Scripture reveals how God has manifested His personality. God knows; God loves; and God chooses, or acts. When God made Adam in His likeness, He endowed Adam with the same essential components of personality that He Himself possesses. When Adam was made in the likeness and image of God, he was given an intellect so that he might know; he was given emotion so that he might love; and he was given a will so that he might choose to obey God.

To be sure, Adam possessed these elements only to a finite degree, because Adam was not God. But Adam could exercise these capacities toward God in fellowship with Him; and in the garden provision was made for exercising these capacities.

Adam, for instance, was given an opportunity to exercise his intellect when he was given the task of naming all the animals. He examined each animal in order to give it a suitable name. Every time he discovered something new about God's creation, Adam exercised his mind and understood something more of God as God revealed Himself to Adam through creation.

When God gave Adam a wife, Adam's emotions became centered on the gift God had given him. He exercised his capacity to love in a new relationship, and he exercised that love toward his wife as a responsibility under God's authority.

And when God placed the tree of knowledge of good and evil in the garden, He gave Adam the opportunity to exercise his will, to choose to obey God or disobey Him. God had said, "Of the tree of the knowledge of good and evil you shall not eat, for in the day that you eat of it you shall surely die" (Genesis 2:17). The tree was placed in the garden as a test of the fellowship between the will of Adam and the will of God.

So we see that when God created Adam and made him a person, endowing him with all the capacities of personality, He made fellowship possible between the mind of Adam and the mind of God; between the heart of Adam and the heart of God; and between the will of Adam and the will of God. For Adam, fellowship was the exercise of these three capacities toward God. For Adam, fellowship was the simultaneous exercise of these three capacities toward God.

Adam could not enjoy full fellowship with God if he exercised his mind and his heart toward Him, but not his will. Likewise, there would be no full fellowship if he exercised his mind and his will, but not his heart. And Adam's fellowship would not be full and complete if he exercised his heart and his will toward God, but not his mind. The essence of fellowship between God and Adam in the Garden of Eden consisted of the mind of Adam in harmony with the mind of God; the heart of Adam in harmony with the heart of God; and the will of Adam in harmony with the will of God.

The Effects of the Fall

The Bible doesn't tell us how long it was before Adam exercised his will in rebellion to the will of God, immediately and completely breaking his fellowship with God. But we do know that sin severed the creature from fellowship with the Creator. The effects of Adam's sin are far-reaching. In Romans 1, in fact, the apostle Paul clearly outlines the effects of Adam's sin.

First, man's intellect was darkened by the Fall, so that man in his intellect could not know God. "What may be known of God," wrote Paul, "is manifest in them [that is, among them], for God has shown it to them. For since the creation of the world His invisible attributes are clearly seen, being understood by the things that are made, even His eternal power and Godhead, so that they are without excuse" (Romans 1:19–20). These verses show us that creation is a revelation of God's wisdom, and that nature is an open book in which everyone may see two things: God's eternal power, and His Godhood, or deity. But even though men were able to know something of God through that revelation, did they respond? "Although they knew God," wrote Paul, "they did not glorify Him as God, nor were thankful, but became futile in their thoughts, and their foolish hearts were darkened" (Romans 1:21).

The same truth is affirmed in Ephesians 4:17–18: "This I say, therefore, and testify in the Lord, that you should no longer walk as the rest of the Gentiles walk, in the futility [or emptiness] of their mind, having their understanding darkened, being alienated from the life of God, because of the ignorance that is in them, because of the hardening of their heart." The heart of the natural, unregenerate person is darkened because of sin. The Bible does not say that the mind is blindfolded; rather, it is *blinded*. If someone is blindfolded, all that is necessary is to remove the blindfold in order to see again. But God tells us that the entire human race has been blinded by sin. We no longer have the capacity to see. Thus the first disastrous result of Adam's sin was that mankind's intellect was darkened.

Not only was humanity's intellect darkened, but our emotional capacity was degraded as well. In Romans 1:24–26 we learn, "God . . . gave them up to uncleanness, in the lusts of their hearts, to dishonor their bodies among themselves, who exchanged the truth of God for the lie, and worshiped and served the creature rather than the Creator, who is blessed forever. Amen. For this reason God gave them up to vile passions. . . ." Ephesians 4:19 likewise describes those "who, being past feeling, have given themselves over to licentiousness, to work all uncleanness with greediness."

The natural man has not totally lost his emotional capacity; but his emotional capacity is so perverted and prostituted that it cannot be directed toward God. Thus the natural person simply cannot experience fellowship between his or her heart and the heart of God.

Romans 1 concludes by showing us yet another result of Adam's sin: the human will was deadened toward God. In verse 32 we learn that people "knowing the righteous judgment of God, that those who practice such things are worthy of death, not only do the same but also approve of those who practice them." Again, in Romans 7:18 Paul wrote, "I know that in me (that is, in my flesh) nothing good dwells; for to will is present with me, but *how* to perform what is good I do not find."

Natural man is marked by the deadness of his will toward God. Romans 8:7 tells us, "The carnal mind is enmity against God; for it is not subject to the law of God, nor indeed can be." Again, in Galatians 5:17 we read, "The flesh lusts against the Spirit, and the Spirit against the flesh; and these are contrary to one another, so that you do not do the things that you wish."

When we put these passages together, we find the Bible consistently teaches that while every person still has a will and can choose, the human will is a will enslaved to sin, a will that cannot and will not exercise itself toward God, a will that wills only that which is centered on self-gratification.

Because of the Fall, we all have been brought under judgment and under a curse. But we continue to be distinctly human. We did not lose our human personality; we have not been degraded to the level of animals. It is impossible, however, for us to exercise our God-given capacities toward God. The unsaved person has an intellect, but it is darkened and cannot know God. The unsaved person has an emotional capacity, but it is degraded and cannot love God. And the unsaved person has a will, but it is deadened toward God and cannot and will not obey God.

Even though God created people for fellowship with Himself, that He might be glorified through our fellowship with Him, that great purpose cannot be attained by unsaved, unregenerate, natural human beings. Though we still bear the image of God and possess all the component parts of personality, we have been so bound and enslaved by sin that we cannot exercise these reflections of His personality toward Him, to His glory.

The New Creation

In order that God's purpose for humanity be attained, God planned a new creation—in Jesus Christ. In 2 Corinthians 5:17 we read, "If anyone is in Christ, he is a new creation; old things have passed away; behold, all things have become new." Through the miracle of new creation, God has so enlarged and energized the believer's capacity that he or she now can enter into fellowship with God and glorify Him.

The Bible repeatedly confirms that God's purpose in this new creation is that we might again manifest His image. Second Corinthians 3:18 tells us, "We all, with unveiled face, beholding as in a mirror the glory of the Lord, are being transformed into the same image from glory to glory, just as by [or from] the Spirit of the Lord." Notice, we are being changed into *His* image. Again, in Colossians 3:10, we find that we who have trusted Christ have "put on the new man who is renewed in knowledge according to the image of Him who created him. . . ." And in Romans 8:29 the Bible tells us that "whom He foreknew, He also predestined to be conformed to the image of His Son."

What has God done for us so that we who are re-created in the image of God might glorify Him through intimate fellowship with Him?

First, God has given us a new mind. In 1 Corinthians 2:16 we read that "we have the mind of Christ." This is not a renovation or "fixing up" of the old mind; rather, it is the implanting of a new capacity in the mind of the Christian, so that he or she might enjoy fellowship with God. Notice, too, that we "are in Christ Jesus, who became for us wisdom from God—and righteousness and sanctification and redemption" (1 Corinthians 1:30). Jesus Christ has become for us wisdom, that we might understand and appropriate the truth that in Him there is righteousness, sanctification, and redemption. God's program for us begins with a new mind, that we might know Him.

Second, we are given a new capacity of heart. God does not try to renovate or purify the old capacity that exists under judgment. Instead, He gives us a new and enlarged capacity, that we might love Him. Speaking to the disciples in the Upper Room, Jesus presented this crucial test of discipleship: "By this all will know that you are My disciples, if you have love for one another" (John 13:35). Later, while writing to his own spiritual children, the apostle John said, "We know that we have passed from death to life, because we love the brethren" (1 John 3:14). And in the same letter, John wrote, "Beloved, let us love one another, for love is of God; and everyone who loves is born of God and knows God. He who does not love does not know God, for God is love. . . . In this is love, not that we loved God, but that He loved us and sent His Son to be the propitiation for our sins" (1 John 4:7–10). We have been given a new capacity of heart in order that the new heart might exercise itself toward God.

Third, we have been given a new will in order that we might obey God. In 2 Peter 1:4, Peter wrote that all believers are partakers of the divine nature. The child of God now has a new relationship to the will of God because of the new nature given to him through the new birth.

In Ephesians 6:6, Paul told his readers that they were to do the will of God from the heart—something that is utterly impossible for anyone who is alienated from God's grace. In Colossians 1:9, Paul prayed that those believers might "be filled with the knowledge of His will in all wisdom and spiritual understanding." In Colossians 4:12, Paul spoke of Epaphras, who prayed that the Christians at Colossae might stand "perfect and complete in all the will of God." And the author of Hebrews closed that great epistle by praying, "Now may the God of peace . . . make you complete in every good work to do His will . . ." (Hebrews 13:20–21).

What we see, then, is that when God made man in His image, He endowed him with the capacities of personality in order that the human race might have fellowship with God. God gave humanity—and humanity alone among His creation—a mind to know God, a heart to love God, and a will to obey God. However, when Adam disobeyed God, the entire race was cursed and cut off from fellowship with God. And though Adam still possessed the traits of personality, his intellect was darkened, his emotions were degraded, and his will was deadened. Such is still the plight of everyone who is born into this fallen world, thus there is no fellowship between the unsaved person and God the Creator.

But through the new birth, he or she who trusts Christ as Savior is given a new mind, a new heart, and a new will. And when you, the child of God, exercise your mind toward God to know Him, your heart to love

Him, and your will to obey Him, then you are in fellowship with God. On the other hand, if any area of your personality is not in harmony with Him, then you are not enjoying fellowship with God. And because fellowship with Him is the reason we were created and then re-created in His image, we cannot glorify God apart from that fellowship.

Therefore in our fellowship with God, there must be growth. We must grow in the area of knowledge. That's why Peter wrote, "Grow in the grace and knowledge of our Lord and Savior Jesus Christ" (2 Peter 3:18). We must grow, or increase, in love. Paul's prayer for the believers in Philippi included the objective "that your love may abound still more and more in knowledge and all discernment" (Philippians 1:9). And believers must continue to choose the way of complete obedience to God's will. The Lord Himself emphasized this when He said, "He who has my commandments and keeps them, it is he who loves Me. . . . If anyone loves Me, he will keep My word; and My Father will love him, and We will come to him and make Our home with him" (John 14:21–23).

We glorify God by our growth and fruitfulness as we abide in Christ, and as our minds, hearts, and wills are in harmony and fellowship with the mind, heart, and will of the Redeemer. This is God's purpose for us.

Notes

1. Some popular philosophies teach that if all things were made by God, humankind enjoys no special status as a unique creation in His image. The Bible, however, teaches that man and woman were a unique creation of God, "in His image." The difference between humankind and the rest of creation, then, might be illustrated in the difference between a man making a chair, and a man fathering a child. The chair is his creation; but the child is his off-spring, an extension of himself.

2. Genesis 1:26–27 clearly sets the human race above and apart from the animal kingdom. In contrast, today's radical environmentalists place the human race and its value below the animal kingdom. While the Bible does not leave room for wanton waste and destruction, it also does not allow the elevation of animals to an equal footing with humanity. Just a few illustrations: God Himself killed animals to cover Adam and Eve's nakedness and guilt; multiplied billions of animals died in the universal flood of judgment; God proclaimed certain animals as clean both for sacrifice and for food for Israel; animal skins were used for the tent of the tabernacle; animal blood was used as an inferior covering of sins until the blood of Christ; and Jesus Himself ate fish following His resurrection.

3. In light of Genesis 2:7, the worth of human life begins with God, not with an arbitrary quality of life standard assigned by others. This means that every

human life—though in need of redemption and accountable to God—is of equal value and potential.

4. If God possesses all knowledge and wisdom, then the knowledge and wisdom He has chosen to reveal to us in His Word is of infinite value! Do we treat it like it is more valuable, more reliable, and more essential than all of our other sources of information (television, newspapers, books, magazines, etc.)? How does the time we spend in the Bible compare with the time we spend receiving input from all the media of the world? Logically, then, which is having the greater effect on the way we think?

5. This view of the human race—that we can experience fulfillment only through a relationship with our Creator—can be the key to effectively sharing Christ with non-Christians. Too often we get sidetracked on discussions of political or moral issues, forgetting that the person with whom we are arguing has a huge void that can be filled only by a relationship with God. In fact, the Bible says unbelievers will understand nothing else of a spiritual nature until they have responded to the gospel by trusting Christ. We would do well to remember the unbeliever's real need for Christ and keep our conversations centered on Him and what He offers them.

6. Concern for our children's intellectual development is an accepted virtue in our culture; yet the Bible shows us that a fallen, blinded human intellect will always be at odds with God. Are we as concerned for our children's spiritual education as we are for their intellectual development? Do we invest as much time and energy ensuring that their minds will be regenerated through faith in Christ as we do ensuring that they perform well academically?

7. If we understand these effects of sin—that we come into this world dead toward God intellectually, morally, and emotionally—then it should come as no surprise when the unregenerate world tries to express these dead aspects of personality in ways that are contrary to God. This is the reason the world's version of intelligence is denial of God; the world's version of morality is unrestrained tolerance; the world's version of love is perversion and self-indulgence. Therefore the only answer to these symptoms is to treat the disease. While we might subdue the symptoms through human effort, the only way the disease can be turned back is through the supernatural work of the gospel.

8. The truth of the new creation and transformation that comes with faith in Christ is sometimes overlooked today by teachers and counselors who focus on the problems of the old man rather than the benefits of the new creation. Human nature is such that we would rather try to solve our own troubles than believe that God has solved them for us. God does not ask us to improve the

old person; He asks us to walk in newness of life, recognizing that He has made us an entirely new creation.

9. How interesting it is that the way our new will expresses itself is through obedience to God! Obedience, holy living, piety, Christian purity, knowing and following the commands of God—these are not among the most popular topics in Christian circles today. But commitment to knowing and obeying God's Word is absolutely *essential* to living out the new life He has given us. Is this the direction your Christian life is going?

10. Knowledge, obedience, and love are inseparable in relation to our walk with Christ. We cannot say we know Him if we do not obey Him; we cannot say we obey Him if we do not possess love; we cannot say we love Him if it is not consistent with knowledge and discernment. If we truly know Jesus Christ and walk in fellowship with Him, our lives will reflect His supernatural regeneration of our intellects, our wills, and our emotions. And we will continue to mature in that well-balanced newness of life.

Questions

1. In light of this chapter, what is your definition of *fellowship* as it applies to your relationship with God? In what area(s) of our lives should we seek fellowship with Him?

2. What do you think it means that God created man in His image? How is this concept sometimes misunderstood? What do you think is most significant about this truth?

3. What are the three aspects of personality that enable us to have fellowship with God? What were the effects of the Fall on these aspects of personality?

4. Read Romans 1:18–32. Can you name some examples in our modern society that illustrate the specific results of man's sin as mentioned in these verses?

5. What is your definition of *a new creation* as it is used in 2 Corinthians 5:17? How does this verse relate to Philippians 3:13–14? What does this mean to a person with a personal history of sin, mistreatment, or hardship? What does it mean to you?

6. Read Colossians 1:9–11. Explain the role of obedience in the Christian life. According to this passage, what is required first in order for a Christian to obey God's will and walk worthy of the Lord?

CHAPTER 3

THE OLD MIND

1 Corinthians 1:18–31

God, as a Person, possesses a mind. With His mind He knows and thinks. As a Person, God possesses a heart; and with His heart, He loves. And, as a Person, God possesses a will; and with His will He moves and decides and acts.

When God created man in His image, God gave him a mind so he could know, a heart so he could love, and a will so he could obey. Further, God intended that with our minds we should receive truth from Him and know Him; that we should receive His love and love Him in return; and that we should understand His will and obey Him. The fellowship which Adam and Eve enjoyed with God in the Garden of Eden was a fellowship of mind, heart, and will with the mind, heart, and will of God.

But according to Genesis 3, the human race enjoyed this intimate fellowship with God for only a limited time. Adam rebelled against God, chose to disobey Him, and translated his inward choice into an outward act of disobedience. Because of Adam's sin, his mind was darkened so that he did not know God; his emotions were degraded so that he did not love God; and his will was deadened so that he did not obey God. Since that original sin, all of Adam's descendants (that's all of us) have been born without the capacity for person-to-person fellowship with God.

Next, then, we will look at the effect of Adam's sin on these three essential components of an individual's personality, and then follow with a study of God's work in re-creating us and providing us with a *new* capacity to again enter into fellowship with God. Our logical starting point is the "old mind," the capacities of intellect with which all people are born as the result of Adam's sin. Because, as someone has said, "the thought is father to the word and deed," we cannot speak without first thinking of what we will say; and we cannot act without first conceiving that act in our mind. The words we speak, and the actions we carry out originate in our minds. To examine the thought life, then, is to consider that which is basic to all conduct.

The Mind of Adam

We should begin by recalling that before the Fall, Adam's mind could enjoy fellowship with the mind of God. And God gave Adam certain responsibilities which would cause him to exercise his God-given intellect. In Genesis 2:19–20 we read, "Out of the ground the LORD God formed every beast of the field and every bird of the air, and brought them to Adam to see what he would call them. And whatever Adam called each living creature, that was its name. So Adam gave names to all cattle, to the birds of the air, and to every beast of the field."

The only way Adam could give a suitable name to each created thing was to exercise his God-given capacity of mind and, by discovering the chief characteristic of each creature, give it a name in keeping with its character. God could easily have named each animal He created, and then required Adam to memorize the list. Instead, however, God told Adam, "You give names to all created things."

As Adam studied each creature to discern its peculiar characteristics, he indirectly was learning more of God as God's handiwork revealed His power, wisdom, and glory. Adam's fellowship with God in the Garden of Eden was a growing fellowship because his intellect was being enlarged, and he was understanding more and more of the Creator.

We also find in the second chapter of Genesis that Adam's mind was exercised not only in respect to naming the animals, but in giving a name to his wife after God formed her from part of Adam's own body. Genesis 2:22–23 tells us, "Then the rib which the LORD God had taken from man He made into a woman, and He brought her to the man. And Adam said, 'This is now bone of my bones and flesh of my flesh; she shall be called Woman, because she was taken out of Man." In calling his wife *woman,* Adam emphasized her origin. He understood that because she had been taken from man and that her physical body had been formed from part of man's body, it was appropriate to call her *woman* as a reminder of her origin. Also, in Genesis 3:20, "Adam called his wife's name Eve, because she was the mother of all living." Adam named his wife Eve because of her destiny; she was destined to be the mother of all men and women. This again was an exercise of Adam's mind. It was the result of using the capacity he possessed because God created him in His own likeness.

Romans 1 reminds us that originally the mind of man was exercised toward God. We read in Romans 1:19, "What may be known of God is manifest in them, for God has shown it to them." However, this knowledge and truth about God was held down, stifled, suppressed. In their ungodliness and unrighteousness, people refused the truth. They did not want to know God. For this reason, "the wrath of God is revealed from heaven against all ungodliness and unrighteousness of men, who suppress the truth in unrighteousness" (Romans 1:18).

Some may wonder, "What right does God have to reveal His wrath against all the unrighteous and ungodly, even those who have never heard the good news of salvation through Jesus Christ?" God is just in His wrath because a revelation has been given to all people. His judgment applies universally because revelation was given universally. But what was the universal revelation that is the basis of universal accountability? We find out in Romans 1:20—"For since the creation of the world His invisible attributes are clearly seen, being understood by the things that are made, even His eternal power and Godhead, so that they are without excuse."

The Bible tells us there are two distinct facts about God everyone could know, which in turn make them subject to divine judgment. These two facts are His power and His Godhood. All that has been created by the hand of God is evidence to rational creatures that God is a God of power and a God who must be obeyed. His power and Godhood were clearly seen from the things that were made. God's revelation to Adam through creation was designed to bring Adam's mind into fellowship with the mind of God. The Garden of Eden with all that God had placed in it was intended to bring Adam into fellowship with God; and as Adam enlarged his knowledge by studying creation, he would enter into deeper fellowship with God through his mind.

Characteristics of the Natural Mind

We discover in Scripture that the Fall brought about a radical change in the human mind. A number of passages in the Bible show the characteristics of the mind of the natural man. First, in Romans 1:21–23 we discover that the mind of the natural person is characterized by *darkness*. "Although they knew God, they did not glorify Him as God, nor were thankful, but became futile in their thoughts, and their foolish hearts were darkened." In other words, their powers of perception were darkened! This same truth is confirmed in Ephesians 4:17–18, where the apostle Paul refers to the Gentiles (those without God's revelation) who walk "in the futility of their mind, having their understanding darkened." The word *darkened* emphasizes that the mind of the natural person, in itself, has no power to receive light. It cannot receive divine revelation. Just as a cave fish born without sight cannot respond to light, no matter how bright, because it has no sensory perception, so people born into this world cannot, of themselves, respond to light from God because the intellect has been darkened in regard to divine truth.

In addition to the human mind being characterized by darkness, Genesis 6:5 reveals that because of the Fall, the human mind is *evil.* "Then the LORD saw that the wickedness of man was great in the earth, and that every intent of the thoughts of his heart was only evil continually." In this passage, the word *heart* signifies the seat of the thought process, or the intellect. Notice how universal is the darkness of the human mind: *every* imagination of the thoughts of man's heart was *only* evil *continually.* Not only is the human intellect darkened in respect to divine truth, what it produces is always evil in God's sight.

Looking again at Romans 1, we also discover that the natural mind is marked by a *distorted worship.* The unregenerate mind recognizes a responsibility to worship *some* god. The darkness of the mind has not totally obliterated this sense of responsibility. But because the natural mind is darkened and has become evil, and cannot exercise itself toward God, it devises gods of its own making. "Professing to be wise they became fools, and changed the glory of the incorruptible God into an image made like corruptible man—and birds and four-footed animals and creeping things" (Romans 1:22–23). They made gods for themselves. They deemed this an act of wisdom, of course; but God says it is an act of absolute foolishness.

This is illustrated perfectly in Genesis 11, where we find the first false religious system organized on the face of the earth. To the huge majority of humankind in rebellion against God, it seemed wise to erect a temple as a gathering place for the unified masses. In their "wisdom," they called that place Bab-el, "the gate of God." God, however, in His divine wisdom called it Babel, or "confusion." Such is the nature of people's distorted worship.

Further, the natural mind is *at war with God.* Paul wrote in Romans 8:6–7, "To be carnally minded is death, but to be spiritually minded is life and peace. Because the carnal mind is enmity against God; for it is not subject to the law of God, nor indeed can be." Notice again that the natural mind is characterized not only by rebellion, but by incapacity. It simply *cannot* be subject to the law of God. Why not? Because of "the ignorance that is in them" (Ephesians 4:18). The Bible pictures those who are at enmity against God as those who, having had a revelation of

God's power and Godhood, have refused to submit to Him. They have declared war on God. They live in a perpetual state of warfare against God, and in their blindness and ignorance have invented gods to suit themselves.

The natural mind is also marked by an *incapacity to receive God's truth.* In 1 Corinthians 2:14 we read, "The natural man does not receive the things of the Spirit of God, for they are foolishness to him; nor can he know them, because they are spiritually discerned." Spiritual truth can only be discovered and acquired by a spiritual nature. But the unregenerate person does not have a spiritual mind, therefore he or she does not have the capacity to receive divine truth. And since the natural mind does not have the capacity to receive divine revelation, it is characterized by ignorance and can never be educated into divine truth. It takes an entirely new capacity to receive divine truth. Apart from that new capacity, the natural mind perceives divine truth as foolishness and nonsense.

In Romans 1:28, God calls the mind of the natural man a *debased* mind: "Even as they did not like to retain God in their knowledge [that is, in the intellectual capacity God gave], God gave them over to a debased mind, to do those things which are not fitting." A debased mind is a mind that not only wanders into evil, it *gravitates* toward evil. The debased mind is entirely given over to evil.

In Ephesians 4:17 we discover that the natural mind is also an *empty* mind. The natural person walks "in the futility [literally, emptiness] of their mind." This doesn't mean that the natural mind is not full. The mind is never a vacuum. Something is always going through the human mind; but when God looks at the mind of the unregenerate person, He says that it is devoid of any content toward God. It does not retain God in its thoughts. And because the true God is left out of all that passes through that mind, it has no spiritual content. In that sense, then, it is empty and is characterized by futility.

"The *carnal* mind" is a phrase used by the apostle Paul in Romans 8:7: "The carnal mind is enmity against God." We find the same thought in Colossians 2:18 where we read, "Let no one defraud you of your reward, taking delight in false humility and worship of angels, intruding into those things which he has not seen, vainly puffed up by his fleshly mind." The carnal, or fleshly, mind is one which is focused only on sensual things, things which concern only this life and this existence. When the natural mind exercises itself, it never exercises itself toward the things of God. Rather, it is always occupied with things that have to do with this body—the gratification of its desires and appetites, the satisfaction of its wants.

In the same passage (Colossians 2:18), we find that the mind is "vainly puffed up." That is, it is a *conceited* mind, a mind that thinks well of itself. This is the characteristic Paul refers to in Romans 12:3: "I say, through the grace given to me, to everyone who is among you, not to think of himself more highly than he ought to think." Paul was warning his Christian readers not to think like an unregenerate person, who is puffed up with self. The conceited mind loves to elevate self above all those with whom he deals. He sees himself in a superior position, and thus reflects the sin of the first sinner, Satan, who was puffed up in mind, rebelled against God, and refused to remain in his place of submission to rightful authority. All those who remain in Satan's kingdom are characterized by the same vain, puffed-up mentality.

The *defiled* mind is mentioned in Titus 1:15—"To the pure all things are pure, but to those who are defiled and unbelieving nothing is pure; but even their mind and conscience are defiled." The defiled mind is so under the blight of sin that it can think nothing clean or pure, and it is driven to think the worst in every situation.

Very similar to the characteristic of the defiled mind is the *corrupt* mind, which is mentioned in 1 Timothy 6:5 in reference to "useless wranglings of men of corrupt minds and destitute of the truth. . . ." The corrupt mind is so perverted it cannot exercise the function for which the mind was originally given to man. To be sure, the natural man may be imaginative in sin, but he cannot be imaginative in the things of God or toward God.

And in Philippians 3:19 we read of the *earthly* mind. Here the apostle speaks of certain sinners "whose end is destruction, whose god is their belly, and whose glory is in their shame—who set their mind on earthly things." Talk to a natural person about material wealth and he can understand you. But begin talking to him about spiritual things, about the things of heaven, about eternity—and you might as well be talking to someone who is dead, because he will not understand that at all. Scientists often try to justify their rejection of God because they say they cannot accept anything they cannot see, feel, taste, touch, or measure. They accept earthly things, but reject heavenly things.

In 2 Corinthians 4:4, we discover that the natural mind has been *blinded*—they "whose minds the god of this age has blinded, who do not believe, lest the light of the gospel of the glory of Christ, who is the image of God, should shine on them." The natural person has not been blindfolded by sin; rather, he is marked by blindness, which is the utter inability to see.

Finally and ultimately, the natural mind is characterized by *death*. Romans 8:6 tells us that "to be carnally minded is death, but to be spiritually minded is life and peace." A person is physically dead when his body cannot perform any physical functions. Likewise, a person is spiritually dead when he or she cannot function toward God. The mind is dead spiritually when it cannot perform the function for which it was given to humankind by its Creator—to receive truth from God, to assimilate that truth, to know God who has revealed Himself in truth, and then to glorify God based on that truth.

Since the mind of a person is marked and designated as reprobate, carnal, empty, puffed up, fleshly, defiled, corrupt, earthly, blinded, and dead, do you begin to understand why it is difficult for you to control your thoughts? Don't be deceived into thinking that your old mind has been changed because you have been born into the family of God. The mind we have read about in Scripture is the mind we receive by physical birth. We possess within ourselves the same capacity for carnality, vanity, fleshly defilement, corruption, enmity, and attention to earthly, material things that characterized us before we were born into God's family. And if that old mind is allowed to exercise itself, that mind will produce words and actions that are in keeping with the corruption, defilement, blindness, and deadness God says characterizes the mind of the unsaved person.

I thank God that this old mind was brought under judgment at the cross. God did not try to improve it, clean it up, change its distortion or purify its perversion. He judged it at the cross. And He imparts to those who believe in Christ the new mind of Christ in order that it might exercise itself toward God in fellowship with Him.

Notes

1. The mind, heart, and will of the Christian are equally important in a vital, vibrant relationship with God. While some believers perhaps put too much emphasis on knowledge of theology and doctrine to the exclusion of love and obedience, it has also become quite popular today to emphasize love and obedience to the exclusion of a sound knowledge of the Bible. As we will see, God has made us new creatures in order that we might experience a full, balanced, well-rounded relationship with Him—in knowledge, love, and obedience.

2. How many disorders and maladies today are diagnosed as psychological, or "of the mind"? Because the human mind was clearly designed to operate properly in fellowship with God, we can assume that it will *always* be dysfunctional when operating apart from fellowship with Him. That, in fact, is the point of Romans 1:18–32. That means that the most we can do for our

own mental health or that of someone else is to concentrate first and foremost on knowing Christ and growing in a relationship with Him.

3. Isn't it interesting that even the secular world refers to uncontrollable natural disasters as "acts of God"? Likewise, earthquakes, tornadoes, and other crises of nature often reduce the unsaved to prayers for mercy. As much as natural man wants to deny God's existence, when His might is reflected in natural occurrences our minds naturally discern something of His eternal power and invisible attributes. The Bible says that this tendency alone condemns those who perceive His existence and yet do not seek to know Him.

4. Secular humanists tell us that the many social ills we face today—illicit sex, youth violence, rampant crime, family disintegration—can be cured through education. But while God's Word speaks highly of the human mind and its capacities, it tells us that apart from God its knowledge is dark, incomplete, and futile. As we evaluate the world's solutions to social problems, we need to do so on the basis of knowing God and understanding that only He can give light to the human mind.

5. From Babel onward, the world's false religious systems have universally denied that God alone can provide sinful people with the only means to eternal life; that the Bible is not the only authoritative written Word of God; and that man is fallen and in desperate need of salvation from God. Look for these hallmarks of false religion in any religious group, whether or not it carries the label "Christian."

6. In a day of evangelical activism, we should not mistakenly think that we can Christianize our culture by trying to convince the unsaved majority about the truth and wisdom of God's precepts and principles. The Bible clearly says that such information is nonsense to unbelievers. Instead, the most we can possibly do to act as salt and light in our society is personally share the gospel of Jesus Christ with the lost and lead as many as possible to faith in Him. Only through the transformation of lives will our culture and country be transformed.

7. An old cliché cautions believers to not be "so heavenly minded that they are no earthly good," yet the Bible tells us the opposite is more likely to be true. Before we come to know Christ, we are entirely earthly minded; and after we come to know Christ, that will continue to be our natural bent. It will always be easier and more natural for our thoughts to revolve around earthly things—money, comfort, security, entertainment, recreation, status, popularity—than heavenly things. Devoting our thoughts to spiritual matters will always require a conscious commitment and mental effort as the Spirit quickens our hearts and minds toward the things of God.

8. If you've ever hit your thumb with a hammer or been cut off in traffic, you may have been surprised at how quickly your thought life went from a godly,

spiritual plane to a debased, carnal, unrighteous level. This is because Christ did not improve or revamp your old mind; He gave you a new mind. That means that our efforts to clean up or improve the old mind, rather than appropriating and walking in the new mind, will get us nowhere spiritually. Unfortunately, too much counseling today encourages believers to dwell on, analyze, probe, relive, and concentrate on the old rather than leaving the old behind and living in the new. Remember, 2 Corinthians 5:17 tells us, "If anyone is in Christ, he is a new creation; old things have passed away; behold, all things have become new."

Questions

1. What does Genesis 2:19–20 tell us about the creative capacities God instilled in the human mind? What does it tell us about man's position in relation to the animal kingdom?

2. Read Genesis 2:22–23. What did Adam's unfallen mind recognize concerning his wife's origin? What does this say about his relationship to her? How should this affect the way Christian husbands view their wives? About the way they treat them?

3. According to Romans 1:20, how has God revealed Himself to all people, whether or not they believe in Him? What can be perceived of God in this way? How have unsaved people tried to ignore and deny this revelation of God?

4. Left to themselves, what course will the people's minds naturally pursue (see Genesis 6:5)? In light of Romans 1:22, will unregenerate people recognize their ignorance of God? According to the next verse (Romans 1:23), what happens to people's perception of God as they continue to deny Him?

5. Read Romans 8:6–7. When non-Christians today react so vehemently and violently against Christians, who are they really battling? What effect might this have on collective human government (see Genesis 11:1–4)?

6. If the fallen mind is incapable of seeing, hearing, or understanding God's truth (2 Corinthians 4:4), how can the body of Christ, or individual Christians, ever hope to affect the world around them (see Acts 1:8; Ephesians 2:13)? In your opinion, what is the most effective way of influencing our non-Christian culture?

CHAPTER 4

THE NEW MIND

1 Corinthians 2:7–16

A new capacity of mind has been given to the person who has experienced the new birth, the person who is a new creation in Christ Jesus. To the one who believes in Christ, God gives new life through that which is called the new birth (John 3) and the new creation (2 Corinthians 5:17). When He makes a person a new creation in Christ, God does not remake the capacities of the natural man, nor does He change the basic characteristics of his personality. Rather, God gives the person a new capacity of mind, heart, and will. With the new mind a person can know God, with the new heart a person can love God, and with a new will a person can obey God.

In the previous chapter we surveyed God's Word concerning the human mind since the Fall; the purpose of this chapter is to examine Scripture concerning the capacity of the new mind God has given to each one who has trusted in Christ as Savior.

God does not try to use the old mind. Through the new birth, God imparts a new mind to the believer—a mind with the capacity to receive divine truth, to exercise itself toward God, and to enjoy fellowship with Him in the realm of spiritual truth. This is emphasized in 1 Corinthians 2:16 where Paul wrote, "We have the mind of Christ." The apostle had been reminding his readers that God had revealed a body of truth through the Holy Spirit. But, according to verse 9, the natural eye had not seen, the natural ear had not heard, nor had there entered into the thoughts of the natural mind the things God has prepared for them that love Him. In verse 14 Paul explained the ignorance of the natural mind by observing, "The natural man does not receive the things of the Spirit of God, for they are foolishness to him; nor can he know them, because they are spiritually discerned." But, the apostle goes on to explain, the revelation which natural minds cannot receive can be received by those who have the mind of Christ. God gives a new capacity to the person who has received Christ, so that as he exercises the new mind, he can grasp the truth of God and appropriate the revelation God has made of Himself. As a result, the believer enjoys fellowship with God—the mind of the believer in harmony with the mind of God.

Romans 12:1–2 tells us more about God's work in the area of mind. It reads, "I beseech you therefore, brethren, by the mercies of God, that you present your bodies a living sacrifice, holy, acceptable to God, which is your reasonable service. And do not be conformed to this world, but be transformed by the renewing of your mind, that you may prove what is that good and acceptable and perfect will of God." The word *renewing* is the same word used in Titus 3:5 where we read, "Not by works of righteousness which we have done, but according to His mercy He saved us, through the washing of regeneration and renewing [that is, the making new] of the Holy Spirit." It means to rejuvenate, to modernize, or to bring up to date. We speak of renewing furniture when we refinish an antique—but that is not the scriptural meaning of the word. The New Testament word translated from biblical Greek into English means "to make new from above." That's what God does when He makes a man or woman a new creature in Christ Jesus. He sees the natural mind as it really is: defiled, evil, reprobate, and dead. Instead of remaking the old mind, God imparts an entirely new mind—a new capacity of mind.

When the Holy Spirit does His work of instructing us in the things of Christ, He never appeals to the old mind. He never addresses truth to the natural man, with his natural capacity. Rather, the new mind in Christ is the channel through which divine truth is learned and lived. The Lord said to His disciples, "The Helper, the Holy Spirit, whom the Father will send in My name, He will teach you all things, and bring to your remembrance all things that I said to you" (John 14:26). Likewise, in John 16:12–15 our Lord said, "I still have many things to say to you, but you cannot bear them now. However, when He, the Spirit of truth, has come, He will guide you into all truth; for He will not speak on His own authority, but whatever He hears He will speak; and He will tell you things to come. . . . All things that the Father has are Mine. Therefore I said that He will take of Mine and declare it to you."

Until the Holy Spirit came on the Day of Pentecost to indwell all believers and to do His work of teaching, there was no new mind in believers. Thus there was no vehicle for receiving divine truth, nor was there a Teacher to impart that truth. But since that time everyone who trusts Christ has been given a new mind, and God—through the Holy Spirit—can teach us the things concerning Christ.

Conflict

Because of the new mind, with its capacity to receive divine truth and respond to it in fellowship with God, every believer is engaged in constant warfare. There is a perpetual warfare between the new mind in Christ and the mind of the natural man. We often refer to the two natures in the child of God; but when we do, we are not suggesting that the Christian has become two persons, or that he possesses two distinct personalities, because that is not a biblical concept. However, it is biblical to understand that in the area of mind, the Christian has two capacities—the capacity for divine things through the new mind, and the capacity for carnal, fleshly, sinful, dead things through the old mind. And there is a constant, cease-less, incessant, unrelenting opposition from the old mind to the new mind as it seeks to glorify God.

This is the conflict we find in Romans 8:5–8 where Paul wrote, "Those who live according to the flesh set their minds on the things of the flesh, but those who live according to the Spirit, the things of the Spirit. For to be carnally minded is death, but to be spiritually minded is life and peace. Because the carnal mind is enmity against God; for it is not subject to the law of God, nor indeed can be. So then, those who are in the flesh cannot please God." In short, the carnal mind is at war with God, but the spiritual mind pursues those things that are characterized by life and peace.

We can also see this conflict in Romans 7:14, where Paul wrote, "I am carnal, sold under sin." Notice, he did not say, "I am *doing* carnal, worldly things." He says, "This is my essential makeup. In the area of my mind I am carnal. That is, although I have the new mind of Christ, I still have the old capacity, the old, natural mind. Therefore I have to be characterized in mind as one who is carnal, because the old mind has not been elimi-nated; it has not been changed."

After Paul speaks of his essential makeup, he writes, "I see another law in my members, warring against the law of my mind, and bringing me into captivity to the law of sin which is in my members. . . . So then, with the mind I myself serve the law of God, but with the flesh the law of sin" (7:23, 25). May I paraphrase the last part of verse 25 to make it plain? Paul says, "With the new mind I serve the law of God, but with the fleshly mind I serve the law of sin."

This is the principle that Paul is laying down for us: Every child of God would have to be classified as carnal in the area of the mind; that is, we have the old capacity which can manifest itself in sin, lawlessness, ignorance, corruption, defilement, and death. We experience a constant battle in the area of the mind—the new against the old, the old against the new. Never will the old mind and the new mind agree on anything in the believer's life. There is never a time when these two capacities agree on any thought, any word, or any action in our lives.

Transformation

Because of this ongoing, unrelenting conflict of the mind, the Bible offers a number of exhortations to believers. Let's look at some of these.

Ephesians 4:23 admonishes believers, "Be renewed in the spirit of your mind." It is important to notice that Paul is not commanding believers to *get* the new mind. As believers we already have the new mind. Now we are to allow the new mind to do its renewing work in transforming our lives. When the old mind is allowed to dominate the child of God, the result will be sin, defilement, and corruption. But when the new mind dominates or controls the Christian, one's life will manifest that which comes from a holy, righteous, and just God.

In Romans 12:2 we read, "Do not be conformed to this world, but be transformed by the renewing of your mind." This speaks of a changed life, a life that comes from the renewing of the mind. The old mind will produce its corrupt fruit, but the new mind will manifest itself in righteousness and true holiness.

Colossians 3:5–8 catalogs a list of heinous sins, every one of which is an outworking of the natural mind. They include "fornication, uncleanness, passion, evil desire, and covetousness, which is idolatry. . . . anger, wrath, malice, blasphemy, filthy language out of your mouth." Don't think such sins are impossible for the child of God! The new mind will never produce these sins—but if the old mind is permitted to control the child of God, this is exactly the fruit it will produce every time.

Having listed the sins the old mind will produce, Paul goes on to say in verse 9, "Do not lie to one another, since you have put off the old man with his deeds, and have put on the new man *who is renewed in knowledge* according to the image of Him who created him" (italics added). As we have already seen, when God made man, He made him in His image and gave him a mind with the capacity to know Him. Since the Fall, the minds of all people born into this world have been darkened and deadened by sin. Thus, in order for us to know Him, we have to become new creatures. When that happens, we are "renewed in knowledge according to the image of Him who created him." The new creature in Christ is a person who has been re-created in the image of God and endowed with the capacity to enter into fellowship with Him.

Therefore, because we have been renewed in knowledge (that is, in the area of the mind), we are to put off the old mind and put on the fruit of the new mind.

In Philippians 2:5 we find another command concerning the new mind: "Let this mind be in you which was also in Christ Jesus." Or, more literally, "have this mind in you." It is not, "*Get* this mind in you." Had the apostle stated it that way, we would have known immediately that he was writing to unbelievers. Instead, from the words he used we know that he was writing to believers, exhorting them to manifest the fruit of the new mind instead of the fruit of the carnal mind.

What characterized the mind of Jesus Christ? This glorious passage speaks of the humiliation of Christ, who, "being in the form of God, did not consider it robbery to be equal with God, but made Himself of no reputation, taking the form of a servant, and coming in the likeness of men. And being found in appearance as a man, He humbled Himself and became obedient to the point of death, even the death of the cross" (Philippians 2:6–8). The mind of Christ was characterized by submission to the will of God—He knew God, perceived the will of God, and willingly submitted to it.

Philippians 4:8 speaks of exercising the new mind, exhorting believers, "Finally, brethren, whatever things are true, whatever things are r oble, whatever things are just, whatever things are pure, whatever thin's are lovely, whatever things are of good report, if there is any virtue and if there is anything praiseworthy—meditate on these things." The new mind should be centered on those things which can be characterized as true, noble, just, pure, lovely, and of good report.

Responsibility

What does God's Word say about the believer's responsibility to use this new capacity?

First, the mind of the child of God should be *occupied with Christ*. In light of Philippians 4:8, Jesus Christ is One in whom all these traits have been fully displayed. "Whatever things are true" certainly refers to Christ, for Jesus could say of Himself, "I am the way, the *truth*, and the life" (John 14:6). "Whatever things are noble" refers to Him as well, for it was said that in His lips was no deceit. "Whatever things are just" must also refer to Him, for the centurion at the cross looked at Him and declared, "Surely this was a righteous man. Truly this was the Son of God!" "Whatever things are pure" refers to Jesus Christ, for He was totally without sin. "Whatever things are lovely" refers to Him, for He is altogether lovely. "Whatever things are of good report" points to Him, for this phrase literally means, "Whatever things are worthy of praise," and we know the Lord Jesus Christ is worthy of all praise and honor.

If we desire to exercise the new mind in such a way that we enjoy fellowship with God, this new mind must be centered upon the Lord Jesus Christ. As soon as the mind turns from Him, the old mind takes over and produces thoughts in keeping with the cesspool it really is. The new mind was given to each Christian so that with it the child of God might know the Father. God did not have to make us new creations so we could understand history, or mathematics, or languages, or physics, or medicine. The old mind was sufficient for that. He gave us a new mind because of our one great mental deficiency, our inability to exercise our minds toward God. If we are not exercising our minds Godward, then we cannot know fellowship with God, and we cannot fulfill the purpose for which we were re-created in Jesus Christ.

Paul is an outstanding example of this exercise of the mind. In Philippians 3:10 he reveals the great impelling, compelling, and propelling force in his life: "that I may know Him." How? With the old mind? God forbid! Rather, he had the new mind, which was occupied with Christ. As Christians, we will never fulfill the purpose for which we were made a new creation in Christ until we exercise our minds toward God.

Second, God's Word reveals that which will *sustain* the new mind. First Peter 2:2 tells us, "As newborn babes, desire the pure milk of the word, that you may grow thereby." God's Word, the Bible, is spiritual food that produces spiritual growth. This is confirmed by Jeremiah, who proclaimed, "Your words were found and I ate them, and Your word was to me the joy and rejoicing of my heart; for I am called by Your name, O Lord God of hosts" (Jeremiah 15:16).

The Christian who saturates his mind with the Word of God will be strengthened from within in such a way that the old mind will be kept from controlling his thoughts and actions. That is why the psalmist said, "Your word I have hidden in my heart, that I might not sin against You" (Psalm 119:11). Notice, too, that it is not the Word you have bound inside a nice book cover that is going to keep you, and it is not the words you have underlined in your Bible that will protect you. It is the Word of God you have stored in your mind that will sustain you in a day of temptation. The mind must be sustained by the Word of God.

Third, we find that the Bible speaks of the *defense* of the mind. Paul wrote, "Be anxious for nothing, but in everything by prayer and supplication, with thanksgiving, let your requests be made known to God; and the peace of God, which surpasses all understanding, will guard your hearts and minds through Christ Jesus" (Philippians 4:6–7). The peace of

God will guard your *minds*! What does this mean? As we who know Christ sustain our minds by God's Word, the knowledge we have gained through the Bible will defend us in a time of temptation, in a time of discouragement, in a time of testing, or in a time of doubt.

We can see this relationship between knowledge and faith in Romans 10:17, where Paul wrote, "Faith comes by hearing, and hearing by the word of God." We cannot believe something we do not know. We cannot trust God in a time of testing unless we know Him. When you are brought into some trying experience, the truth of God that has been revealed through the Bible to your new mind will sustain you, defend you, protect you, and uphold you. Many believers have walked confidently into a valley of dark shadows with God's Word upon their lips. Why? Because the Word of God sustains and defends the new mind of God's own children.

Fourth, we find that the new mind has been *set free from the dominion of the old mind.* In 2 Timothy 1:7 we read, "God has not given us a spirit of fear, but of power and of love and of a sound mind." God has given us a *sound mind.* The sound mind God has given us is the new mind, for the new mind is characterized by soundness. Soundness means the new mind can function as God intended at creation, that is, knowing God and having fellowship with Him. Paul illustrated this in Romans 7:25: "I thank God—through Jesus Christ our Lord! So then, with the mind I myself serve the law of God, but with the flesh the law of sin." Fellowshiping with God, receiving divine truth from His Word, and enjoying God because we have come to know Him are the wonderful possibilities available to everyone who is a new creature in Christ Jesus.

Fifth and finally, we find in 2 Corinthians 10:3–5 some very practical words concerning the use of the new mind. "Though we walk in the flesh, we do not war according to the flesh. For the weapons of our warfare are not carnal [of the flesh] but mighty in God for pulling down strongholds, casting down arguments [thoughts that would originate from the old mind] and every high thing [every manifestation of the old mind] that exalts itself against the knowledge of God, bringing every thought into captivity to the obedience of Christ. . . ." We are to bring into subjection to Christ every expression of the old mind with its sin, sensuality, greed, hatred, and corruption. We are to bring every thought into subjection to the obedience of Christ.

We recognize, of course, that of ourselves we cannot do this. Only the Spirit of God can restrain the evil nature within each one of us. But God has given us the responsibility of bringing our thoughts into captivity to Jesus Christ, and bringing them into subjection to Him. Our minds dart so rapidly from one thing to another, and today we are bombarded with continual stimuli from television, movies, billboards, magazines, newspapers, music, and conversations around us. Each of us experiences countless appeals to the old mind. But God says we should not retain or harbor these thoughts, but subject every thought to the authority of Christ, in order that we might manifest Jesus Christ in and through our minds.

It is extremely important to realize that it is not the heart that is the primary receptacle and repository of divine truth—it is the mind. If our minds are so cluttered with expressions of the old mind that the new mind cannot manifest itself, we will continue in carnality, we will be ignorant of divine truth, and even though we have been born into God's family, we will continue to limp and stumble along in our walk with Christ. We will be babies in Christ until we allow the mind of Christ to control us.

Notes

1. In understanding the capacity and potential of the new mind, it may help us to remember that the primary purpose of the new mind is to know God. That means that our relationship with Him should not be just one of many areas of equal interest, but rather should be the focus of our thoughts from which our ideas about everything else flow. This is the idea behind 1 Corinthians 2:15: "He who is spiritual judges [appraises, evaluates] all things." Are the things of God the focus of your new mind, shaping your thoughts about everything else?

2. One miracle of nature that illustrates what God does for our minds is the process of *regeneration.* Some animals possess the capacity to create entirely new body parts to replace those that are lost to predators. Obviously, they cannot rebuild what is not there; rather, they *regenerate* something entirely new. Rather than overhauling our old, fallen minds, God creates something new—the "mind of Christ"—in us.

3. Someone has said, "Every Christian is only one thought away from sin." In other words, we do not grow or mature beyond our ability to choose the old mind over the new, or to submit to the old capacity of our minds. If you are struggling with your thought life, it may be because you are not saturating your mind with food and fuel for the new capacity—specifically, with the Word of God. That is why Bible study, personal devotions, and memorization of Scripture is so beneficial for any Christian, no matter how long he or she has known Christ.

4. We live in a culture of self-help. Everywhere we turn we are told the how-to's of successful living. Yet the Bible tells us that our lives will be transformed

only as our minds are renewed through our relationship with Christ, and as the Holy Spirit works in our lives through His Word. Though our old nature might want all the control and credit for a transformed life, we need to remember that it is our submission to Christ, not our human effort, that will change us from the way we used to be into the image of Christ.

5. How shocked we are when sins like those listed in Colossians 3:5–8 appear in our lives! Our natural tendency is to either excuse these attitudes and actions, or to try and make it up to God somehow. The best plan, however, is to recognize these things for what they really are (manifestations of the old nature), confess them (1 John 1:9), and submit ourselves to the Spirit's control in order to manifest the new mind He has created in us.

6. Whether or not you have a personal plan for Scripture memorization, committing Philippians 4:8 to memory could be a giant step toward purifying your thought life. It is, in fact, just the opposite of the things we read in Colossians 3:5–8, which probably include at least one or two areas you may struggle with.

7. Perhaps we too often think of prayer only in terms of supplication—asking God for what we want or need. However, the Bible indicates that prayer will have a marked effect on our thought life. Does your day include time spent on your knees before God, not only letting Him know what you want, but letting Him invade your thoughts?

8. Obviously, Christians who exercise the new mind will find themselves at odds with popular thought as it is reflected in the media and repeated by unbelievers. Rather than fearfully adjusting our convictions to avoid this conflict, we can use it both as an opportunity to either validate or reject the media's presentation of "truth," and to determine when we have an opportunity to share the gospel with an unbeliever. Remember—winning a person to Christ is far more significant than winning an argument!

9. If all our thoughts were tangible packages we could handle and carry, how many of those would we actually bring before our Lord Jesus Christ? If a specific thought or attitude is not something we can bring to Him, we should probably not entertain it ourselves. Bringing our thought life into subjection to the obedience of Christ means that we are willing for every thought, all the time, to be tested by the standards of His Word as we submit ourselves to the scrutiny and control of His Spirit in our lives.

Questions

1. What do you think it means to possess the mind of Christ? What process is a part of this, according to Romans 12:1–2? In light of Colossians 3:9 and 1 Peter 2:2, how is this process accomplished?

2. Do you think that the natural condition of the fallen mind prevents it from producing any type of useful knowledge (such as mathematics, science, medicine, etc.)? If not, what does it lack? Can you give some specific examples from our modern world of what the natural mind can do, as well as what it cannot or does not do?

3. Read Romans 12:2. What forces or influences do you think are at work to conform us to the world? What outside factors can work in our favor, that we might be transformed by the renewing of our minds? Which of these two categories receive the greater amount of your time and attention? Which, then, will probably have the greater impact on your thoughts?

4. From the list found in Colossians 3:5–8, which are areas you are struggling with, or have struggled with in the past? Where do these problems originate? What, according to Philippians 4:8, is the answer to this broad area of difficulty?

5. What role do you think the Word of God should play in sustaining your thought life? How—*specifically*—might that come about? Do you have a plan to see this happen?

6. What does 2 Timothy 1:7 reveal about the power behind a victorious thought life (also see Romans 8:1–2)?

CHAPTER 5

THE OLD HEART

Romans 1:18–32

In our previous studies, we examined the old mind and the work God has done to give us a new mind in Christ, that we might enjoy fellowship with Him. Now we will move on to the second aspect of the new creation: the heart.

As used in the Word of God, the term *heart* is a very broad term that may describe any part of the total personality. First, for example, Scripture refers to the heart as the source of one's *intellectual capacity*, or the mind. Second Corinthians 4:6 says, "It is the God who commanded light to shine out of darkness who has shone in our hearts to give the light of the knowledge of the glory of God in the face of Jesus Christ." The light shining in our hearts has brought us knowledge of God's glory. Reception of knowledge is the function of the mind—yet this passage tells us that our hearts have received the revelation of knowledge of God. This illustrates that the terms *heart* and *mind* may be interchangeable.

This is also true in 1 Corinthians 2:9–12, which says, "Eye has not seen, nor ear heard, nor have entered into the heart of man the things which God has prepared for those who love Him. . . . Now we have received, not the spirit of the world, but the Spirit who is from God, that we might know the things that have been freely given to us by God." In this passage, "the heart of man" refers to that part of the personality which receives knowledge, for with the heart we know the things that are "freely given to us by God." So we see that *heart*—in its broad sense—is used first of all to describe the mind of the personality.

Second, the term *heart* is used of the seat of the *affections* of one's personality. Paul wrote in 2 Thessalonians 3:5, "Now may the Lord direct your hearts into the love of God and into the patience of Christ." Likewise, Peter wrote in 1 Peter 1:22, "Since you have purified your souls in obeying the truth through the Spirit in sincere love of the brethren, love one another fervently with a pure heart." In both of these passages, the heart is that part of the personality that feels emotion and love.

Third, we find in 2 Corinthians 9:7 that *heart* is used of the seat of the will: "So let each one give as he purposes in his heart, not grudgingly or of necessity; for God loves a cheerful giver."

We see, then, that the word *heart* can refer to the seat of the mind, the seat of the affections, or the seat of the will. Thus, when the Bible speaks of the heart, it speaks of the whole personality. The main thought seems to be this: The affections control the whole person's actions. What a person knows, he loves or hates; and what he loves or hates results in an action of the will. Therefore, the seat of the affection may be used of the total person. When we discuss the capacity of the heart old, we need to understand that the word *heart* cannot be restricted to emotions alone. Rather, it encompasses the whole being.

We know from God's Word that God loves. In 1 John 4:8 we find the simple statement, "God is love," which provides us with a great categorical affirmation about our God. He is not only infinite in His intellect, but He is also infinite in His compassion. God is love.

One expression of God's love is His love for His Son. At the time of Christ's baptism by John the Baptist, the heavens opened and the voice of God was heard saying, "This is my *beloved* Son, in whom I am well pleased" (Matthew 3:17). At the time of the Transfiguration of Christ, God's voice again was heard saying, "This is My *beloved* Son . . . . Hear Him" (Matthew 17:5). From eternity past, God the Father has loved His Son. God did not begin to love the Son at the time of His incarnation, His baptism, His transfiguration, or His crucifixion. The eternal Father has eternally loved His Son.

Not only did God love the Son, who was worthy to be loved, but He also loved sinful humanity, which was *not* worthy of His love. Jesus Himself bore witness to this love when He said, "God so loved the world that He gave His only begotten Son, that whoever believes in Him should not perish but have everlasting life" (John 3:16).

The Heart of Adam

When God created Adam in His own image, He gave to him not only a mind so he could think, but also a heart so he could love. In Genesis 2:21–25, we read about the creation of Eve. "The Lord caused a deep sleep to fall on Adam, and he slept; and He took one of his ribs, and closed up the flesh in its place. Then the rib which the Lord God had taken from man He made into a woman, and He brought her to the man. And Adam said: 'This is now bone of my bones and flesh of my flesh; she shall be called Woman, because she was taken out of Man.'

Therefore a man shall leave his father and mother and be joined to his wife, and they shall become one flesh. And they were both naked, the man and his wife, and were not ashamed."

In that last statement, in which God gives us His divine principle of marriage, we find that Adam's heart was responding to Eve, and Eve in turn responded to Adam's affection. Man and woman were able to use their God-given capacity to love.

As we continue through the Word of God we find that Adam's sin not only darkened his mind, but also had an effect on his heart. Adam's emotional capacity was degraded by his sin. Romans 1 gives us a glaringly clear description of this degradation of human emotional capacity. It is a candid description of the old heart. As we read through this passage carefully and understand the truth God has given us there, we may well feel guilty or defiled. One cannot look at this portrait of the natural person's heart without drawing back in revulsion from its description of the heart's capacity for evil. But we will not truly understand some of the thoughts, some of the desires, some of the affections that grip our hearts until we see the effect of Adam's sin on the area of human emotion.

The Effect of the Fall

In Romans 1:21, Paul wrote, "Although they [that is, those who had received revelation concerning God] knew God [with the mind], they did not glorify Him as God, nor were thankful." In other words, unregenerate human beings received revelation from God, but they were blinded in the area of the mind and could not receive, accept, and respond to that revelation. Instead, they "became futile in their thoughts, and their foolish hearts were darkened." In verse 21, *heart* may refer to the person's capacity to receive truth, or it may refer to the person's emotional capacity to respond to that truth. In either case, this verse's first description of the natural heart is that it is *foolish*. In Scripture, a fool is not necessarily someone who is marked by a low IQ, but rather is someone who leaves God out of his thought processes (see Psalm 14:1: "The fool has said in his heart, 'there is no God.' ") The fool is the person who does not take God into consideration in every area of life. Therefore when Paul speaks of "their foolish hearts," he is referring to hearts that leave out God and are perfectly willing to continue without God's presence, without feeling God's love.

Further in Romans 1 we read, "Professing to be wise, they became fools, and changed the glory of the incorruptible God into an image made like corruptible man—and birds and four-footed beasts and creeping things" (1:22–23). Notice that the human race did not become demented because of the Fall. People were not deprived of their reasoning ability. Human beings could reason; and they reasoned that they were responsible to some deity. However, they refused to worship and serve the God who had revealed Himself. So they made false gods. By manufacturing deities that resembled corruptible man, and birds, and four-footed beasts, and creeping things, human beings showed that their reasoning processes were functioning; but they were not functioning properly.

Next, Romans shows the emotional result of this corrupted thinking: "God also gave them up to uncleanness, in the lusts of their hearts, to dishonor their bodies among themselves" (1:24). Here we see a double characterization of the heart—it is a *lustful* heart, and it is an *unclean* heart. The perpetual desires of this lustful heart do not include a desire for God, a desire for godliness. Rather, this degraded heart has insatiable immoral lusts.

In verse 25 we read that they "exchanged the truth of God for the lie, and worshiped and served the creature rather than the Creator, who is blessed forever." And in verse 26 we find that "for this reason God gave them up to vile passions." This clearly shows that the old heart is the seat of *vile passions*. At the creation of the marriage relationship, God intended that a husband and wife should express their God-given capacity to love. But Romans 1:26–27 shows that as a result of the Fall and because of the degradation of the natural heart, men and women did not exercise this capacity of affection as God intended. Instead they invented perverted ways of manifesting the capacity of emotion in the most degraded forms and practices. And from what we read in this passage, it is very clear that the sodomy, homosexuality, and perversion so rampant today is a direct result of the degradation of the human emotional capacity.

In verses 29–32 we find a list of some specific things that are manifestations of this degraded emotional capacity: People are "filled with all unrighteousness, sexual immorality, wickedness, covetousness, maliciousness; full of envy, murder, strife, deceit, evil-mindedness; they are whisperers, backbiters, haters of God, violent, proud, boasters, inventors of evil things, disobedient to parents, undiscerning, untrustworthy, unloving, unforgiving, unmerciful; who, knowing the righteous judgment of God, that those who practice such things are worthy of death, not only do the same but also approve of those who practice them."

Today's public complacency toward the open display of these traits is even further evidence of the filthiness of the human heart.

Characteristics of the Natural Heart

Other aspects of the natural heart are described elsewhere in the Bible. In Romans 2:5 Paul wrote, "In accordance with your hardness and your impenitent heart you are treasuring up for yourself wrath in the day of wrath and revelation of the righteous judgment of God." The human heart is *hard* and *impenitent.* The word translated "hard," when used in reference to the heart, literally means "calloused." Perhaps you have seen someone with a calloused hand that seemed impervious to the sensation of pain. Why is this so? Because something that is calloused is not sensitive to external stimulation. The heart of the natural man has become hardened in that same way and is not subject to any stimulation concerning righteousness, nor conviction concerning sin. The result is that it has become impenitent.

The Word of God may be declared, the righteousness of God may be revealed, the judgment of God that will be poured out on sinners may be proclaimed, but sinners are not affected at all. They are not convicted of the enormity of their sin, and they complacently continue in their degradation, perversion, and immorality. Why? Because their hearts are characterized by hardness.

Why is it so difficult to reach some people with the gospel of Jesus Christ? Perhaps you have lived righteously, testified to people of God's grace, given them God's Word—yet they brush it all aside. Why? Because they are utterly insensitive to external stimulation, and resisting the truth of God simply builds up the callous even further, making their hearts even harder and more impenitent. Therefore we should not be surprised by those who reject the gospel of Jesus Christ when they have hearts characterized by hardness and an unwillingness to repent.

In Ephesians 4:18 we read that unbelievers have "their understanding darkened, being alienated from the life of God, because of the ignorance that is in them, because of the hardening of their heart." This verse indicates that this hardening of heart means that unbelievers' hearts are *blinded.* Notice that they are blinded, not merely blindfolded. As ambassadors of Jesus Christ we do not seek to take blindfolds off of people. Rather, we present the gospel of Christ to those who cannot see the truth of God because of the blindness, the hardness, of their hearts. We cannot make them see, nor can we convince them of Christ's power to save. Only Jesus Christ can perform the miracle that causes hardened, blinded hearts to perceive who Christ is and thus receive eternal life through Him.

In Hebrews 3:10–12 we find two additional descriptions of the natural heart. Quoting from the Old Testament, the writer of Hebrews tells that God said about the children of Israel when they were in the wilderness: "I was angry with that generation, and said, 'They always go astray in their heart, and they have not known My ways.' " The natural heart is a heart that goes astray. When people follow the natural tendencies of the heart, they go astray and follow ways which are far from God's ways.

Then the writer of Hebrews warns in 3:12, "Beware, brethren, lest there be in any of you an evil heart of unbelief in departing from the living God." The natural heart is an *evil* heart. Our Lord characterized the human heart as evil when He was questioned by the Pharisees because some of His disciples had not followed the traditional hand-washing procedure. The Pharisees' philosophy was that a person was clean within, and that defilement was external. People were defiled by contact from outside, not by what was within. Christ corrected this erroneous idea by pointing out that defilement is not external, but internal. In Mark 7:21–23, Jesus very clearly delineated what proceeds from an evil heart: "From within, out of the heart of men, proceed evil thoughts, adulteries, fornications, murders, thefts, covetousness, wickedness, deceit, licentiousness, an evil eye, blasphemy, pride, foolishness. All these evil things come from within and defile a man."

Remember, Christ did not need anyone to tell Him what was in man, for He knew what was in man. What He said is a divine revelation of what God sees in the human heart. The natural heart is an evil heart, and it is this kind of heart the apostle had in mind in Hebrews 3:12.

James referred to a *deceived* heart when he wrote, "If anyone among you thinks he is religious, and does not bridle his tongue but deceives his own heart, this one's religion is useless" (James 1:26). A deceived heart sets a false standard, and then convinces itself that it measures up to the standard it has adopted. Can you imagine a person daring to think that he or she has measured up to the righteousness of God? Or a sinner persuading himself that he is as holy as God? It happens all the time. The natural person can deceive himself into believing that even in his sinful state he can be acceptable to God through his own works. But this is the ultimate self-deception, for "the heart is deceitful above all things, and desperately wicked; who can know it?" (Jeremiah 17:9).

Finally, in Romans 1:31 Paul wrote that the heart is *devoid of natural affection*. He used the same expression in 2 Timothy 3:2–5, where he wrote, "Men will be lovers of themselves, lovers of money, boasters, proud, blasphemers, disobedient to parents, unthankful, unholy, unloving, unforgiving, slanderers, without self-control, brutal, despisers of good, traitors, headstrong, haughty, lovers of pleasure rather than lovers of God, having a form of godliness but denying its power."

This may create a problem for some Christians who know unsaved people who deeply, devotedly love their spouses, love their children, love their country. We might ask, "What does this passage mean when it says men are without natural affections, when unsaved people do display affection?"

What the Bible refers to in these passages is that the human heart, because of the degradation by the Fall, cannot perform the function for which emotional capacity was given at creation. Remember that the primary function of emotion was not to love wife, children, country, or home. The primary purpose of emotional capacity was to love God. And so people are indeed without natural affection; that is, the capacity to exercise love toward God.

When we put all these passages together, we might recoil and rebel against the revelation God has given us concerning the human heart. In that case we should remember that even if we have been made a new creation in Christ Jesus and have been given a new capacity of heart, the old capacity of heart has not changed. All that we have covered concerning the natural heart characterizes each of us, even though we have been made new creatures in Christ. Our natural hearts still are lustful, vile, foolish, hard, impenitent, blind, erring, evil, deceived, and without natural affection. Because we have been made new creatures in Christ does not mean we no longer have the capacity to manifest the old lusts, the old desires, the old immorality—for those capacities are still there.

But we have been given a new capacity of emotion, and we can submit ourselves to the control of the Spirit of God. Unless our new capacity is energized by the Spirit of God, however, the old capacity will manifest itself. We cannot have victory over the old heart until we understand its capacities, and until we accept and appropriate God's provision for victory.

Notes

1. Understanding how strongly our affections control our actions is a genuine key to godly living. While an intellectual knowledge of Christ and His Word can definitely change the way we think, act, and live, it is not until He becomes the object of our affections that we begin to obey God from the heart and take genuine pleasure in doing His will. Is He the object of your affections?

2. When we have difficulty grasping God's personal love for us, we would do well to keep in mind the Father's love for the Son. Imagine how much a human parent can love a son or daughter; then amplify that by God's infinite and perfect nature, remembering that we are completely identified with His Son, Jesus Christ. Although it becomes easy to doubt God's love when we face difficult or seemingly impossible circumstances, He does love us infinitely because we belong to Him through Jesus. We can trust His love.

3. Too often Christians in a "rocky" marriage postpone their total commitment to Christ, reasoning that they cannot get on with spiritual things until their personal lives are straightened out. Actually, the opposite is true. Just as Adam and Eve were designed to experience an ideal love relationship as their hearts enjoyed unbroken fellowship with God, the depth and quality of a marriage relationship will always be in direct proportion to the husband's and wife's relationship with Christ. The closer we draw to Him, the more our hearts will be enabled to love others with His quality of love—especially our spouses.

4. Notice that the Bible presents this downward spiral as inevitable. Once a society denies God, it will eventually elevate animals to a status above human beings. The only solution to today's unnatural emphasis on nature above humanity is spiritual revival—the turning of people's hearts back to God as His children who are faithful pray, obey, and share the gospel with everyone they can.

5. The homosexual movement attempts to justify its "vile passions" (the Bible's terminology) by calling for understanding and tolerance, or by accusing Christians of homophobia and hate mongering. The point is that God indeed hates homosexuality; but He loved homosexuals (and murderers, and adulterers, and all people) enough to die for them. God's love never compromises His holiness; and His holiness never compromises His love. Our view of both must be steadfast and unmoving.

6. Psychological treatment or counseling that rids the heart of guilt over present, willful sin is no solution to the sin problem. Guilt is to our hearts what pain is to our bodies. Ridding our bodies of the ability to sense pain when damage occurs would be disastrous. The same is true of callousness of the heart. Feelings of guilt warn us of spiritual and moral damage that is occurring in our lives, and call us to repentance and obedience before Him.

7. When we share the gospel with someone who is especially hard-hearted, remember that the task of drawing a person to Jesus Christ is God's, not ours. One organization has well said that "successful witnessing is taking the initiative to share Christ in the power of the Holy Spirit, leaving the results to God."

8. While we may recognize non-Christians' tendency to follow their feelings and thus be misled, we may not see that we Christians can commit the same error by indulging our feelings or even "letting the Spirit lead" without a sound knowledge of Scripture to keep us in check. The Bible teaches that there is no emotional shortcut to spiritual maturity, and that God has given us the Spirit of a "sound mind" to guide us better than our natural feelings can.

9. Sometimes even we Christians deceive ourselves concerning personal sin, based on how we compare with other Christians. "It can't be that bad," we

reason, "because so many other Christians do things that are so much worse." Our point of comparison is not other Christians, but Jesus Christ Himself. Anything in our lives that is contrary to Him or His Word is sin, no matter how it compares with other Christians' behavior.

10. As we understand that the Holy Spirit empowers our new capacity of heart, we can see how important it is to consistently walk in submission to Him. Of course, this requires that we consciously seek Him, that we "hunger and thirst for righteousness" (Matthew 5:6). Personal devotions, weekly worship, Bible study, prayer alone and in groups, witnessing, and regular fellowship all will enhance our understanding and practice of submission to the Holy Spirit, who in turn empowers our new capacity of heart.

Questions

1. Read Romans 6:17 and Ephesians 6:6. What role does the heart play in obedience to God? What is necessary before someone can obey God from the heart?

2. Write down three examples of the ways in which we naturally translate our affections into actions. Based on these examples, in what ways might our actions be different if Jesus Christ is the object of our affections?

3. What would be your answer to someone who says that it is not possible to simultaneously love someone and condemn their actions? How might you relate this to Christ's death on the cross?

4. According to Romans 1:26–27, what is the cause of homosexuality? What appears to be the natural outcome of this path? What, in light of 1:16–17, is the only real solution to this problem, as well as to the other sins mentioned in 1:18–32?

5. In light of Romans 2:5 and Ephesians 4:18, do you think it is possible for someone to become less sensitive to the gospel and spiritual things as they continue through life? What might this imply about the importance of sharing Christ with children and teens? Does it mean we should cease communicating the gospel to those who are unresponsive? Why or why not?

6. Can you recall an area of emotional expression or action from your heart that changed when you trusted Christ as Savior? In your opinion, why did that area change?

CHAPTER 6

THE NEW HEART

1 John 4:7–21

A new heart has been given to the child of God. Through the new creation, a new emotional capacity has been given to the believer that makes it possible for us to fulfill the purpose for which we were created.

First John 4:19 tells us, "We love Him because He first loved us." Until this new capacity was given, man was without natural affection. He could neither know God's love, nor respond to it—yet John could affirm in 1 John 4:19, "We love Him." This is a result of the new creation. The fact that we love Him demonstrates that we have received new hearts, a new capacity for emotion. This is affirmed in a number of other passages.

For example, Romans 5:5 says, "Hope does not disappoint, because the love of God has been poured out in our hearts by the Holy Spirit who was given to us." God's love is poured out *in our hearts*. This does not so much emphasize that God's love has been manifested *through* us as it emphasizes that God's love has been manifested *to* us by the Holy Spirit who is God's gift to us.

In 2 Corinthians 4:6 Paul asserted the same truth as he wrote, "It is the God who commanded light to shine out of darkness who has shone in our hearts to give the light of the knowledge of the glory of God in the face of Christ." Scripture frequently presents the thought that God makes His entrance into one's life through the mind, then from the mind into the heart, and then from the heart into the will. But this verse suggests that God makes His entrance into one's life through the heart. The heart receives God's love, and then through the heart enlightenment is given to the child of God. Notice that God commanded the light to shine out of darkness and shine *in our hearts* to give the light of the knowledge of the glory of God in the face of Jesus Christ.

Paul writes in 2 Corinthians 1:22 that God "also has sealed us and given us the Spirit in our hearts as a deposit." This seal is the Spirit of

God, who comes to dwell in the believer's heart, the seat of emotions. As a result, the person who formerly had only a vile, lustful, foolish, hard, and impenitent heart now has a new heart.

Again, 2 Corinthians explains, "You are our epistle written in our hearts, known and read by all men; you are manifestly an epistle of Christ, ministered by us, written not with ink but by the Spirit of the living God, not on tablets of stone but on tablets of flesh, that is, of the heart" (3:2–3). Here Scripture confirms that the truth that came to these believers through the gospel penetrated their *hearts*. Their transformed lives were evidence they had received the truth the apostles presented to them.

A New Capacity to Love

Speaking to His disciples in the Upper Room, our Lord anticipated their new capacity to love as a result of the new birth. He said, "This is My commandment, that you love one another as I have loved you. Greater love has no one than this, than to lay down one's life for his friends. You are My friends if you do whatever I command you. No longer do I call you servants, for a servant does not know what his master is doing; but I have called you friends . . ." (John 15:12–15). When Christ used the word *friend*, He was emphasizing that He had established a new heart-to-heart relationship. The disciples had been His servants, and He had been their Master. Now, however, that servant/master relationship was superseded by an intimate relationship based on affection.

This love described by God's Word is not a purification of the old heart; it is not the remodeling, the remaking, or the refurbishing of the old capacity. Rather, God—through the new birth—has given us a new emotional capacity with which we may love God, receive God's love, and love others.

God's Word contains two different Greek words translated into English as "love." The first word is the word *phileo*. *Phileo* love responds to that which is attractive. The natural person, with an unregenerate heart, may respond naturally to that which is attractive. He may love his wife, his children, his home, his country, his luxuries, and so on.

However, when the Bible refers to God's love, it uses—almost without exception—a second Greek word: *agapao*. *Agapao* is not love that responds to what is attractive; rather, it is love that manifests itself because the lover wills to love. Remember: "God so loved the world." Why? Because the world was attractive to Him? Never! A sin-cursed people could not be attractive in His sight. But God loved us because He willed to love us. While the concept of *phileo* emphasizes receiving, *agapao* emphasizes giving.

With these words in mind, we discover why love is evidence of being born into God's family. The proof that one has been born into God's family is to love as God loves—not responding to what is attractive, but loving even those who may be unattractive, because one wills to love. Such love manifests the new capacity to love which God gives every believer.

A New Conflict

Because both the old capacity and new capacity are present within the believer, there is a constant conflict going on inside the child of God. This conflict is absent in the unbeliever, because the unbeliever does not have a second, new capacity warring against the first. The unbeliever may have conflicts *within* this area of life, but he cannot have conflicts *between* the old capacity and the new.

Because we, as new creatures in Christ, have been given this new capacity, we are engaged in a continual warfare within the emotional realm, determining whether the old heart or the new heart will manifest its fruit. In 1 John 2:9–11 we see this conflict spelled out for us: "He who says he is in the light, and hates his brother, is in darkness until now. He who loves his brother abides in the light, and there is no cause for stumbling in him. But he who hates his brother is in darkness and walks in darkness, and does not know where he is going, because the darkness has blinded his eyes." Again, in 1 John 4:20 we read, "If someone says, 'I love God,' and hates his brother, he is a liar; for he who does not love his brother whom he has seen, how can he love God whom he has not seen?"

Notice that these verses mention two manifestations of the capacity of affection. First, 1 John 2:9 refers to the person who says he is in the light and hates his brother. This hatred comes from the old capacity. Hatred will never, under any circumstances, come from the new capacity we receive at the new birth. The Bible says that he who hates his brother is in darkness, because that person is manifesting the fruit of the old nature, the old capacity. In contrast, the person who loves his brother abides in the light. This love comes from the new capacity, not the old.

So then, each of us who knows Christ has within us two capacities: love and hate. Both come from within the same realm of the heart. But while the old heart manifests itself in hatred, rancor, bitterness, and maliciousness, the new heart manifests itself as the love of God is revealed through the individual.

Understanding our conduct, our thinking, and our feelings can help us with the problems we face in the realm of our affections. We should trace every manifestation of our affections to its source. If it springs from the old heart, then we immediately know that it is wrong. If it can be traced to the new heart, then we know that the Holy Spirit is manifesting His fruit through us. But we should never mistakenly believe that somehow the old heart will be changed, so that it will no longer reveal its corrupt fruit. As we already have seen, we face a continual battle of our old mind against our new mind. Likewise, then, in the area of emotion we face a daily battle between the old heart and the new. And—as we will see later—we also face a battle between the old will and the new. Every person who becomes a Christian through the new birth faces a continuous warfare in every area of personality, though victory is available to each one of us.

New Affections

Since God's Word has a great deal to say concerning the Christian's affections, we would do well to examine some of the many passages of Scripture that exhort us in the realm of the heart.

First, there are certain negative commandments, that is, things we are *not* to do or are to *stop* doing. For example, 1 John 2:15 commands concerning the believer's relationship to the world, "Do not love the world or the things in the world. If anyone loves the world, the love of the Father is not in him." This tells us that if anyone loves the world, it is because he manifests the old capacity. It is not the new heart doing the loving; it is not the love of the Father loving the world through him. Thus the negative command, "Do not love the world."

This same truth is presented in James 4:4—"Adulterers and adulteresses! Do you not know that friendship with the world is enmity with God? Whoever therefore wants to be a friend of the world makes himself an enemy of God." What James was communicating in this verse, and John in the passage before, is that the God-given capacity to love may be prostituted. Through the old heart, the Christian may focus his affections on that which is displeasing and distasteful to God. Therefore believers are commanded to abstain from such spiritual prostitution, which is an evidence of perverted affection.

Ephesians 5:3–6 commands all Christians concerning a second great area in the realm of affection: "Fornication and all uncleanness or covetousness, let it not even be named among you, as is fitting for saints; neither filthiness, nor foolish talking, nor coarse jesting, which are not fitting, but rather giving of thanks. For this you know, that no fornicator, unclean person, nor covetous man, who is an idolater, has any inheritance in the kingdom of Christ and God. Let no one deceive you with empty words, for because of these things the wrath of God comes upon the sons of disobedience." In these very clear words we see that no child of God has any right to manifest his or her affections in any immoral act, word, or thought. We all have the potential within our hearts to practice all these things. But Christians are not to give a place to the adversary or to manifest his capacity of affection in these directions.

In 1 Thessalonians 4:3–7 we read, "This is the will of God, your sanctification: that you should abstain from sexual immorality; that each of you should know how to possess his own vessel in sanctification and honor, not in passion of lust, like the Gentiles who do not know God; that no one should take advantage of and defraud his brother in this matter, because the Lord is the avenger of all such, as we also forewarned you and testified. For God did not call us to uncleanness, but in holiness."

Again, it is very plain that believers should abstain from fornication. Many people to whom this was written had practiced immoral acts in the name of religion before they met Jesus Christ as Savior. They especially (as is true of many in our day) still had the potential to manifest the old affection in all kinds of immorality. But for Christians, such acts are now unthinkable, because God has called us to holiness.

Second, the Bible offers many positive exhortations which call for a response from believers. For example, Colossians 3:2 commands us, "Set your mind on things above, not on things on the earth. For you died, and your life is hidden with Christ in God." And Romans 12:9–10 says, "Let love be without hypocrisy. Abhor what is evil. Cling to what is good. Be kindly affectionate to one another with brotherly love, in honor giving preference to one another." Here we see that a genuine evidence of the new capacity to love will be a love that is without hypocrisy. No empty profession of affection, no empty endearing words like those salespeople use to establish rapport with a customer; but rather a genuine manifestation of the love of Christ toward those whom Christ loves. This is love without hypocrisy, true brotherly love.

Again, Romans 13:8 puts every child of God in debt: "Owe no one anything except to love one another, for he who loves another has fulfilled the law." This is one obligation that cannot be met or reduced through monthly payments! It requires weekly, daily, hourly, and moment-by-moment payments to discharge the debt God has put upon us. He commands us to constantly live out the new heart that has been given to us. How? By loving one another.

In 1 Thessalonians 4:9–10, Paul first forbids all manifestations of uncleanness, then writes, "Concerning brotherly love you have no need that I should write to you, for you yourselves are taught by God to love one another; and indeed you do so toward all the brethren who are in all Macedonia. But we urge you, brethren, that you increase more and more." Paul's desire for those who had walked in uncleanness, licentiousness, and lust, who had been the embodiment of the fruits of the old heart, was that they might now live out the fruits of the new creation by their love for one another.

Peter wrote in much the same vein when he said, "Since you have purified your souls in obeying the truth through the Spirit in sincere love of the brethren, love one another fervently with a pure heart, having been born again, not of corruptible seed but incorruptible, through the word of God, which lives and abides forever" (1 Peter 1:23). Again God commands His children to love one another. In what way? With a pure heart, and fervently. Here is a vibrant love, a love that purifies the person by his very affection for those who are bound to him in the ties of the gospel (see also 1 Peter 2:17).

The apostle John is sometimes known as the apostle of love, because he devoted so much of his writings to the subject. For example, in 1 John 2:10 he wrote, "He who loves his brother abides in the light, and there is no cause for stumbling in him." Then in 3:11–12 of the same letter he wrote, "This is the message that you heard from the beginning, that we should love one another, not as Cain who was of the wicked one and murdered his brother. And why did he murder him? Because his works were evil and his brother's righteous." In verse 14 we find, "We know that we have passed from death to life, because we love the brethren." Notice that the first biblically recorded public crime committed after the Fall was a crime against love. Cain murdered his brother, Abel, and in so doing sinned against love. John, therefore, conscious of that first outworking of the old heart, says that we who have been born into God's family must be very careful lest we repeat in one form or another Cain's sin. Positively stated, the evidence that we have passed from death into life is that we love one another.

Five New Testament epistles close with an exhortation to believers to greet or salute one another with a holy kiss. Why? In that day, Christian brothers greeted Christian brothers, and the sisters greeted the sisters, with a kiss. It was evidence that they loved one another fervently from pure hearts. It was not enough to simply say to someone, "I love you." Love was to be expressed. Christians often fail to express their affection for one another in Christ, and they may be hesitant to express their affection to God as well. But God has given each one a new heart with which to love, that it might manifest itself toward God and toward other believers.

The Word of God assumes that the Christian will love God "first" (1 John 4:19), and it also commands "that he who loves God must love his brother also" (1:21).

Since we are engaged in a warfare every moment of every day, the old heart seeks to express everything of which it is capable. The old heart wants to focus its affection on that which God hates. But the Holy Spirit has been given to us to energize us as new creatures in Christ and to produce His fruit of love in us, that we might realize His purpose for us as we enter into fellowship with His heart and manifest His love toward one another.

Notes

1. Some teachers today deny or ignore the fact that our old heart is utterly devoid of capacity to know and love God. They believe that is too bad to believe, or too harmful to our self-images. Yet the Bible clearly shows that the bad news concerning our old hearts pales alongside the good news that we can receive new hearts through faith in Jesus Christ.

2. As spelunkers (cave explorers) know, no matter how dark a cave may be, one small light is enough to dispel the darkness. In the same way, no matter how great the darkness was in our lives before knowing Christ, the light that has shone in our hearts can dispel everything that preceded it. Of course, that means we must be willing to leave all that darkness behind—not reliving it, retelling it, or reveling in it.

3. The concept of Messiah as a *friend* probably was quite revolutionary to the Jewish believers to whom Christ spoke. They looked for Messiah to come and rule as King, which He will do, but to be as lofty and unapproachable as King David or King Solomon had been. If we can understand the privilege and prestige of a personal friendship with a celebrity or sports star, we may begin to understand the unthinkable privilege that has been given to us in a friendship with Christ.

4. Are we learning to love as God loves—not based on the worthiness of the one being loved, but on the infinite love of God? If you are hurt when you initiate kindness toward another person and he or she doesn't reciprocate, that's a good clue that you are still expecting something in return for the emotional energy you have spent "loving" that person. On the other hand, when we allow Christ to express His love through us, looking to Him for our fulfillment, we are free to expect nothing in return.

5. As the old saying goes, "Talk is cheap." The Bible repeatedly draws a line of distinction between what believers say with their lips and what they prove through their actions. First John 2:9–11 says that if we voice love with our mouths but express the opposite with our attitudes and actions, we are walk-

ing in the same darkness that characterized our old condition of not knowing Christ. We must be careful not to become so caught up in the so-called "big" issues of the faith that we ignore those "little" things—gossip, slander, back-biting, quarreling, bitterness—that turn our lives into a lie.

6. Notice that the Bible does not present the inward conflict as an even fight between a "black dog and a white dog," as some might misrepresent it. It is a conflict between that which is old, dead, inferior, natural, powerless, unrighteous, and of the flesh; and that which is new, alive to God, superior, supernatural, empowered by God's Spirit, righteous, and of the Spirit. When we appropriate the new capacity of heart by willfully submitting to God's Spirit, there is no fight or contest at all. The superior will always prevail over the inferior.

7. If ever there has been a world-loving culture, it is ours. Every day we are bombarded with a mandate to love things, love money, love pleasure, love self, love sensory excitement, love the world. Besides distraction away from the things of God, loving the world allies us with an entire system that has been opposed to God and under the control of Satan ever since the Fall. To set our affections on the world is to be in love with a system that will ulti-mately and inevitably express itself in opposition to God and the things of God. We cannot remove ourselves from the world—but we can certainly decide that we will not allow our affections to become enslaved to it. We love God and simply live for a time in the world.

8. Ephesians 5:3–6 soundly condemns "filthiness . . . foolish talking . . . coarse jesting, which are not fitting." Now that these things have become common-place not only in restricted movies but on prime time television, we must be even more wary of the way they can creep into our lives and destroy our walk as well as our witness. What decisions can we make to ensure that the media's electronic programming does not become our internal programming? Hitting the "off" button is one sure key! But that will take tremendous com-mitment and self-control.

9. Enslavement to sex and our modern sex culture can be one of the most diffi-cult areas with which young believers struggle. More mature Christians, there-fore, have a distinct responsibility to set a proper example of pure living; to avoid creating obstacles that might cause the weaker brother or sister to stum-ble; and to encourage these believers along in their process of maturity. The issue of purity and impurity not only affects us directly, but can greatly influ-ence those around us.

10. One theme that permeates all these passages is the visible, tangible evidence of brotherly love that should be present among Christians. Though we say we are members of God's family, and may even call one another "brother" and

"sister," is our genuine love, concern, self-denial, sincerity and purity toward one another *visible* to those within our fellowship as well as to those on the outside? More specifically, is your personal behavior toward other believers something that is distinctly different, something that causes unbelievers to take notice?

11. One area of our lives that certainly brings out the conflict between the old capacity of heart and the new is how we relate to other family members—husband, wife, children, siblings. Not only are our family relationships the most dominant in our lives, they often are the last place we live out the love of Christ. Do any family relationships in your life need the touch of Christ's love today? If we yield ourselves to His control in even the most difficult situations, we will begin to see great changes as He lives—and loves—through us.

Questions

1. Read John 15:12–15. List some of the things people may turn to as substitutes for God's love and friendship. What specific substitutes were present in your life prior to your becoming a Christian? What changes has Christ's friendship made in your life since then?

2. List some specific ways in which Christians' love for one another might be lived out in sharp contrast to the world's usual way of doing things. What are some ways in which believers have shown you that kind of practical love? What are some ways you can show Christ's love to other believers within your own local fellowship?

3. According to 2 Corinthians 3:2–3, where do all outward expressions of Christ's transforming power begin? What enables or empowers these outward actions?

4. Looking back on this chapter, what are the two Greek words translated "love" in the New Testament? What characterizes each? What does each term emphasize?

5. Based on 1 John 2:9–11, what is the relationship between a Christian's words and actions? With which is God most concerned? What are the consequences of living the kind of hypocrisy described here? What do you think is the solution to this problem?

6. Relate Colossians 3:2 to the Christian's new capacity of heart. How would you describe an ideal relationship to the world? In light of 1 John 2:15, how do you make sure you are "in the world but not of the world"?

CHAPTER 7

THE OLD WILL

John 6:35–40, 60–65

It seems that every teacher has some idiosyncrasies—some teachers more than others. And I'm sure that one class at the seminary where I teach thought I had gone beyond all bounds when they read one of the questions on a final examination. The question was: "Wherein do you differ from a horse?" I was not trying to be facetious. I wanted the students to recall that when God created man He set him apart from all the animal creation. God endowed man with all the capacities of personality so that he could enter into fellowship with God. God did not give to animals a mind that can respond to the mind of God; a heart that can respond to the love of God; nor a will with which to obey God. But to human beings God gave a mind, a heart, and a will—and when Adam fell, humankind suffered the effects of the Fall in each of these aspects of the total personality.

Having looked at the mind and the heart, we now examine the issue of the will. First we will consider the will at the time of creation, and then we will examine the results of the Fall in the area of the will, so that we can understand those things that characterize the will of the natural man apart from the experience of new birth in Jesus Christ.

The Will of Adam

Again we look first at the record of creation provided for us in Genesis, where God said, "Let Us make man in Our image, according to Our likeness . . . . So God created man in His own image; in the image of God He created him; male and female He created them" (1:26–27). In Genesis 2:15–17, we also read, "The LORD God took the man and put him in the garden of Eden to tend and keep it. And the LORD God commanded the man, saying, 'Of every tree of the garden you may freely eat; but of the tree of the knowledge of good and evil you shall not eat, for in the day that you eat of it you shall surely die.' "

In previous chapters we have seen that God gave Adam the capability of exercising each part of his capacity toward God so that Adam might enjoy fellowship with Him. Adam, for example, was given the responsibility of naming all the animals, which was an exercise of his mind. Through his mind Adam knew more and more of the greatness of God's power and wisdom, and thus entered more deeply into fellowship with God. It was also God's custom to come to the garden in the cool of the day, giving Adam an opportunity to exercise his heart toward God. Adam enjoyed fellowship with God heart-to-heart as well as mind-to-mind.

But if Adam, in his total person, was to enjoy fellowship with God, there must be some way in which Adam would subject himself to the will of God, so that the will of God and the will of Adam might enjoy fellowship together. This is the precise reason we read in Genesis 2:15–17 that God set apart one particular tree, forbidding Adam to eat of its fruit.

God's creation was a perfect creation. There was nothing poisonous in the fruit of that tree that would harm Adam physically. There was nothing in it which of itself could defile Adam. Rather, God prohibited Adam from taking of its fruit in order to test Adam's obedience to God's will, so that through the exercise of his will Adam could enjoy fellowship with God in the area of the will. If Adam's *mind* was in fellowship with the mind of God, and Adam's *heart* was in fellowship with the heart of God, but Adam could not exercise his *will* toward God, there could not have been full fellowship between the creature and the Creator. Therefore, in order for Adam and God to enjoy the fullest fellowship together, God set apart the tree of the knowledge of good and evil and forbade Adam to partake of it.

It is extremely important to notice that when God prohibited Adam's eating of the fruit of this tree, He did not do this to withhold from Adam something that would have been a blessing or benefit to him. Rather, He did it to bring the greatest possible blessing to Adam, and to bring him into complete fellowship with God.

In Genesis 3 we find the record of how Eve was dissuaded from the path of perfect obedience to God's will, and as a result lost all fellowship with God. In Genesis 3:1 we discover that this temptation appealed first of all to the mind of Eve. Satan began by raising a question in her mind: "Has God indeed said, 'You shall not eat of every tree of the garden'?" This raised a question of fact. This was a challenge in the area of mind. Next, Satan moved from the mind to the heart, saying, "God knows that in the day you eat of it your eyes will be opened, and you will be like God, knowing good and evil" (3:5). This was a subtle temptation to doubt the love of God, to doubt the goodness of God. Satan's subtle seed, planted in the mind of Eve through his original question, was that God was not the loving, good God that He set Himself forth to be—for if He really loved Eve, He would not withhold that which would make her like Himself. When we are jealous, we reserve for ourselves something which we claim exclusively. Jealousy is a sin against love—and Satan was saying to Eve that God was jealous, that He was selfish. Satan further implied that in being jealous and selfish God had withheld from her something that would be for her greater good. Thus Eve was led to doubt the love of God.

When we entertain a thought in the mind, and then let that thought penetrate to the heart so that we love that thought or idea, that love soon moves upon the will. So "when the woman saw that the tree was good for food, that it was pleasant to the eyes, and a tree desirable to make one wise, she took of its fruit and ate. She also gave to her husband with her, and he ate" (Genesis 3:6). Notice that the Fall did not come when the woman exercised her mind and recognized that the tree was good for food. Nor did the Fall occur when Eve's emotions were stirred and she saw that it was pleasant to the eyes. The Fall did not even take place when the woman entertained Satan's suggestion that she eat of the fruit to become wise. The Fall *did* take place, however, when Eve took the fruit and ate it. The sin was not in Eve's looking, evaluating, and considering—but in exercising her will to stretch out her hand, pluck the fruit, and then eat it in disobedience to the commandment of God.

The Effects of the Fall

Because of this one act of the will in which both Adam and Eve were involved, there were far-reaching effects. We have already discovered that because of this sin the human mind was darkened; and while people did not lose the ability to think, they could not *know* God. Also, in the realm of the heart, the emotions were degraded, so that while human beings did not lose the capacity to love, their emotional capacity was so degenerated they could not love God. But even as great as were the effects of the Fall in the realms of the mind and heart, the Bible indicates that the greatest effect of Adam's sin was in the realm of the will. Because of Adam's sin, the will of man is a will that is enslaved to sin, a will that lives for sin and loves sin. It is a will entirely under the dominion of sin.

Romans 6:14 tells the Christian, "Sin shall not have dominion over you." The word *dominion* is the word for a master or sovereign ruler who exercises authority and control over an individual. This verse tells believers that sin should no longer have dominion over them as it formerly had. This statement clearly reveals the relationship between the unbeliever's sin and his will. Sin has absolute dominion over the unbeliever. It is the overlord of unbelievers, their taskmaster. They are in bondage to it. Romans 6:16–20 confirms this: "Do you not know that to whom you present yourselves slaves to obey, you are that one's slaves whom you obey, whether of sin to death, or of obedience to righteousness? But God be thanked that though you were slaves of sin, yet you obeyed from the heart that form of doctrine to which you were delivered . . . . For when you were slaves of sin, you were free in regard to righteousness." These verses describe the basic principle of the individual's relationship to sin. The individual is a servant of sin; he is not free to do as he pleases; he is a bondslave of sin.

A true servant sets his own will aside and is expected to do the will of his master immediately and implicitly. He has no right to question an order given by his master. Thus the Bible tells us that before we met Jesus Christ as Savior, we were in bondage as servants to sin, without any will of our own, without any choice in the matter, following whatever it dictated to us.

Freedom of the Will

We often hear debates concerning the freedom of the will. It is helpful, therefore, to understand what the Bible has to say on this subject. First, we must define what is meant by *freedom of the will*. With our lawless natures, we like to define freedom as the right to do whatever we please, with no restraint on us from the outside, with no obligation to anyone but ourselves. However, that concept of freedom is not found anywhere in Scripture. In essence, it is the philosophy and practice of Satan.

In the scriptural sense of the word, a creature is free when it can move in its native element, fulfilling the function for which it was created. A fish is free when it can move about in the water; but when we remove that fish from the water, it loses its freedom. Likewise, a bird is free when it can move in the air, because that is its native element, the sphere in which it was designed to function. And a person is free when he can move in his native element, the sphere for which he was created. That sphere, as God created it, is one of continual fellowship with God. But because of the Fall, mankind was expelled from its native element and consequently is no longer free. Fallen man is "free" only in the sense that a bird in a cage is free; a caged bird is free to move within that cage, but its life is defined and bounded by that cage. What a mockery it would be to take a free-flying bird out of the air, confine it in a cage, and then say to the bird, "You are free."

In the same way, the natural person is free to move about within the element of sin. But our lives are circumscribed by sin. Sin is the foundation under us, and the canopy over us. A person's total life apart from Jesus Christ is lived in the element of sin and in the sphere of sin. And since we are not free to live in our native element of fellowship with God, we cannot say we are free. We are not free until we can move within that area for which we were created—and that area is the area of pleasing God, because all things, including humankind, were created for God. "By Him all things were created that are in heaven and that are on earth, visible and invisible, whether thrones or dominions or principalities or powers. All things were created through Him and for Him" (Colossians 1:16).

Every person enjoys a certain amount of freedom. For example, when you get dressed, you may choose to put on a blue tie, a black tie, or a red tie. You are free to choose the color of the car you buy, or the location of the house you live in. But that is not freedom in a biblical sense of the word. Dr. Donald Grey Barnhouse used to say that a man is free to jump from the fifteenth floor of a building—but he does not have the freedom to jump back up again. This is a perfect illustration of the limits on our freedom.

Various passages of Scripture also show us restrictions on human freedom. In Galatians 5:17 we read, "The flesh lusts against the Spirit, and the Spirit against the flesh; and these are contrary to one another, so that you do not do the things that you wish." Notice the last part of the verse: "You do not [literally, cannot] do the things that you wish." There are some things the will cannot do. A little farther on, in verse 19, we read, "The works of the flesh are evident, which are . . . ." The list that follows enumerates the works of the natural person's will. When the non-Christian wills, acts, chooses, or decides, he chooses in the realm of sin, for all the works of the flesh listed in verses 19–21 are sins.

In Romans 7:23 Paul wrote, "I see another law in my members, warring against the law of my mind, and bringing me into captivity to the law of sin which is in my members." The phrase *bringing me into captivity to the law of sin* shows that each one of us is a captive, a slave to sin. Sin is our lord. Romans 5:12 reminds us that "through one man [that is, Adam] sin entered the world and death through sin, and thus death spread to all men, because all sinned." We are dead in that we cannot fulfill that for which we were created by God: to enjoy fellowship with Him. Then, in verse 17 of the same chapter, we read, "By the one man's offense death reigned through the one." And in verse 20–21 we read, "But where sin abounded, grace abounded much more, so that as sin reigned in death, even so grace might rein through righteousness to eternal life through Jesus Christ our Lord." Notice the word *reigned* in verses 17 and 21. Here the Bible portrays sin as a mighty ruler, a dictator, who manifests an unopposable will in giving commands to all the serfs under him. Sin has dominion over all the unsaved in the same way a monarch reigns over all his subjects.

In Ephesians 2:2–3 we read that we "once walked according to the course of this world, according to the prince of the power of the air, the spirit who now works in the sons of disobedience, among whom also we all once conducted ourselves in the lusts of our flesh, fulfilling the desires of the flesh and of the mind, and were by nature children of wrath, just as the others." The expressions *walked* and *conducted ourselves* show that when the will acted within the individual, it produced the lust of the flesh and desires of the flesh and mind which were contrary to the nature and character of God.

It is very clear from these passages that because of Adam's sin, the human will was entirely deadened toward God. The unregenerate person cannot obey God. The natural person has no desire to obey God. We are by nature rebels against God. We are lawless, and we manifest our lawlessness and rebellion against God by living under the dominion of sin, serving as sin's vassals.

This is precisely our Lord's view of man's will as revealed in John 6. In that chapter, Jesus had presented evidence that He was the Son of God, the Messiah. Through His words and works, He had sought to convince an unbelieving nation that He had come to bring light and life to the world. But those to whom He came rejected Him. They did not believe Him. Therefore Christ pointed out that Israel's unbelief was not because Christ had not authenticated His Person and had not validated His words. There was another explanation for the nation's unbelief. In John 6:38 Jesus said, "I have come down from heaven, not to do My own will, but the will of Him who sent Me." In this verse Christ contrasts His will to the will of those unbelievers. They wanted to do their own will, which was in rebellion to the will of God. But Christ's will was not like the will of fallen humanity, for He came to do the will of the One who sent Him.

Then, in John 6:44, Jesus said, "No one can come to Me unless the Father who sent Me draws him." He also said in verse 65, "I have said to you that no one can come to Me unless it has been granted to him by My Father." Why does our Lord speak of the utter impossibility of a person coming to Him unless God the Father draws him? It is because Christ knew that the will of the natural man is deadened toward God, that the natural man is bound and enslaved by sin, that the natural man lives under dominion of sin, takes his orders from sin, and serves sin.

Sin will never point a person toward Jesus Christ, and sin will never relax its reign over an individual. It is only as Jesus Christ breaks the shackles of sin and sets the captive free that an individual will respond to Christ's invitation to come to Him for light and life.

A person, in the deadness of his will toward God, may do things that morally or ethically are acceptable and approved by society. But he can never do anything that is pleasing to God because all that he does, he does in response to the commands of sin, which is his master. And God cannot and will not accept obedience to sin as acceptable to Himself. This should strike in us a very dark and somber note. There is no joy in proclaiming the truth of God's Word that all people are the bondslaves of sin—but there is great joy in the message of the gospel that all those who believe in Christ will be made a new creation and will be given a new will in order that they might obey the Word of God.

Notes

1. One "no-no"—that's all God gave Adam and Eve in the garden, and yet they focused on that one prohibition as though it was all they knew of God. Isn't it interesting today that those who do not know Jesus Christ focus their resentment on all the prohibitions God has graciously given us, as though that is all He has said. They see nothing of His love, care, grace, mercy, or provision in the warnings He has given us. Once we come to know Christ, this is a difficult habit to break. But as our hearts and minds are enlightened by His Spirit, we can begin to see how perfect His commandments really are. Most important, we are now free to obey them.

2. How quickly doubts about God's love can lead us into sin! Unpleasant circumstances, illness, death of a loved one, financial struggles, career pressures, difficult relationships—any of these can cause us to doubt God's love for us, which in turn opens the door for us to take matters into our own hands, resulting in sins of attitude or of actions. It may be a cliché to say we should "never doubt in the dark what God has shown us in the light," but the continual encouragement from His Word that He is perfectly sovereign and faithful is not a cliché. Both in good circumstances and in bad, we would do well to periodically review what we know to be true about His faithful love, and to remind ourselves of these things when the next crisis comes up.

3. The process Eve went through before she took the fruit and ate is very revealing. Although the act itself was the sin, the process of looking, evaluating, and deciding should be familiar to all of us. How often do we fall into sin simply because we wanted to get close enough to it to look, evaluate, and then decide? There is in one of our national parks a rocky outcrop from which numerous people have fallen hundreds of feet to their deaths—even though

it is ringed with a fence and large warning signs. None of the individuals who went beyond the fence and signs intended to die; they just wanted to get a little closer look at the danger. Some sins can be the same kind of trap for us. If we want to avoid them, we need to stay as far away as possible—not creep up for a closer look.

4. Although it is already enslaved to sin, our fallen human will resents the prospect of God exercising His will over ours as unfair, unjust, and uncalled for. The unsaved person believes he is master of his own fate—yet apart from the enablement of God's Spirit is entirely incapable of choosing God's righteousness over his own selfish desires. Do we see the world around us as enslaved, chained to a corrupt, fallen human will? And do we envision for these slaves the great joy that comes with freedom in Christ? This perspective could give us an entirely new urgency in our efforts to take the gospel to others.

5. In today's political climate, we could easily get the false impression that "freedom" is an absolute absence of restraint. Yet those who talk loudest about freedom of expression and unrestrained diversity are the first to put limits on others who disagree with them. This is the nature of the fallen human will. Even when it claims to be free from outside influence or control, it is compelled to set its own new, self-serving limits. In our lost state, we intuitively know we need limits. But in our spiritual deadness, we do not want those limits to reveal our sinfulness or condemn us. And according to the Bible, in our lost condition we are not even capable of obeying the rules we set for ourselves. Therefore we must liberalize them even further. The result is the downward spiral described in Romans 1. The only answer to this vicious cycle is the new will that Christ gives us when we give our lives to Him.

6. This concept of the human condition is extremely distasteful to non-Christians; yet it can be illustrated by simply asking them what kind of success they have had in fulfilling New Year's resolutions, keeping secrets, or obeying the posted speed limit. If we are not naturally inclined to obey even the simplest human constraints, we certainly are not going to be capable of taking seriously the commandments of God!

7. This should remind us of the difference between our responsibility and God's responsibility in witnessing to unbelievers. Our responsibility is to share a clear message of God's love; His responsibility is to draw men, women, boys, and girls to Himself.

8. A proper understanding of the will of the unsaved should strike a note of caution in our minds. Not only does a Christian have nothing in common spiritually with a non-Christian, but the two are in opposite camps morally. This means that Christians who insist on dating non-Christians or becoming romantically involved with unbelievers are not going to grow and mature in the new capacity of will God has given them. Likewise, Christian business people who do not make allowance for the fallen, unregenerate will of unbe-

lievers may open themselves up to fraud, financial deception, or worse. As Jesus said, His disciples should be "wise as serpents and harmless as doves" (Matthew 10:16).

Questions

1. Why do you think God created human beings with a will? What light does Genesis 1:26–27 shed on this?

2. In Genesis 2:15–17, what allowance did God make in contrast to His prohibition against eating of the tree of the knowledge of good and evil? In addition to the consequences Adam and Eve suffered for their sin, what privilege did they lose when they chose to sin (see Genesis 3:22–23)?

3. What examples of our natural bent toward disobedience can you give from everyday life? In what ways do you see this arise in your own life?

4. Briefly describe the relationship between obedience and blessing in the Christian life. How does this relate to the internal arguments that might convince us not to obey God? Where should we look for the encouragement to obey God even when it seems illogical?

5. Look again at the rationalization Eve went through before she ate the fruit (Genesis 3:6). How does this compare with 1 John 2:15–17? Can you give examples of the way we are tempted daily in the three areas mentioned in those verses?

6. How would you describe a non-Christian's personal freedom? According to the Bible, what are some of the limits on that freedom? Can unrestrained moral freedom coexist with the Holy Spirit in the life of a Christian (see Romans 5:17)? Why or why not?

7. If an unbeliever is in bondage to sin and cannot choose God, how does anyone ever come to know Christ personally (John 6:44–45)?

CHAPTER 8

THE NEW WILL

Colossians 3:1–15

The natural man is a bondslave to sin. According to Romans 6:14, the unregenerate person is under the absolute dominion of sin. Romans 6:16–17 tells us that people are enslaved to sin. But, through the work of new creation (2 Corinthians 5:17), the believer in Christ is brought into a glorious freedom. The chains of sin which bound him as a slave have been broken. The door that confined him within certain prescribed limitations has been opened, and he has been liberated from sin as a master he is obligated to obey. And this is the wonderful truth we will examine in this chapter.

Liberty in Christ

Romans 6 deals with the glorious liberty that belongs to the children of God. We discover in verses 12–13 that God has given the believer freedom from bondage to sin as master over him. Paul writes, "Do not let sin reign in your mortal body [that is, as it used to], that you should obey it in its lusts. And do not present your members as instruments of unrighteousness to sin [as you used to have to do], but present yourselves to God as being alive from the dead, and your members as instruments of righteousness to God."

Paul could make such appeals as "do not let sin reign" and "do not present your members as instruments of unrighteousness" only because of the freedom from bondage given to us when we become new creations in Christ Jesus. The appeal to not let sin continue to reign in your mortal bodies, as it used to is based on a liberation that is the result of God's imparting a new capacity in the area of the will.

In fact, whenever the Bible appeals to believers to do something that will please God, it is never an appeal to the old will. God never makes an appeal to the old mind, to the old heart, or to the old will. God never asks the old mind to receive spiritual truths or divine revelation.

He never appeals to the old heart to receive and respond to the love of God. He never makes an appeal to the old will to do something that will be acceptable to God, or to obey God. God knows the limitations of the old capacities and never makes an appeal to them. So when the Bible admonishes the child of God, as in this passage, it is an appeal to a person with a new capacity imparted by the miracle of new creation.

In Romans 6:18 Paul begins, "Having been set free from sin . . . ." We must be very careful here. Paul did not say, "You have been made free from any possibility of committing sin again." Nor did he say, "You have been made free of the possibility of the old will obeying sin further." Rather, he did say, "You have been made free from the obligation to obey the sin nature and to obey the dictates of the old will."

How are we made free from sin? Only as we are given freedom by the new creation in Jesus Christ. Then we are made free from enslavement to the old will, because an entirely new capacity is imparted to us. This fact is affirmed in Romans 6:22, where we read, "Having been set free from sin, and having become slaves of God, you have your fruit to holiness, and the end, everlasting life." We were bondslaves of sin, which we served voluntarily. But now we have been made free from sin and have become servants, literally slaves, to God. There is now a choice within the capacity of will. A choice pleasing to the old capacity will result in sin; a choice conforming to the new capacity will result in obedience and righteousness and holiness.

Romans 8:2 teaches us the same truth: "The law of the Spirit of life in Christ Jesus has made me free from the law of sin and death." The principle which operated within us as unsaved individuals here is referred to as the principle, or law, of sin and death. It is called the principle of sin and death because sin is its character and death is its result. Though I once served this principle as master and lord because I had no other option, now by the Holy Spirit (which Paul calls "the law of the Spirit of life in Christ Jesus") I have been made free from the law of sin and death. Again, this does not propose that we have been removed from the possibility of sinning. That would mean that the old mind, the old heart, and the old will have been eradicated—a misconception that cannot be supported from Scripture.

Rather, the Bible says that there is an emancipation from servitude to the old capacity, because a new capacity has been imparted through the new birth. "What the law could not do in that it was weak through the flesh, God did by sending His own Son in the likeness of sinful flesh, on account of sin: He condemned [or judged] sin in the flesh, that the righteous requirement of the law might be fulfilled in us who do not walk according to the flesh but according to the Spirit" (Romans 8:3–4). God's purpose is to produce righteousness in his children. But righteousness never comes from the operation of the old mind, the old heart, and the old will. Instead, righteousness comes as the Holy Spirit energizes the new mind, the new heart, and the new will.

In Galatians 5:1 we find a principle concerning the law in relation to the old capacities the child of God still possesses. Galatians 4 deals with the relationship of the individual to the law of Moses. The law cannot save; neither can it sanctify. Then, having shown that faith in the Lord Jesus Christ liberates from bondage to the law, Paul gives this appeal: "Stand fast therefore in the liberty by which Christ has made us free, and do not be entangled again with a yoke of bondage" (Galatians 5:1). Paul addressed a question to those who were considering the idea of submitting to the Law of Moses as a guiding principle for fulfilling God's requirements for the Christian life. He asked, "Why would those who have been liberated from the bondage of the law seek to put themselves back into bondage again?" And then he affirmed the glorious truth of liberation from any obligation to serve the law of Moses or the law of sin (the old capacity) that dwells within us.

Continual Conflict

Because God has imparted a new capacity of will to the child of God, the believer is in constant conflict. There is an unrelenting and ceaseless warfare going on within him all the time. This warfare is vividly described in Galatians 5:17: "The flesh lusts against the Spirit, and the Spirit against the flesh; and these are contrary to one another, so that you do not do the things that you wish." The word *flesh* in this verse refers to the sum total of the individual's personality—mind, emotions, and will—all of which has been corrupted by the Fall. The word *Spirit* in Galatians 5:17 refers to the Holy Spirit living in the child of God and expressing Himself in the new creation—the new capacity of mind, the new capacity of heart, and the new capacity of will.

In the area of the mind, there is constant warfare. What the old mind loves, the new hates; and what the new desires, the old despises. That same warfare is true in the realm of the heart. What the old heart desires and lusts after, the new capacity hates and despises; what the new seeks, the old utterly repudiates. That same warfare is true also in the area of the will. What the old will delights to serve, the new will resists obeying; the old utterly hates what the new desires to do.

So in every area of the total personality there is constant warfare. The old capacity and the new will never, under any circumstances, agree on a thought, word, or deed. Never will the old mind agree with the new mind. Never will the old heart agree with the new heart. Never will the old will agree with the new will. If the old purposes one thing, the new contradicts it; and if the new would set something into operation, the old immediately seeks to counter it. Therefore Christians are facing constant, ceaseless, unrelenting warfare in the areas of mind, heart, and will every moment we live.

In Romans 7 we find Paul's testimony concerning this warfare within himself. He wrote in verses 22–23, "I delight in the law of God according to the inward man. But I see another law in my members, warring against the law of my mind, and bringing me into captivity to the law of sin which is in my members." Again the fact of constant warfare is emphasized. When he says, "I delight in the law of God according to the inward man," he is referring to the sum total of the capacities given him in the new creation. Paul says that his new mind revels in the truth of God, his new heart loves the Person of God, and his new will delights to obey the will of God. But when with his new mind he knows, loves, and serves God, immediately war is declared by the old against the new. Thus the old mind fights against the truth of God, the old heart against the love of God, and the old will against obedience to God.

We will never understand the conflict Christians face day by day and moment by moment until we grasp this truth concerning the warfare that goes on within us. Again and again we face discouragement, defeat, and frustration, just as the apostle Paul did. He wrote in Romans 7:15–20 concerning his experience in conflict, "What I [the old] am doing, I [the new] do not understand. For what I [the new] will to do, that I [the old] do not practice; but what I [the new] hate, that I [the old] do. If, then, I [the old] do what I [the new] will not to do, I agree with the law that it is good [for it condemns me]. But now, it is no longer I [the new] who do it [this wicked thought, false affection, or disobedient act], but sin [the old capacity] that dwells in me. For I know that in me (that is, in my flesh [the old mind, heart, and will] nothing good dwells; for to will is present with me [because I have a new capacity of will], but how to perform what is good I do not find. For the good that I [the new] will to do, I [the old] do not do; but the evil I [the new] will not to do, that I [the old] practice. Now if I do what I [the new] will not to do, it is no longer I [the new capacity] who do it, but sin [the old capacity] that dwells in me."

Thus Paul explains the origin of this conflict. It is not a conflict from without, but it is a conflict from within. He says in verse 23, "I see another law in my members, warring against the law of my mind [the new capacity], and bringing me into captivity to the law of sin [the old capacity] which is in my members."

According to human reason, it would be wonderful if, at the moment we are saved, this old capacity would be eradicated; or when we reach a certain state of maturity or sanctification, this old capacity would be eliminated, leaving us with only a new heart, will, and mind. Some even teach that this is, indeed, what happens. But that is not consistent with Paul's experience, nor with the balance of Scripture. The Bible teaches that until the time of our translation into Christ's presence and our glorification, we will continue through life with both the old capacity and the new capacity. As a consequence we face a lifelong conflict. Though some claim that this fact is discouraging and defeating to the Christian, we actually can be grateful that the Word of God gives us very, very clearly the principles upon which we may experience victory over the old capacity. There is no question that the Bible teaches that we can, indeed, walk in triumph.

Appeals to the Will

In the chapters that follow, we will examine those portions of Scripture that give us instruction concerning the power provided by the Holy Spirit so that we who know Christ might live in a way that pleases Him. But before we move on we need to look at several places where the Bible makes a specific appeal to the Christian. These passages will emphasize that the Christian life is not a passive life, but an active one. It is true that the Christian life is a life of rest, a life of trust. But God also has given us a new will that He expects us to exercise. And we are commanded to exercise the new will toward God.

Romans 6:13 commands us, "Do not present your members as instruments of unrighteousness to sin, but present yourselves to God as being alive from the dead, and your members as instruments of righteousness to God." When you "present" yourself, you turn yourself over completely to another's control. The believer, then, is commanded to turn himself over to the Lord Jesus Christ, to be controlled by the Holy Spirit, so that righteousness might be reproduced in him by the Spirit's power. When Paul gives the command, "Present yourselves to God . . . and your members as instruments of righteousness to God," he is making an appeal to the new capacity of will. This is something the child of God can now do which he could not do before he was saved. He now has a new capacity, and can exercise that capacity in a Spirit-directed choice.

So when God's Word commands believers not to let sin continue reigning, and not to continue yielding their members to sin's control but to yield themselves to God, and to present their members as instruments of righteousness—it is calling for an act of the new will. In verse 16, Paul affirmed the same truth when he asked, "Do you not know that to whom you present yourselves slaves to obey, you are that one's slaves whom you obey, whether of sin to death, or of obedience to righteousness?" This shows us the capacity the child of God has, the capacity to present oneself as an obedient servant to God so that the fruits of righteousness may be reproduced in one.

In Ephesians 4:24, the Bible has another word to say concerning righteousness as God's objective in the new creation: "Put on the new man which was created according to God, in righteousness and true holiness." In this passage, Paul has already exhorted the child of God to put off the former manner of life (4:22). That putting off is an act of the will. But he is not to be left naked. He is to put on the new man so that instead of lying he will speak the truth; he can be angry and not sin; he will stop stealing; he will stop gossiping; and so on. This act of putting off and putting on is an act of the new will. The old will can never put off the things of the flesh—but the new will may obey God in this.

Colossians 3:9–10 addresses the same truth. It tells us of the divine work done for us through the new birth: "You have put off the old man with his deeds, and have put on the new man." The old man we have put off is the old mind, heart, and will. The new man we have put on is that which was imparted as the result of new creation. What are we to do since we have become new creatures in Jesus Christ? Paul says, "Put off all these" (3:8); then he mentions some of the sins of the flesh we are to put off. Next, in verse 12 he says, "As the elect of God, holy and beloved, put on . . . ," and then mentions the fruit that the Spirit will produce through the new creature. When Paul says "put off" and "put on," he is making an appeal to the new will, which can be in subjection to the Spirit of God. Through His power the righteousness of Christ will be reproduced in the believer.

Mentioning these verses in which an appeal is made to the will does not imply that the Christian life is lived out as we—through our own determination and our own strength—manifest the new mind, the new heart, and the new will. Not at all! Apart from the power of the Spirit of God, the child of God cannot perform this putting off and putting on. But when the Bible gives a command or an exhortation to the child of God, it is being given because sin's bondage has been broken through faith in Christ, because we have been freed from servitude to sin, and because we have received a new capacity, a new will, that we may fulfill that which God commands. Those who once were bondservants and slaves have been liberated. Sin's chains have been broken! Not only has the condemnation of sin been removed through the death of Christ, but the confining shackles of sin have been taken away. Now we may enjoy the liberty that belongs to the child of God, and enjoy full fellowship with Him!

Notes

1. One Bible teacher describes this choice between the old will and the new will as "catching a sin in mid-air." We see the temptation coming; we know it is an area of weakness; we have fallen victim to this sin time and time again; but because we can choose to exercise the new will in the power of the Holy Spirit rather than trying to fight off sin with the old will, we can catch it in "mid-air." We need to remember that our old will is powerless against sin and will never win that battle. Only the new will—exercised as we walk in the Spirit—will choose God's righteousness over the momentary pleasures of sin.

2. The misconception that Christians have been removed from the *possibility* of sinning has destroyed more than a few well-meaning believers who dropped their guard only to be blindsided by sin of a magnitude they had never known before. If there was no longer any possibility of sin, the New Testament would not repeatedly warn the Christian against sin. The freedom to now choose holiness over sin is a far greater miracle than removal from the possibility of it!

3. The New Testament often uses the Greek word *doulos,* translated "bondservant," to describe the believer's new relationship to Christ. Prior to trusting Christ, we are unwilling slaves to sin, born into servitude. *Doulos,* however, denotes a "slave by choice." This servant was someone who had been set free, but then chose to live in servitude to his master. Our enslavement to Christ is a servitude of choice, and is the only way we can experience true freedom from sin.

4. A sure sign of maturity in Christ is the amount of time we spend cultivating the new will through learning and obeying the Word of God. Let's face it— time is on the side of the old will. We have years and years of practice obeying its impulses. Moreover, even if we do nothing and remain passive in our relationship with Christ, the old nature will prevail in our thoughts and actions. It is only as we actively seek to foster the new will, in the power of the Holy Spirit, that we will begin to experience spiritual victory on a consistent, day-to-day basis.

5. How do we know that the conflict Paul describes in Romans 7:15–20 is not a thought process of the unsaved, dealing with the conflict between seeking God and remaining in sin? Because the Bible is very clear that the non-Christian does nothing to seek God (Romans 3:10–12). In the unregenerate heart there is no desire to do good or to seek God. Only *after* God has supernaturally drawn a person to faith in Christ is there a conflict between the old will and the new.

6. One of the things that makes the idea of eradication of the sin nature so attractive to the human heart is that it does away with spiritual lukewarmness or carnality. If eradication is true, then there are only Christians and sinners—there are no sinning Christians. However, God's Word and real life both tell us otherwise. In this life there is no such thing as instant spirituality, a cessation of sin's hostilities against us, or a point of maturity beyond which the believer no longer struggles against sin. That's why the admonitions of God's Word never lose their value!

7. In our American economy we are called on once every year to present a certain amount of our income to the government as its "instruments." By law, we present our resources to the government for it to use as it pleases. The idea behind Romans 6:13 is that we voluntarily turn over our entire lives to God rather than to sin, and that we present or yield our physical bodies (hands, arms, legs, feet, brains, ears, eyes, tongues) to Him to use as He pleases. Rather than our physical members fulfilling the purposes of sin, they will now fulfill the purposes of God. This is a conscious choice, and one that should be seen in the way our bodies are used from day to day.

8. It is easy to say, "I am a Christian; I belong to Jesus Christ," but many who do are living their lives as slaves to sin, according to Romans 6:16. A Christian who claims to be the property of Christ but lives like a bondslave of Satan is as conspicuous and misfit as a plumber in a dress shop, or a computer programmer in the middle of a corn field.

9. One of the rites of passage at any military academy is the process of taking away all semblances of personal identity and blending new recruits into the whole. Uniform haircuts, dress, housing, schedules, drills, and treatment all reinforce the idea that the person has ceased to be his or her own individual, and has now become a part of something bigger. Daily these cadets are required to "put off" the old individual they used to be, and to "put on" the new person the institute has created. They can choose to disobey this mandate; but the consequences will not be pleasant! The same is true of our new position in Jesus Christ. God calls us to "put off" the old person, who served sin and fulfilled its wishes, and to "put on" the new creation in Christ, who is now free to obey God from the heart. We can choose to disobey this admonition; but the consequences will never be pleasant.

10. The prospect of our sin nature waiting in the wings would be grim indeed, if not for the supernatural power of the Holy Spirit. Rather than being intimidated by the possibility of the old will exercising itself, we can seek to walk daily, moment-by-moment in the power of the Holy Spirit, recognizing that only God Himself can keep us from sin. The presence of the old will and the new will in our lives does not present us with an unwinnable war we must fight; rather, it presents a situation for which the victorious power of the Holy Spirit is more than sufficient. We can walk in victory!

Questions

1. Was Romans 6:12–13 written to Christians or non-Christians (6:11)? In this passage, what do the words *let* and *present* show us?

2. If we are free to choose obedience to sin or obedience to God, can we choose God in our hearts but still enjoy a few sinful practices in our lives (see Romans 6:15–16)? Explain your answer as you would to a young Christian.

3. What does Galatians 5:1 reveal about the difference between religion and a personal relationship with Christ? Do you think liberty means no more restraints at all on our behavior? If not, what does it mean?

4. Compare Galatians 5:17 with Romans 8:1–2. If there is continual conflict between the old will and the new in the Christian life, does this mean we are doomed to a life of frustration and spiritual defeat? Why or why not?

5. What does Galatians 5:16 tell us about the "how to" of not obeying the will of the flesh? What does this mean?

6. The next time you experience the conflict between the desires of the flesh (the old will) and obedience to God (the new will), how will you face it? Which of the verses we have examined in this chapter will be helpful to you? Why?

CHAPTER 9

WHAT IS MAN?

Romans 8:1–8

One of the major secrets of victory in any conflict is knowing your enemy. No commanding officer would send his troops into battle without first learning all he could about the adversary he is going to fight. No team engaged in an athletic contest would think of going into a game without trying to discover the tactics the opposing team might use. No businessperson would introduce a competitive product into the marketplace without first trying to discover what competitors are offering to the public.

To succeed in any enterprise, we must be informed about our competitors or our adversaries. Yet many of God's children are totally defeated in the Christian life because we do not understand the conflict in which we are engaged, nor the adversary whom we fight. We have been betrayed by divisive tactics. We have focused all-out attention on Satan, the evil one. We are mindful of the wiles of the devil. But we have failed to realize that the greatest enemy we face is ourselves, the adversary within.

The New Testament uses three words or phrases to describe man. First, he is referred to as "the flesh." Second, he is referred to as "the old man." And third, he is referred to as "sin." We want to examine these words one at a time in order to understand ourselves and, understanding ourselves, see the nature of the conflict in which we are engaged. This kind of study is not popular for one reason: Who can find any enjoyment in looking at the evil forces within? But we are not trying to present a popular message. We are trying to present the Word of God so that each one of us might understand the nature of the conflict within us. Only then can we fully appreciate the glorious provision God has made for His children to triumph over the enemy—ourselves.

The Term *Flesh*

The first and most important word we need to look at is the term *flesh*. In the New Testament, this word has three non-theological usages, and four theological usages.

In its first non-theological usage, the word *flesh* refers to the physical body in which a person dwells. Through this body of flesh a person expresses the mind, the emotions, and the will which constitute his personality. For example, 1 Corinthians 15:39 says, "All flesh is not the same flesh, but there is one kind of flesh of men, another flesh of beasts, another of fish, and another of birds." In creation God did not give every being the same kind of body. In this usage of the word, there is no ethical connotation at all; it refers to a body made up of flesh and blood.

In its second non-theological usage, the word *flesh* is used to describe, or differentiate, classes of human beings. We find that it is used of both Jews and Gentiles as classes or groups. For instance, in Romans 1:3 Paul referred to God's "Son Jesus Christ, our Lord, who was born of the seed of David according to the flesh." Here *flesh* refers to a national designation. In His incarnation, Jesus Christ was born of the seed of Abraham and was a Jew by race. In Ephesians 2:11 Paul wrote to Gentiles, "Remember that you, once Gentiles in the flesh—who are called Uncircumcision by what is called the Circumcision made in the flesh by hands . . . ." Paul's usage of the word again has no ethical connotation. He refers to "Gentiles in the flesh" as a division of the human race.

The third non-theological use of this word refers to humankind as a whole. Romans 3:20 says, "Therefore by the deeds of the law no flesh will be justified in His sight, by the law is the knowledge of sin." In this passage, *flesh* refers to all mankind, the whole human race, created by God, possessing of flesh and blood. Though once again the word has no ethical connotation, when mankind is referred to as flesh, the term emphasizes his weakness, his corruptibility, his mortality—characteristics of a body which, because of sin, is passing away.

When we examine the theological uses of the word *flesh*, we find that it is used to show us what we are in the sight of God as a result of Adam's sin. From these theological applications of the word we gain a clear picture of what we are and an understanding of the nature of the enemy that dwells within.

First of all, the word *flesh*, in its theological or ethical sense, refers to one's own effort independent of God. It refers to that which a person does apart from divine aid, divine guidance, or divine empowerment. In Romans 4:1 we read, "What then shall we say that Abraham our father has found according to the flesh?" We might rephrase this question this way: "What shall we say then that Abraham our father, by his own power and strength, unaided by God, accomplished or achieved?" The answer, of course, is "nothing." Again, in Philippians 3:3, the word *flesh* is used in the same sense: "We are the circumcision, who worship God in the

Spirit, rejoice in Christ Jesus, and have no confidence in the flesh." We have no confidence in the flesh. Why not? Because the flesh represents man's effort apart from divine help or assistance. Galatians 3:3 uses this word with the same force: "Are you so foolish? Having begun in the Spirit, are you now being made perfect by the flesh?" Notice that in this passage, the flesh stands in contrast to the Holy Spirit. The flesh represents all that man does by himself, apart from divine aid.

The flesh, then, is human nature, the sum total of all man's personality that, as a result of the Fall, is corrupt—a mind darkened, an emotional capacity degraded, and a will that is dead toward God. The phrases *according to the flesh* and *by the flesh* describe work, merit, or righteousness produced by the natural man out of his own mind, emotion, or will, apart from God's help. Of necessity, all that is of the flesh is under divine judgment.

The second theological use of the word *flesh* emphasizes infirmity, weakness, and helplessness. In Romans 8:3 we read, "What the law could not do in that it was weak through the flesh [that is, it was weak because it depended on flesh, which is weak in itself], God did by sending His own Son in the likeness of sinful flesh, on account of sin: He condemned sin in the flesh. . . ." Again, in Romans 6:19 Paul wrote, "I speak in human terms because of the weakness [or impotence] of your flesh." This characterizes the flesh as the seat of weakness and inability. This refers to man not as he was created directly by the hand of God, but to man after the Fall. Because of the Fall, the strength given to man at creation was stripped away, and man—because he is flesh—was characterized by weakness, impotence, and helplessness.

A third characterization of the flesh is found in Romans 7:5, which says, "When we were in the flesh, the passions of sins which were aroused by the law were at work in our members to bear fruit to death." Paul says "when we were in the flesh" not to mean "when we were alive," as if we have passed beyond the land of the living. Rather, he is using the term *flesh* as a sphere of existence, a state in which we had our existence. To be in the flesh is to be in sin. To be in the flesh is to be in an unsaved or unregenerate state. To be in the flesh is to be controlled by sin that uses this mortal body as the vehicle through which it translates its desires into action, and its affections into deeds. Not only does the flesh, then, represent our natural effort apart from God, characterized by weakness and impotence, but the flesh is a state; it is a condition in which all the unregenerate live.

A fourth concept of *flesh* we observe is presented in Romans 7:18: "I know that in me (that is, in my flesh) nothing good dwells; for to will is present with me, but how to perform what is good I do not find." Here the apostle Paul is using *flesh* to describe the sum total of the old capacity we have as a result of the Fall. The flesh represents the old mind, the old heart, the old will. Notice that in this verse the apostle makes a distinction between the flesh and himself. He is not his flesh; but he is characterized by flesh. Because he had been saved, Paul was a new man in Christ Jesus, and he was not to be equated with the flesh (for the flesh has no personality). But a man is fleshly because he is dominated and controlled by the flesh.

In Romans 8:3 we find another reference to the word *flesh*. Here Paul says that God sent His own Son in the "likeness of sinful flesh." Sin is not inherent in the flesh—that is, in the physical body we possess. Because of a philosophy prevalent among Greeks at the time—the belief that all material things are corrupt and evil, and that only the spirit is uncorrupted—the Gnostics of Paul's day taught that Jesus Christ could not have had a material body, because sin dwelt in the flesh itself.

Therefore, in Romans 8:3 Paul showed that Christ's physical body was not sinful flesh. Christ was sent in "the *likeness* of sinful flesh." Adam was created with a physical body, but Adam was not created a sinner. Adam lived in a physical body in the Garden of Eden before the Fall, but Adam did not have sin because he had a body. When Jesus Christ came into the world through the miracle of virgin birth He possessed true, complete humanity. He possessed a man's body—but He did not have a sinful body.

What we need to understand is that our physical bodies of flesh are not sinful, but they are the vehicles through which sin operates, translating its desires into deeds. Possessing a physical body does not mean a person must practice sin, for sin is not inherent in the flesh. But sin operates through this body, as other passages make clear.

For example, in Romans 13:14 we read, "Make no provision for the flesh, to fulfill its lusts." How does sin operate? It operates through the body. We find the same thing in Romans 6:12–19: "Therefore do not let sin reign in your mortal body, that you should obey it in its lusts. And do not present your members as instruments of unrighteousness to sin . . . . For sin shall not have dominion over you . . . . For just as you presented your members [that is, the physical parts of this human body] as slaves of uncleanness, and of lawlessness leading to more lawlessness, so now present your members as slaves of righteousness for holiness."

Galatians 5 makes it very clear that the fruits of the sin nature manifest themselves through the physical body. This does not mean that there are no sins of the mind, for pride is a sin of the mind, as are covetousness and lust. But the Bible teaches that when these sins of the mind demonstrate themselves, they do so through some member of one's physical body.

That leads us to the conclusion that this fleshly body is the vehicle through which sin operates, and apart from this body, apart from this flesh, sin cannot make an overt expression. Thus we rejoice in the redemption provided for us in Christ Jesus! But redemption is not yet complete. That does not mean we are not saved—but, as Romans 8:3 points out, redemption is still incomplete, for while "God . . . condemned sin in the flesh," the believer has not yet been set free from the possibility of sin. Romans 8:22–23 reminds us, "For we know that the whole creation groans and labors with birth pangs together until now. And not only they, but we also who have the firstfruits of the Spirit, even we ourselves groan within ourselves, eagerly waiting for the adoption, the redemption of our body [that is, the redemption of our flesh]."

Here Paul was anticipating our resurrection. Not until we receive our glorified, resurrected bodies will redemption be complete. As long as we are in our mortal bodies, we are living in unredeemed vessels; we are living in flesh which is the vehicle of sin.

In Romans 7:14, Paul made a very perplexing statement. He wrote, "We know that the law is spiritual, but I am carnal, sold under sin." The phrase *I am carnal* can be translated "I am fleshly." What did he mean by that? Some say Paul had experienced salvation (as he himself says in Romans 6), but he did not come into a full salvation experience until after the seventh chapter. This argument asserts that in Romans 7 Paul was living in weakness, ignorance, and immaturity; that he was living in sin and did not know the secret to victory over sin. However, this view has a serious flaw, since it suggests that a person cannot come to spirituality except by a long, difficult, and tedious process. It also suggests that carnality is an essential part of our development and growth.

Paul was not speaking of his *experience* in Romans 7:14. He was not *practicing* carnality, or doing something that would be classified as carnal. Rather, he was telling his readers what he *is* when he said, "I am carnal." By that Paul meant that he has experienced redemption from sin and is free from bondage to sin, but he still dwells in a body of flesh with all of the weakness, impotence, and helplessness to which the flesh is prone—and as long as he lives on this earth, he will be a carnal being. He did not say, "As long as I live on the earth I will practice carnality." But he did say, in essence, "As long as I live in this body, I am carnal; I am a fleshly being with all of the potential and possibilities to which the flesh is susceptible."

We need to realize exactly the tendency of the flesh with which we are so intimately associated, because apart from resurrection, there will be no deliverance from this fleshly body. While the person has been redeemed, the flesh has not been redeemed. Thus we have to say, as Paul said, "We are carnal." We live with the flesh every moment of the day; it is impossible for us to put it off. It is something with which we must learn to live, and the provision God has made for us in our victory in Christ takes into full account what the flesh is. Yet God's provision is sufficient to enable us to triumph over the flesh.

The Old Man

The second word or phrase the Bible uses to describe unregenerate man is the "old man." Paul wrote in Romans 6:6, "Knowing this, that our old man was [has been] crucified with Him, that the body of sin might be done away with, that we should no longer be slaves of sin." Our old man has been crucified! Paul again uses the expression "the old man" in Ephesians 4:22, where he exhorts believers to "put off, concerning your former conduct, the old man which grows corrupt according to the deceitful lusts." Again, in Colossians 3:9 we read, "Do not lie to one another, since you have put off the old man with his deeds."

The old man refers to the old sinful nature, the total personality, corrupted by the fall of Adam. It emphasizes the source of the corruption and takes us back to Adam, our first father, whose nature was corrupted by his disobedience and who passed on his nature to all his descendants. *The old man* refers to the total unregenerate person, and the nature he has received because of his connection with Adam, because he is Adam's descendant. Like the term *the flesh*, the term *the old man* refers to the old unrenewed self—the old mind, the old heart, the old will—which is corrupt, reprobate, blind, and lawless. It refers to what we were, before God in salvation made each believing sinner a new creation in Christ Jesus. *The old man* relates us to Adam, just as *the new man* relates us to Jesus Christ.

The Term *Sin*

The third word used to describe an unregenerate person is the word *sin*. Obviously, on many occasions the word *sin* refers to the acts which flow from the sin nature, though we usually refer to these in the plural as *sins*. The word *sin* may also refer to the state in which all are born because of Adam's sin. David wrote, "In sin my mother conceived me" (Psalm 51:5).

But the word *sin* also refers to the basic nature we have as human beings. Romans 6 uses this word a number of times to refer to the quality of a person's nature, to the kind of person he is apart from the saving work of Jesus Christ. In Romans 6:6 we read, "Knowing this, that our old man was crucified with Him, that the body of sin might be done away with, that we should no longer be slaves of sin." Here the apostle Paul is not talking about a state, because we cannot serve sin as a state. Neither is he talking about individual acts, because we do not become servants to individual acts. Rather, he is talking about the essential nature that is within each one of us; and he uses the word *sin* to describe the quality, or kind, of nature we possess.

In Romans 6:7 we read, "He who has died has been freed from sin [that is, freed from necessary enslavement to the sin nature]." In verse 10 we read, "For the death that He died, He died to sin [that is, to control by the sin nature] once for all." And in verse 11 we read, "Reckon yourselves to be dead indeed to sin." Paul is not saying that we cannot commit a sin; rather he is saying, "Consider it true that you died to necessary or obligatory control by the sin nature." And in 1 John 1:8, we read, "If we say that we have no sin, we deceive ourselves, and the truth is not in us." Here John uses the word "sin" the same way Paul uses it in Romans 6, to emphasize the fact that we have a nature within us that God calls sin, which we can refer to as "the sin nature." Again and again the Bible teaches the fact that God calls the unbeliever "sin."

When we put together the concepts contained in these three expressions—*flesh, the old man,* and *sin*—we get a picture of the adversary against which we are called to war. We dwell in a corrupted body, a body characterized by weakness. We have flesh that is the instrument through which sin works. We inherited it from Adam, our first father, so that it can be called *the old man.* God calls the nature within us *sin,* because all that flows from that nature is sinful.

That is why Galatians 5:19–21 calls the sins that manifest themselves in a person's life "the works of the flesh." First, the works of the flesh are sensual—adultery, fornication, uncleanness, and lasciviousness. Second, the works of the flesh are perverted in regard to spiritual things (for men gave themselves over to idolatry and sorcery). Third, the works of the flesh are basically selfish—hatred, contentions, jealousies, and selfish ambitions. Fourth, the flesh is essentially intemperate, giving itself over to drunkenness, revelries, and the like. Notice that some of these works of the flesh are material, while others are immaterial. Some are deeply rooted in the mind, while others are translated into action. Some works of the flesh are mental; others are physical.

This is indeed a dark picture. It is enough to bring about discouragement and despair if we agree with God's assessment of the individual.

But the Word of God does more than accurately portray what we are in ourselves. It also brings us to the glorious message of liberation from the flesh, from the old man, and from sin. And it is that liberation we want to study in detail in the following chapters. The subject of this chapter is neither comforting nor complimentary. But it is essential, for unless we realize that we live every moment of every day with an adversary within, one that seeks to express its basic nature through our flesh, we will not be prepared to turn to God and receive from Him the provision He has made through Christ's death and the Holy Spirit's power. It is a provision that can provide us a life of victory and triumph over the flesh, the old man, and sin.

Notes

1. Besides its obvious contradiction to the biblical account of creation, the theory of evolution teaches a view of humankind far different from that found in the Bible. Atheistic anthropology tells us that the human race has developed upward from base, unintelligent beginnings into the human beings we know today. The Bible, on the other hand, teaches that our beginning as a unique creation of God—innocent and untainted by sin—was the peak of our existence, and that the Fall degenerated the entire race. Evolution also tells us that we have within ourselves the capacity to improve ourselves, develop, and evolve into a higher state of being. The Bible, however, makes it clear that only through redemption in Christ can we begin to experience the higher level of existence for which we were created. Understanding the Bible's view of the human race is essential to understanding ourselves and our position in Christ.

2. When the word *flesh* is used in reference to the entire human race, it stands in sharp contrast to Almighty God, who is Spirit (John 4:24). If nothing else, this should remind us of how small, powerless, and limited we are compared to the God we seek to know and obey. When we become defiant or bitter toward God because of difficult circumstances, are we keeping this view of ourselves in mind? Do we who are merely flesh and blood dare pass judgment on Him who is infinite, perfect, and all-powerful? The thought is ridiculous, yet it is an area of struggle for all of us.

3. "No confidence in the flesh"—this is hard to accept in our culture of self-help, self-confidence, and self-reliance. Where do you place your confidence? In the flesh—your own strengths, abilities, assets, status, position, popularity— or in the Spirit?

4. As almost any weight training coach will confirm, the biggest obstacle that keeps young athletes from beginning a weight-training program is the process of finding out how weak they are to begin with. For some, it is too humiliating to admit they are weak; therefore they become trapped in their

weakness and never get any stronger. Spiritually, it can be just as humiliating to admit the weakness of the flesh—that we cannot please God in our own power. But admitting that weakness is the only way we can begin to experience the power of the Holy Spirit working through us. This is why Paul wrote, "I take pleasure in infirmities, in reproaches, in needs, in persecutions, in distresses, for Christ's sake. For when I am weak, then I am strong" (2 Corinthians 12:10).

5. As Christians we may encounter two extreme, unbiblical views of the flesh. The first teaches that the flesh in itself is always wicked, and that the only way we can be spiritual is to deny the flesh at every opportunity by forbidding all pleasure, recreation, enjoyment, and so on. The second teaches that since the flesh is sinful anyway, and since we have been redeemed spiritually, we are free to indulge the flesh all we want without any consequences or future accountability. Both of these views are in error. The Bible tells us we are now free from an obligation to obey the clearly sinful compulsions of the flesh; and that we should exercise that freedom by living righteously before God. Are you experiencing both aspects of this truth—freedom from sin, and freedom to serve God in the flesh?

6. A helpful way to envision our relationship to sin as it expresses itself through our flesh is to remember three things: (1) At salvation, Christ permanently saved you from the *penalty* of sin; (2) Through the Holy Spirit, Christ can daily save you from the *power* of sin; and (3) Jesus Christ ultimately will save you and all believers from the *presence* of sin for all eternity.

7. One aspect of our nature as fleshly beings is that we are subject to disease, difficulties, and all the other negative circumstances that go with life in a mortal body. But God can work even these things for our good (Romans 8:28), and through them teach us more about Himself. David—someone who knew firsthand the highs and lows of life in the flesh—wrote in Psalm 119:71, "It is good for me that I have been afflicted, that I may learn Your statutes."

8. Our old self has been crucified with Christ! What a wonderful, comforting thought for believers whose old lives possess emotional scars, haunting memories, or enslaving habits of sin. Jesus is not asking us to revamp something old and imperfect, or to carry that old baggage into our new life with Him. The old you has been nailed to the cross with Jesus so that the new you can walk in all the good things God has prepared for you (see Ephesians 2:10).

9. The next time you are faced with temptation, imagine how much power that temptation would have on a dead person. That's how much it will influence us when we actively consider ourselves to be dead to sin.

10. If you ever doubt how consumed with self the flesh is, think back to the last time you looked at a group picture that included you. Whom did you look at first, longest, and most critically? Yourself, of course. Though we may learn to control our basic self-centeredness to some degree as we grow older, only Jesus Christ can set us free from its domination over our lives.

Questions

1. What are some specific ways the Bible's view of humanity differs from the world's view? In what ways is the world's view of humankind reinforced in the media? In education?

2. Read Romans 8:3. What does it mean that Jesus Christ was sent "in the likeness of sinful flesh"?

3. What are the capabilities of the flesh before God (see Romans 6:19; 7:18)? According to Galatians 3:3, what should be our attitude toward our own abilities to please God apart from the Spirit's power?

4. In what two ways can a believer respond to the flesh, in light of Romans 6:12–19?

5. According to Romans 7:14, can a Christian mature enough to be entirely uninfluenced by sin's power through the flesh? What does this mean to you and your walk with Christ?

6. In what way might your daily walk with Christ be affected by the truths expressed in Romans 6:6–7, 11? Can you give specific examples?

CHAPTER 10

THE JUDGMENT AT THE CROSS

Colossians 2:9–17

How is it possible for a person to know freedom from sin, freedom from the dominion of a sin nature, freedom from the practice of sin, and deliverance from the power of Satan, who is the prince of the power of the air? The answer is, through the threefold judgment of the cross.

Scripture portrays the cross of the Lord Jesus Christ not only as the way we often consider it—an emblem of the love of God—but more as the emblem of God's judgment on sin. When God's love for the world is presented to us in Scripture, that love is described in terms of the giving of a Son, the coming of a Savior, and the offer of salvation through the Lord Jesus Christ. But the cross stands as an emblem of God's holiness, righteousness, and justice. It was on the cross that Jesus Christ was judged in our place that we might be set free from sin and delivered from the power of Satan.

In this chapter we want to focus on three aspects of the judgment accomplished at the cross, which became the basis for believers' liberation from sin in their daily experience. If we, as the children of God, are to live the life of Jesus Christ through the power of the Holy Spirit, we must be delivered from Satan's domain; we must be delivered from the domination of the old sin nature; and we must be delivered from the consequences of our sin. It was at the cross of Christ that God so dealt with Satan and the sin nature that believers can be set free to walk in newness of life.

For, as we will see, there was a threefold judgment at the cross: a judgment on Satan, a judgment on sins, and a judgment on the sin nature.

Judgment on Satan

In John 12, Christ anticipated His death and resurrection. In verse 24 He told His disciples that it would be necessary for Him to die in order that through His death He might produce new life. According to verse

31, Christ's death was also necessary so that He, by His death on the cross, might pronounce judgment on the prince of this world. Jesus said, "Now is the judgment of this world; now the ruler of this world will be cast out."

John 16:11 also refers to the judgment of Satan, the prince of this world. In that passage, Christ—again anticipating the fruits of His death—says that the Spirit will convict the world of judgment because the prince of this world is judged.

When we were born the first time through physical birth, we were born into a world that is Satan's domain. How did it become Satan's domain? Let's review. At the time of creation, God entrusted to Adam sovereign authority over this earth. But Adam, by willful disobedience against God, forfeited his right to rule. And Satan, the tempter, usurped that rule and took it for himself, becoming "the god of this age" (2 Corinthians 4:4). In Ephesians 2:2, Paul refers to Satan as "the prince of the power of the air." In the spiritual realm, Satan—as a king—has innumerable hosts of fallen angels arranged in hierarchies under his authority (Ephesians 6:12). Thus apart from Jesus Christ, all people are under the dominion of Satan. And even though he is a usurper, Satan rules over his subjects as an absolute monarch.

The question may arise, "Does Satan have a right to rule?" Because Satan has ruled from the time of the fall of man to the present day, does it mean he has attained a permanent right to rule? If Satan does have an absolute and irreversible right to rule, then we have no right to expect to be delivered or set free from bondage to him. If he indeed has attained a permanent right to reign, then we are wrong to rebel against him and wrong to seek to live a life pleasing to God rather than pleasing to him.

But the fact is that the Old Testament anticipated a time when the Lord Jesus Christ, as God's King (Messiah), would come to institute His kingdom on this earth, putting down every rebel and subjecting all authority to Himself. The prophets looked forward to a time when righteousness would cover the earth as the waters cover the sea. Their prophecies anticipated the judgment of Satan, the overthrow of his reign, and the liberation of his subjects. But the human race did not understand how this liberation would be accomplished until after Jesus Christ came into the world and went to the cross. When the Lord Jesus Christ died, God passed His righteous judgment on the usurper, Satan. And through those who preached Christ's death and resurrection, God declared that anyone can be set free from the one who had held the human race captive in his kingdom for so long. Satan did not acquire a permanent right to humanity's obedience, nor did he acquire a permanent right to rule.

Colossians 2:15 makes very clear that by His death Jesus Christ "disarmed principalities and powers." The word *disarmed* literally means to take a prey or to relieve someone of his possessions. By the judgment of the cross, Jesus Christ removed from Satan that scepter he professed to have as a permanent possession. Christ stripped the principalities and powers under Satan's authority of their professed rights. He made a show of them openly, triumphing over them. When Jesus Christ went to His death, He robbed principalities and powers of their authority; when He was raised from the dead, He demonstrated that the judgment was a valid judgment, because He triumphed over the powers of hell and death. Though all the powers of Satan were concentrated on Christ's tomb to try and keep Him in death's grip, death could not hold its prey. Thus Christ, by His resurrection, demonstrated the validity of the judgment of the cross as it fell on Satan.

At this point we need to understand something very crucial: Although Satan was judged at the cross, the execution of God's judgment was postponed and will not take place until Jesus Christ comes to this earth a second time to reign as God's Messiah. Then Satan will be bound and will remain bound for the thousand years of our Lord's reign on earth (Revelation 20:1–6). Not until after Satan is released for a brief season at the end of Messiah's millennial reign will the judgment of the cross be finally executed, when Satan will be cast into the lake of fire forever.

Although he has been righteously judged, Satan is still active today. He is as active and vigilant in his reign over his kingdom today as he has ever been. The great difference, however, is that before judgment was passed on Satan, no one had any assurance that they could be delivered from his dominion. But ever since God passed judgment on him at the cross, anyone who trusts Jesus Christ as Savior can be sure that Satan has no right to compel the child of God to obey his evil edicts. When Satan comes to tempt a child of God, the Christian has the right and the authority to rebuke him as a tempter, because judgment has been passed on him. Further, the believer can remind the Enemy that, as a judged and deposed monarch, he has no right to continue issuing orders to the redeemed as though they are still in his kingdom and under his domination.

In short, the believer's deliverance from sin in his or her daily life rests, first of all, upon God's judgment on Satan, passed at the cross.

Judgment on Sins

Second, at the cross God passed judgment on the sins of the world. We have already discovered in our study that people are not only in bondage to Satan by natural birth, they also are in bondage to sin. All of the fruits that flow from our natural lives are characterized and categorized by God as sinful. The works of the flesh are sinful in the sight of God. And when Jesus Christ went to the cross at Calvary, He went there in order that judgment might be passed by God on the sins of the world. Sins as acts, sins as deeds, sins as transgressions—all were brought under divine judgment.

John the Baptizer made this clear when he pointed to Jesus Christ and said, "Behold! The Lamb of God who takes away the sin of the world!" (John 1:29). The apostle John wrote that Jesus Christ is "the propitiation [that is, the covering over, the rendering of satisfaction] for our sins [the sins of believers], and not for ours only but also for the whole world" (1 John 2:2). In Hebrews 2:9 we read, "We see Jesus, who was made a little lower than the angels, for the suffering of death crowned with glory and honor, that He, by the grace of God, might taste death for everyone." The value of Christ's death is for those who personally accept Him as Savior. But when Jesus Christ went to the cross so that sins might be judged in His body, the sins of the world were judged by God.

When the apostle Paul defined the gospel he preached, he said, "For I delivered to you first of all that which I also received: that Christ died for our sins according to the Scriptures. . . ." (1 Corinthians 15:3). The first point of Paul's gospel was that Christ died for our sins. Every sinner had incurred an indebtedness which he could not possibly pay. Eternity itself would be too short for a man to be able to discharge his indebtedness to God. But when Jesus Christ went to the cross He bore our sins in His own body (1 Peter 2:24). And as He hung on the cross, He said, "It is finished" (John 19:30). The Greek word translated "It is finished" was a word used in business transactions to mean "paid in full." Archeologists once uncovered an ancient tax collector's office where they found a number of tax statements with this same word written across the face of each statement. It indicated that the tax bills had been "paid in full." When Jesus said "It is finished," He was saying that our debt of sin has been paid, and our indebtedness has been canceled.

Colossians 2:14 brings out this truth when it says that Jesus Christ, in His death, blotted out "the handwriting of requirements that was against us, which was contrary to us. And He has taken it out of the way, having nailed it to the cross." No Roman citizen could be put in prison until an indictment containing a list of his crimes had been filed and the person had been tried to determine if the indictment was true. If a man was found guilty as indicted and was put in prison, that indictment would be nailed over his prison cell so that anyone going through the prison would look at the indictment and know exactly why the prisoner was in prison. That indictment was the "handwriting of requirements."

Now, after the citizen had served his time and had paid the penalty for his crime, the chief jailer would take that indictment from over the cell and would write across the face of it the words to indicate that the debt had been satisfied through the man's imprisonment. Then that satisfied indictment would be given to the released prisoner, who would return to his home and post the satisfied indictment on his door. If anyone should question his right to be out of prison, he could point to the satisfied indictment and show that he had the right to be free.

The Bible tells us that an indictment has been filed against us, an indictment that carries the record of our sins, transgressions, iniquities, and unrighteousness. Because we could not pay that debt, the Lord Jesus Christ took it to the cross so that if one were to pass by and ask the Lord Jesus, "Why are you there?" He could refer to your indictment and mine and say, "That is why I am on this cross." Further, when Christ died, God wrote across your indictment and mine, "It is finished. It has been paid in full." Therefore all believing sinners have a right to post a satisfied indictment, signed in the blood of Jesus Christ, declaring that they are free because Jesus Christ has paid the price.

Because sins were judged at the cross, the believer is delivered from sin in his daily life in order that he may walk in newness of life.

Judgment on the Sin Nature

The third great area of judgment at the cross is that a judgment was passed upon the sin nature itself. Romans 8:3 states, "For what the law could not do in that it was weak through the flesh, God did by sending His own Son in the likeness of sinful flesh, on account of sin: He condemned [judged] sin in the flesh." At the cross God judged sin (that is, the sin nature) in the flesh (that is, in the Lord Jesus Christ). Romans 6:6 presents this same truth: "Our old man [the sin nature] was crucified with Him, that the body of sin might be done away with, that we should no longer be slaves of sin." The sin nature has not been eradicated; but it has been rendered inoperative. It has been nullified. Its sovereign control over us has been broken.

The question we face is this: Does the old sin nature with which I was born have an inflexible, inalienable right to control my thoughts, words, and deeds? The sin nature operated without opposition in untold multitudes of Adam's descendants. We might conclude that the authority of the sin nature could never be broken, that no one could rebel against its control. But when Jesus Christ died on the cross, God passed judgment on our sin nature. Therefore God can say to all the redeemed that the right of the sin nature to reign and rule has been broken, and that those who believe in Christ need no longer submit to its authority.

In light of this truth, we need to make several key observations.

First, just as God's judgment on Satan does not mean Satan is no longer active, and God's judgment on sins does not mean we can no longer sin, so God's judgment on the sin nature does not mean that the sin nature can no longer operate in our lives. It is tragically true: the old sin nature can still operate and can still control us. Yet for the child of God, the *necessity* to obey the sin nature has been broken, because God has passed judgment on it through Christ's death on the cross.

God's judgment on the sin nature did not change its essential character, did not rehabilitate it, did not alter it one bit. But God's judgment on the sin nature has changed my relationship to it. Before I became a child of God I was obligated to obey the sin nature. But now, because I am a child of God, I know I do not need to obey the sin nature. Its power has been nullified and its right to rule has been broken. To be sure, the sin nature—although judged—is still active. There is no motivation of the will, no affection of the heart, no thought of the mind which the sin nature does not seek to control. But even though the sin nature is active, we have been released from obligation to obey it.

As an illustration, some decades ago the president of the United States saw fit to remove General Douglas MacArthur from his command in the Pacific. When that happened, General MacArthur did not lose his position as a general; but his removal did mean that those who formerly had obeyed him no longer had a responsibility to him. They now were responsible to the general who assumed MacArthur's former command. If those who had been under MacArthur submitted to his authority after he was removed, they did so because they chose to, not because they were obligated. In the same way, the sin nature once was our master and commander; but now its authority has been broken, and we who are children of God have been delivered from enslavement to it, even though it continues active in our lives. We may choose to obey the old commander, but it is not necessary to do so.

Second, we were delivered from an obligation to obey the sin nature so that we might be brought under the authority of Jesus Christ. We are not set free from the sin nature's control in order to embark on a course of lawlessness and independence in which we seek to please ourselves. Rather, we were delivered from bondage to the sin nature in order that we might be brought into bondage to Jesus Christ. Paul made this clear in Romans 6:13 where he wrote, "Do not present your members as instruments of unrighteousness to sin, but present yourselves to

God as being alive from the dead, and your members as instruments of righteousness to God." We have been set free to be brought into bondage—bondage to Jesus Christ.

Third, we were delivered that we might not continue in sin. The purpose of this deliverance was not simply to deplete the ranks of those who follow Satan, nor to depopulate his kingdom. We have been delivered from Satan, and from sin, and from the sin nature in order that we might practice righteousness. Romans 6:12 says, "Do not let sin reign [continue to reign] in your mortal body, that you should obey it in its lusts." We should instead become servants of righteousness.

Fourth, this release from bondage to sin does not in itself give us the power to live a righteous, holy, God-pleasing life. Galatians 5:16 reminds us, "Walk in the Spirit, and you shall not fulfill the lust of the flesh." The wonderful fact of our liberation from Satan, from sin, and from control by the sin nature does not provide for us the power to live the life of Christ. This life can be lived only by the power of the Holy Spirit, who can produce in us the righteousness for which we were set free. It is a common error among Christians to believe that having been saved we have in ourselves the power to live a life of godliness and holiness. But the truth is that only as we walk by means of the Spirit of God that Christ's righteousness can be reproduced in us.

Fifth and finally, we discover in Romans 8:4 that this freedom from control by Satan, sins, and the sin nature is what makes victory possible in the Christian life. This passage tells us that at the cross sin was judged in the flesh in order that "the righteous requirement of the law might be fulfilled in us who do not walk according to the flesh but according to the Spirit." Our victory, our triumph, our reproduction of the life of Christ in our daily experience is inextricably tied in with the death of the Lord Jesus Christ for us. It is the cross of Christ that gives liberty—liberty from Satan's dominion, liberty from the condemnation of sin, liberty from control by the sin nature. The cross of Christ is God's means of victory, and all that the Holy Spirit can do in and through the child of God has its basis in the judgment passed by God at the cross.

We can never appropriate the power of the Spirit of God to live a life of holiness until we have first appropriated the freedom that is ours through the judgment accomplished when God offered up Jesus Christ for our sin. In light of this we understand what Paul meant in Galatians 6:14 when he wrote, "God forbid that I should glory except in the cross of our Lord Jesus Christ, by whom the world has been crucified to me, and I to the world." Paul, like us, had no basis for deliverance apart from the cross of Christ.

We can well sing, "In the cross of Christ I glory, towering o'er the wrecks of time," because all the freedom we enjoy is a freedom based on the judgment at the cross.

Notes

1. One idea to keep in mind as we look closer at all that God accomplished through Christ's death on the cross is that Satan thought the crucifixion would be his greatest moment of victory. Instead, God used it to ensure his demise. This display of God's perfect control and sovereignty should encourage us at times when it seems as though Satan has been victorious in our lives. God is in control, and He has a perfect plan.

2. If the world and the world system are indeed Satan's "turf," we must understand that we can never Christianize the world—though a society's moral condition might reflect how much the church has spread the gospel in that society. The best answer to the worldliness of the world is the transformation of hearts through the gospel of Jesus Christ.

3. For scores of generations the Jews looked forward to the time when Messiah would come and set up His righteous rule on earth. We can see this hope reflected even in the words of many familiar Christmas hymns. Has this happened? Not yet, because the Israel of Christ's day rejected Him as Messiah. Even so, those of us who by faith in Him have become citizens of His future kingdom can still look forward to the time when this great prophetic event will take place. Today, when it seems as though man's wickedness and Satan's rule are prevailing over the earth, we can take great hope and encouragement in knowing that a time is coming when Christ will return and reign over all the nations of the earth!

4. The Bible tells us that mankind was made lower than the angels—in power as well as in position. That means that apart from Christ there is no way we can hope to defeat the plan and purpose of Satan and his host of fallen angels. On the other hand, when we abide in Christ, Satan's power and the influence of his messengers is ineffective in our lives. We have perfect protection in Him, and have nothing to fear from the Enemy.

5. Because Satan still reigns over the world today, we can expect him to hate and oppose anything and every expression of God's righteousness. The Bible is God's Word; Satan will do everything he can to undermine its authority and trustworthiness. God created human beings as the pinnacle of all creation; Satan works to place people at the bottom of the created order. God still loves Israel and has a plan for its future; Satan hates Israel and seeks to destroy it. God instituted the family; Satan hates the family. God values human life above animal life; Satan does just the opposite. You get the picture. We would be wise to evaluate every modern philosophy and ideal in light of God's revelation—not peoples' popular opinions.

6. For some people, their most vivid realization at the point of salvation was God's forgiveness—the lifting of the heavy burden of sin. If the burden of our own sins is so great, imagine what it must have been like for the perfect Son of God to bear the sins of the entire world on Himself so that God might judge them.

7. One problem faced by Christians who have walked with the Lord for many years involves assurance of God's forgiveness after they have sinned, perhaps worse than they ever thought possible. They carry guilt feelings with them long after they have confessed their sin and repented, as 1 John 1:9 tells us to do. The good news for anyone wondering if Christ can forgive sins they commit as Christians is that when Christ paid our sin debt in full, all our sins were future. His payment was complete for all sinners for all time. When we come to Him for forgiveness, we need not wonder if His death was adequate. He Himself said, "It is paid in full."

8. The reason many carnal Christians are afraid to yield their lives to Jesus Christ is because they think they will lose control that they now have over their goals, their direction, their happiness. The truth of the matter, however, is that they have no control over their lives as long as they continue to serve their old master, the sin nature. They are enslaved to its fickle wants and insatiable desires, and they are robbed of the blessing God wants them to have. How much better to serve our new Master with a whole heart so that we might experience life as God intends it to be lived.

9. The art of holy living—joyfully practicing personal righteousness—has been supplanted in our day by a longing to see how much we can do, how far we can go, and still be considered acceptable as Christians. Not only does this stunt our spiritual growth, it dilutes our joy and pollutes our witness. God's desire for us is that we completely turn our backs on sin's enticements and aggressively pursue personal righteousness.

10. Is there a marked line of distinction between you and the world around you? Do you stand apart from the world's empty philosophies and self-serving ideals? Do your thoughts begin with God and His Word? Does your life evolve around knowing Jesus Christ and serving Him? This is what Paul meant in Galatians 6:14. It is the greatest freedom we can know.

Questions

1. Read 1 Corinthians 1:17–18. What does the message of the cross offer that human wisdom can't? What will be the world's response to the message of the cross? What is the cross to believers?

2. In light of Ephesians 2:2, under whose authority do all people live their lives if they have not trusted Christ? Under whose authority were we created to live?

3. What is Satan's present status in light of the crucifixion and resurrection (John 16:11)? When will this be executed on him (Revelation 20:1–6)?

4. What are some more subtle, inconspicuous evidences that Satan is active in the world today? How do you know that these demonstrate his work and not God's?

5. Explain in your own words what Christ's death on the cross accomplished for us. What is the importance of Christ's statement, "It is finished!" (John 19:30)?

6. Based on Romans 6:6, what effect might salvation have on chronic, compulsive, or habitual behavior? Why? In what ways has this affected your life?

CHAPTER 11

CRUCIFIED WITH CHRIST

Galatians 2:15–21

The Christian life is the life of Christ reproduced in the child of God, by the power of the Holy Spirit. "Christian living" is Jesus Christ living His life in and through the believer. In previous chapters we have seen the difficulties of the Christian life—the nature within us, the curse of the Fall, the blindness of our minds, the degradation of our emotions, the deadness of our wills toward God. All put enormous difficulties before the child of God in the quest to live a Christian life.

Having examined the biblical teachings concerning the difficulties we face, it is fitting that we should move on to the practical teachings concerning the Christian life. It is at this point that many of God's children fall far short of the provision God has made for them in His Word. Just as there are doctrines that pertain to salvation by grace through faith, so there are doctrines that pertain to living a victorious Christian life. Only after we have grasped the doctrines of the Christian life will we be ready to move into the area of practical conduct in the outworking of these crucial truths in our daily experience.

The child of God needs to recognize that certain responsibilities, obligations, and requirements are laid upon him by God. He needs to see himself under a divine edict to fulfill the injunctions to put off the old man and to put on the new (Colossians 3:8–10) in daily life. But what is the basis on which we can fulfill these injunctions? What has God done in order that we might be set free in our experience from sin and from domination by the sin nature?

Many different solutions are proposed today to answer such questions. For instance, there are those who have suggested that the best way to deal with this problem is to practice what might be called sanctified suppression—through our own will power, suppressing or denying the sin nature that is within us and preventing it from manifesting itself through us. This approach to the Christian life inevitably leads to legalism. In order to prevent the sin nature from expressing itself, we must set up an endless series of laws, rules, and restrictions. But this is not God's answer to the problem of sin in the believer's life, because no individual has the power to control the sin nature. We cannot control sin through our own willpower.

Also popular today is the teaching of those who propose the doctrine of eradication. Those who accept this teaching believe a person's sin nature is eradicated, or removed, at the moment of spiritual birth, or that the Christian may eventually come to the place where he or she no longer has a battle with the sin nature, because the sin nature has been eliminated. Although we sometimes wish this were true, or perhaps covet the idea of a second blessing that would completely eliminate our battle with sin, this is simply a longing to be removed from the battle completely rather than equipping ourselves with the whole armor of God. The idea of eradication is simply not taught in Scripture, and it is certainly no solution to the problems of the sin nature.

Others deal with the whole subject of sin in the believer's life by giving it the silent treatment. That is, they treat the problem as though it does not exist. The idea seems to be that somehow a child of God, apart from instruction in the Word of God, will drift into a Christian life, and that by some mysterious process of osmosis, he or she will absorb the truths of the Bible concerning the new life in Christ. Many Christians today are struggling against insurmountable difficulties because they are basically ignorant on the subject. And ignorance is certainly no solution to the problem of the sin nature.

Then there are those who teach self-crucifixion. They exhort Christians to crucify themselves as Christ crucified Himself, so that by putting themselves to death, they will end the problem of the sin nature. Many prominent teachers go astray at this point, giving repeated exhortations to an individual to crucify himself. But self-crucifixion is a physical impossibility. Jesus Christ could not crucify Himself; it had to be done to Him. The Word of God never asks any believer to put himself to death.

The Principle of Identification

God's solution to the problem of the sin nature in the believer's life is found in Romans 6:11: "You also, reckon yourselves to be dead indeed to sin, but alive to God in Christ Jesus our Lord." God's solution is not suppression, nor eradication, nor self-crucifixion, but rather a reckoning, a believing, an acceptance of an accomplished fact. God's solution to the problem of sin in the believer's life is based on one's identification with Christ.

Paul was referring to identification with Christ when he wrote in Galatians 2:20, "I have been crucified with Christ; it is no longer I who live, but Christ lives in me; and the life which I now live in the flesh I live by faith in the Son of God, who loved me and gave Himself for me." The key phrase in this verse is *I have been crucified with Christ.* Identification with Christ in His crucifixion is a fact Christians are to believe. When Jesus Christ died, we died together with Him. Identification with Christ, therefore, involves not only crucifixion with Christ, but burial with Christ, resurrection with Christ (Romans 6:4–5), ascension with Christ (Ephesians 2:6), and glorification with Christ. We have been so identified with Him that God reckons us as having experienced co-crucifixion, co-burial, co-resurrection, co-ascension, and co-glorification.

How can this be? How can it be said that we—living nearly 2,000 years after Christ lived—have been crucified with Him? How can it be said that we have been resurrected with Christ? How can it be said of us that we have ascended and have been glorified with Christ when we are still very much alive on this earth?

The answer to these questions is found in the great truths involved in the baptizing work of the Holy Spirit. Here we do not need to develop this doctrine at length, but instead affirm what Paul disclosed in 1 Corinthians 12:13, that "by one Spirit we were all baptized into one body—whether Jews or Greeks, whether slaves or free—and have all been made to drink into one Spirit." According to this passage, the baptizing work of the Spirit joins those who have accepted Jesus Christ as personal Savior to the body of which Jesus Christ is the living Head. As a result, all that is true of the Head is also true of each member in His body.

What does it mean to have been baptized into His body? That question brings us to one of the most debated words in the Bible—a word much misunderstood because of the questions that inevitably arise concerning mode of baptism. The Greek word *bapto*, from which we get the word *baptize*, literally means "to dip," "to plunge," or "to immerse." It is the word that was used by the fuller (or dyer) who prepared cloth. The fuller took raw cloth and put it into the dye vat; and when that cloth was taken out of the dye vat, its entire appearance was changed. The fuller was said to have "baptized" the cloth.

This word, like many words, had both a literal and a symbolic usage. When it was used literally, it had to do with dipping, plunging, or putting something into something else. But in its symbolic usage, it meant "to change identity"; that is, to change the outward appearance. This metaphorical usage of the word was common in the Greek of New Testament times. So when Paul used the same word in reference to our relationship with Christ, he was using it in a widely accepted, symbolic way. Obviously, Paul was not saying that we have been dipped into dye. Rather, his point was that we have changed our identity by forming a new union with Jesus Christ.

Our English word *iron* well illustrates how a word can have both a literal and a symbolic meaning. The word *iron* literally refers to a metal, and we commonly use the word in that way. But it also has a metaphorical usage, such as our reference to a physically overpowering athlete as an "iron man," a person's willpower as a "will of iron," or a firm-handed ruler as having an "iron fist." In fact, in our language this word probably is used more often in its metaphorical sense than in its literal sense. This is also true of the biblical word translated "baptize."

The thought of identifying one thing with another appears very early in the Bible. For example, in Leviticus 16 we read about an act by which someone could identify himself with something else through the ritual of the Day of Atonement. In the first portion of the ritual, a priest killed a goat which was the sin offering, and presented the blood. He then moved to the second portion of the ritual, the separation of the scapegoat. We read in verse 20, "When he has made an end of atoning for the Holy Place, the tabernacle of meeting, and the altar, he shall bring the live goat; and Aaron shall lay both his hands on the head of the live goat, confess over it all the iniquities of the children of Israel, and all their transgressions, concerning all their sins, putting them on the head of the goat, and shall send it away into the wilderness by the hand of a suitable man."

Notice that Aaron was to lay both his hands upon the head of the live goat. And while his hands were on the goat, he was to confess all the sins of the nation Israel. What did that contact by Aaron's hands signify? It signified that the one making the confession was identifying himself with the one upon whose head those sins were being confessed. The priest, representing the whole nation, confessed the sins of the nation. Then, by laying his hands on the scapegoat, identified the nation Israel with this sin bearer. By that act the nation was identified with the sacrifice.

We find a similar use of symbolism in Acts 13, where the church at Antioch is preparing to send out Barnabas and Paul to the work of evangelizing the Gentiles. In Acts 13:2–3 we read, "As they ministered to the Lord and fasted, the Holy Spirit said, 'Now separate to Me Barnabas and Saul for the work to which I have called them.' Then, having fasted and prayed, and laid hands on them, they sent them away."

Again we see the imposition of hands. Why? Because the believers at Antioch were identifying themselves with their emissaries, who were going out to preach the gospel. The laying on of hands was an act of identification in which the church assembly united themselves with their representatives. In 1 Timothy 4:14 we find something similar when Paul writes to Timothy, "Do not neglect the gift that is in you, which was given to you by prophecy with the laying on of the hands of the presbytery." In 2 Timothy 1:6 Paul again referred to this laying on of hands: "I remind you to stir up the gift of God which is in you through the laying on of my hands." The laying on of hands was an act by which Paul and the church were identified with Timothy as a minister of the gospel.

Matthew 3 describes another act of identification. John the Baptizer (or John the Identifier) appeared in the wilderness to call out a separated people, to set apart to Messiah a believing remnant of Israel who anticipated His coming. John proclaimed, "Repent, for the kingdom of heaven is at hand!" His message was, "Turn! Turn from your sin, for Messiah is coming to offer God's kingdom!" Then John said, "I indeed baptize you with water unto [or, with a view to] repentance, but He who is coming after me is mightier than I, whose sandals I am not worthy to carry. He will baptize you with the Holy Spirit and fire" (3:11). John was practicing identification by baptism, identifying a people separated to Messiah and separated from the false system of Pharisaism. The sign of identification was water. When Jesus came to be baptized by John, He also received the sign of identification. The identifier put his identifying mark on all those who were the identified, or baptized, ones.

In Acts 2, Peter also uses baptism as an identifying sign. Following the death and resurrection of Christ, Peter stood up before the nation that was now guilty of asking for the crucifixion of God's Messiah, and he proved to them that Jesus was both Lord and Messiah because God had raised Him from the dead. Peter told them that their nation was under judgment and that they needed to save themselves from that "perverse generation." They responded by asking, "What shall we do?" And Peter replied, "Repent [that is, change your mind about this Jesus whom you deem to be a blasphemous, insane man] and let every one of you be baptized [be identified] in the name of Jesus Christ for [with a view to] the remission of sins" (2:38). What would their baptism do? It would change their identity. It would separate them from the old nation, the old citizenship, the old religion. It would separate them *from* that generation that was under judgment (Luke 21:24), and separate them *to* the Lord Jesus Christ. Thus baptism was an identifying sign.

Identification With Christ

When 1 Corinthians 12:13 refers to the baptism of the Holy Spirit and teaches that all believers were baptized into one Spirit, it is saying that we have been identified with Jesus Christ; we are united with Him in all He experienced. The question arises, then, "To what have we been joined? With what have we been identified?" Here is a mystery so deep that we would be in complete ignorance if the Word of God did not reveal it to us. The Bible teaches that when believers were baptized into one body by one Spirit, they were baptized into Christ's death, burial, resurrection, ascension, and glorification. Let's look at some of the great facets of Christ's redemptive work with which we have been identified.

In Galatians 2:20 Paul wrote, "I have been crucified with Christ." What does that mean? When Jesus Christ died, I was so identified and united with Him that I died also. Colossians 1:21–22 likewise affirms that when Christ died, we died with Him: "You, who once were alienated and enemies in your mind by wicked works, yet now He has reconciled in the body of His flesh through death, to present you holy, and blameless, and irreproachable in His sight." Colossians 3:5 reads, "Put to death your members which are on the earth: fornication, uncleanness, passion, evil desire, and covetousness, which is idolatry." Why? Because you "have put off the old man with his deeds" (3:9). The putting off is death, and the putting on is resurrection. In Romans 6:3 Paul writes, "Do you not know that as many of us as were baptized into Christ Jesus were baptized into His death? Therefore we were buried with Him through baptism into death, that just as Christ was raised from the dead by the glory of the Father, even so we also should walk in newness of life."

This is the first great fact: We were identified with Christ in His death, so that when Christ died, we died. This is not something we can put to the test and prove experientially; rather, it is a fact of divine revelation we are called on to believe. We were not consciously present at the cross. We have no sensory perception of our death with Christ; but it was nevertheless a real death. When we were baptized by the Holy Spirit into Christ Jesus, by that act we were also baptized into—identified with—His death.

Second, Romans 6:4 tells us that believers were also identified with Christ in His burial: "We were buried with Him through baptism into death." Colossians 1:21–22 asserts the same truth. Burial removes the deceased person from the sphere into which he was born. We are born once into this world, a world over which Satan is ruler. But through our identification with Christ's death and burial, we who have died with Christ have been buried with Him, and have been removed from this sphere. We were not conscious of our burial; yet this burial is nonetheless real, a fact we are to believe, a truth on which we can depend.

The third great fact is that we were identified with Christ in His resurrection. Romans 6:4–5 tells us that "just as Christ was raised from the dead by the glory of the Father, even so we also should walk in newness of life. For if we have been united together in the likeness of His death, certainly we also shall be in the likeness of His resurrection." In Ephesians 1:19, Paul prays that believers might know "what is the exceeding greatness of His power toward us who believe, according to the working of His mighty power which He worked in Christ when He raised Him from the dead . . . ." This affirms that we, too, have been raised by God's power. How? We were identified with Christ in His resurrection—as affirmed again in Ephesians 2:5–6: "Even when we were dead in trespasses, [God] made us alive together with Christ (by grace you have been saved), and raised us up together, and made us sit together in the heavenly places in Christ Jesus." In Philippians 3:10, Paul expressed the desire of his heart that he might "know Him and the power of His resurrection." Colossians 3:1 exhorts Christians, "If then you were raised with Christ, seek those things which are above, where Christ is, sitting at the right hand of God."

Any believer can experience the power that raised Christ from the dead and was experienced by Paul and the first century church, because we have been resurrected with Christ.

The fourth thing we discover from these passages is that not only have we experienced co-death, co-burial, and co-resurrection, we have also experienced co-ascension and co-glorification. Ephesians 2:6 tells us that God has "raised us up together, and made us sit together in the heavenly places in Christ Jesus." Romans 8:30 reminds those who have been predestined and called by God that "whom He predestined, these He also called; whom He called, these He also justified; and whom He justified, these He also glorified." This is not speaking of the future glory awaiting God's children, but of our present position before the Father as those who have been identified with Christ in His ascension and glorification.

These wonderful truths may already be very familiar to us. But we can know the facts without realizing the purpose of our co-crucifixion, co-burial, co-resurrection, co-ascension, and co-glorification. Romans 6:8–10 tells us, "Now if we died with Christ, we believe that we shall also live with Him, knowing that Christ, having been raised from the dead, dies no more. Death no longer has dominion over Him. For the death that He died, He died to sin once for all; but the life that He lives, He lives to God." The reason we have been identified with Christ in His death, burial, and resurrection is that we might live for God. We have been baptized into Christ Jesus so that we might be dead to control by the old sin nature, just like a corpse which no longer needs to respond to any command to it or authority over it.

The power of sin has not been canceled; the practice of sin has not become an impossibility. But through our death with Christ, we are delivered from the obligation to obey the commands of the sin nature. We have been set free from slavery to sin. Of course, it is still possible to sin, to obey the old regime. We may obey the defeated dictator; but if we do, we do so by choice and not by necessity. Before we were born into God's family we could hear only the commands issued by the old sin nature. We were like a radio tuned to just one wave length, the wavelength of the sin nature. But by the new birth we have been given a new capacity, a new wavelength; and now we must choose whether we will obey the commands of the old wavelength, or of the new. Because we have been crucified with Christ, we have the option of allowing Christ to live His life through us.

Paul presented this same fact in Romans 6:4, where he stated that we are buried with Christ so that "just as Christ was raised from the dead by the glory of the Father, even so we also should walk in newness of life." The purpose of identifying us with Christ in His resurrection was that we might be delivered from sin's domination in order to walk in newness of life. When God gave Jesus Christ to die for us, He was interested in far more than our salvation from sin's penalty. As we have already seen, Christ's death was God's judgment on sin and the sin nature. Through the death of Christ, God not only provided for our salvation but also provided for our walk in newness of life by identifying us with Christ in His death, burial, and resurrection.

In order to put an end to sin's control over your life, God put you to death with Christ. To remove you from the old sphere in which you lived, God put you into the grave with His Son. And to bring you into a new kind of life, God raised you from the grave with Jesus and elevated you to glory with Him. All these are yours so that Christ, who lives in you, might live His life through you. Romans 6:11 offers us the only correct response to this great truth: "You also, reckon [count it to be true] yourselves to be dead indeed to sin, but alive to God in Christ Jesus our Lord."

God is asking you who have been identified with Christ to believe that you have been liberated from an obligation to serve sin. Your Christian life, therefore, is based upon a fact to be believed. You have died with Christ, you have been buried with Christ, and you have been resurrected and glorified with Christ in order that you might walk in newness of life. And this becomes your experience only when you count it to be true.

Notes

1. It is too bad that the word *doctrine* has become all but taboo in Christian circles today, conjuring up images of inscrutable precepts set forth in obscure language. The fact of the matter is that until we *know* something is true, we cannot put our faith or confidence in it. Doctrine is simply what we know about God and God's truth. Ideally, doctrine presents plain facts, in plain language, for plain people. And by understanding an area of doctrine, or truth about God, we can grow in how much we trust Him and how He works in our lives.

2. If the sin nature was eradicated at the moment of salvation, then complete maturity in Christ would simply be a matter of ridding ourselves of a few leftover habits or behavior patterns. The old nature could not produce in us any sins comparable to those we knew before trusting Christ. But any Christian who has struggled with personal sin knows that we are as capable of the same sins—or worse—twenty years down the road as we are the day we come to know Christ. The sin nature is always with us. But when we trust Christ we are set free from an obligation to obey its lusts.

3. If indeed "it is no longer I who live, but Christ lives in me," what effect should that have on the places we go, the entertainment we pursue, the conversations we have, the people with whom we spend our time, the way we live our lives every moment of every day? If you are unsure or feel convicted about something in your life, ask yourself, "Does this reveal Christ living in me?" If not, it may well be something that you can leave behind with the old, crucified self.

4. It appears that God takes seriously our allegiances, or identification with a particular way of thinking. The logic is this: our inward convictions will be revealed by our outward allegiances. If we identify ourselves with Jesus Christ, our close associations and loyalties will reflect, not contradict, Him and His Word.

5. John's ministry of calling the people of Israel to repentance prior to Messiah's public ministry reminds us that one cannot simply "try Jesus" while clinging to the old way of life. Coming to Christ means that we make a 180-degree turn from self and sin, and trust Him to save us. Likewise, once we have trusted Christ as Savior, we must be willing to repent of (forsake) the sins His Spirit reveals in our lives as we grow in our relationship with Him.

6. If we sense a lack of direction in our Christian lives, perhaps it's because we consider ourselves separated *from* the world around us, but do not really live our lives separated *to* the Lord Jesus Christ. Many Christians take seriously their salvation *from* sin's consequences; but too few take seriously their sal-

vation *to* holy living, careful study of God's Word, diligent prayer, and aggressive witnessing. Do you have this kind of direction in your Christian life?

7. Our identification with Christ in His death, burial, and resurrection is the key to understanding our freedom from sin's power in our daily lives. How much power can sin have over a dead person? And how much power can sin have over you, if you have died with Christ and have been buried with Him? What's more, through identification with Christ's resurrection, you are free to live in an entirely new sphere of existence. This is life-changing!

8. U.S. military planes flying into South Korea must carefully follow broadcast landing instructions to avoid crashing into the mountains. The trouble is, communist North Korea sometimes broadcasts bogus landing instructions to try to make the incoming planes crash. The only way U.S. pilots can tell the difference between the two is to validate each message according to a code book. In other words, they interpret each message "by the book." Is this how we interpret the mixed signals our hearts and minds feed us about the many temptations around us? Do we try to figure out all the angles, all the results, all the consequences? Or do we go to God's Word and play it "by the Book"?

Questions

1. In light of Galatians 2:20, how would you summarize your personal potential for Christlikeness in your day-to-day life? What does this verse imply about the need to probe or relive our pre-salvation lives and improve the old self?

2. What point is being emphasized in Romans 6:1–4? What is the basis of Paul's argument (see 6:7)?

3. What does Ephesians 2:6 tell us about the security or certainty of our salvation? Does this mean we should not be concerned with whether we live righteous lives? Explain.

4. Read 1 Corinthians 12:13. What is the *one body* into which we have all been baptized? Does this mean there should be no variety among Christians (see verse 12). What do you think will be true of all those who are in the one body?

5. What do you think is meant by the phrase *newness of life* in Romans 6:4? Can you give examples from your own life?

6. In light of this chapter, why do some Christians fail to walk in the "newness of life" of Romans 6:4? What encouragement could you give to someone who knows Jesus Christ but is not walking in newness of life?

CHAPTER 12

DEAD WITH CHRIST

Romans 7:1–14

In the cross of Christ, an infinite God has made provision for all the needs of sinners. All that anyone could ever need has been provided for in the death of Jesus Christ. Christ died to pay the price for our sins; to discharge the debt we owe to God; to set us free from spiritual death and make us alive; to liberate us from control by the sin nature.

The basic doctrines of the Christian life must begin with the recognition that when we were born into this world the first time, we were born into the kingdom of Satan. He was our god, and we served him as such, either knowingly or unknowingly. We were members of his family, we were by nature children of disobedience, and we were bond-slaves of sin. Sin was a ruthless, domineering master, and we obeyed its commands.

But Romans 6–7 sets forth for us the glorious liberty that is in the gospel of Jesus Christ. There the Bible reveals to believers the benefits of Christ's death in respect to the Christian life. After the writer tells believers that they were baptized into Jesus and that being joined to Him they were joined to His death, he goes on to show that death with Christ sets believers free from domination by the sin nature. Our slavery to sin has been broken, and our obligation to obey sin has been canceled.

Emancipation

Over a hundred years ago, slaves in America were set free by a proclamation of emancipation, a judicial pronouncement by the chief executive of our country. God, who might have set the sinner free by a divine edict, by an emancipation proclamation, chose another means of liberation—death. And in order that we might be set free from bondage to sin, God put us to death with Jesus Christ.

Romans 6:6–7 says, "Our old man [that is, all that we were by nature through our first birth; all that we were because we were in Adam; all that we possess because we possess a sin nature] was crucified with Him, [for the purpose] that the body of sin might be done away with, that we should no longer be slaves of sin. For he who has died has been freed from sin."

When the Bible says that we died with Christ that the body of sin might be done away with, it is not teaching that the sin nature has been eradicated, nor that the sin nature is no longer able to operate within us. If this were true, scores of admonitions in the New Testament would be totally unnecessary. Rather, God's Word teaches that we died with Christ in order that the body of sin, or the sin nature, might be set aside as the master that controls us, the master we are obligated to obey. It deals with this question: "Does the sin nature have the exclusive right to dominate and control us?" The Bible says that because we died with Christ, because we were joined to Christ in His death, we are no longer obligated to serve the old master.

Romans 6:7 says positively, "He who has died has been freed from sin." This verse does not teach that the person who has died with Christ can no longer commit a sin. Indeed, we often see that the child of God can respond to temptation and succumb willingly to mastery by sin. What this verse does teach may be paraphrased this way: "He that has died with Christ is freed from the obligation to obey sin, a deposed master, when it issues orders to him."

These verses show us that our death with Christ delivers us from compulsory obedience and submission to the sin nature that once dominated and controlled us. Just as by resurrection Jesus Christ was delivered from the power of death, so by our resurrection with Christ, death and sin have no right to lay hands on us, for we have been made alive in Christ Jesus. We were brought into death and resurrection with Christ in order that the power of the sin nature over us might be broken. It was not eliminated. It was not eradicated. It was not rendered incapable of tempting us. But now we are not compelled to submit to it as we were before we experienced death and resurrection with Jesus Christ.

Romans 7 again takes up the theme of the believer's death with Jesus Christ and its practical effects in our experience. Paul writes, "Do you not know, brethren (for I speak to those who know the law), that the law has dominion over a man as long as he lives?" (7:1). When Paul introduces a thought with the words, "Do you not know?" he assumes the ignorance of those to whom he is writing. Then he continues on to dispel their ignorance on that subject. Thus we present-day believers can learn a great deal from the ignorance of first-century believers.

In this case, Paul recognized his readers' slowness to understand the twofold value of Christ's death for the believer and the believer's death with Christ as that which liberates from sin's control. Therefore he went into great detail to provide an explanation before he applied this truth to their daily experience. The doctrine Paul taught is simply stated, "The law has dominion over a man as long as he lives." By "the law," Paul meant any law principle, whether it is the Mosaic Law, the law of Rome, the law of marriage, or the physical laws by which our lives are governed day by day. It is evident and obvious that a law can operate in reference to a person only as long as that person is living. When a person dies physically, he is no longer under the laws that formerly applied to him. Even those to whom Paul was originally writing would recognize that the laws of Rome did not extend into the cemetery. When someone died, Rome's law over him was canceled and broken. In the same way, the Law of Moses had authority over a man only as long as he lived. The Law could not descend into a grave to control a man after he had departed from this life.

In verses 2–3, Paul went on to use the familiar illustration of marriage to emphasize the same thing—that the law operates for those who are living, and death terminates the control of any law over any person. Even a law predating the Law of Moses—the law of marriage—operates continuously only as long as both people are living. Death, and death alone, breaks the control of the law of marriage over a wife, according to verses 2–3.

In verse 4, Paul applies this principle: "My brethren, you also have become dead to the law through the body of Christ, that you may be married to another, even to Him who was raised from the dead, that we should bear fruit to God." Paul is not referring to physical death, but to our death through identification with the Lord Jesus Christ. When we were baptized into the body of Jesus Christ, so that we participated with Him in His death, the old law (the sin nature which operated within us) was broken and its power was terminated. By our death with Christ, we have been set free from the obligation to serve the sin nature, in the same way that a wife whose husband has died is set free to marry another.

Our good, well-meaning resolutions do not break the control of the sin nature over us; joining a church doesn't break sin's control; fellowshiping with good Christians does not terminate the sin nature's control; enacting more laws, expanding the rules of legalism, or affixing penalties for misbehavior does not end sin's control. Only one thing can break sin's control over us. Death. When Jesus Christ died, you—as a believer in Jesus Christ—died with Him. That death broke sin's control over you that you, through resurrection with Christ, might walk in newness of life. As Romans 6:4 tells us, "We were buried with Him through baptism into death, that just as Christ was raised from the dead by the glory of the Father, even so we also should walk in newness of life."

A Fact To Be Believed

The real challenge of this study is that we should see how great is our deliverance, our emancipation. We who were born as slaves to sin have no power whatever to break the shackles by which we were chained. There is no power within us that can enable us to utter even the weakest "no" to any order the sin nature might issue to us. But since we were joined to Jesus Christ in His death and resurrection, God can announce that sin's dominion over us has been broken. By death we have been freed from our obligation to serve sin.

This does not mean it is impossible for us to succumb to the entice-ments of sin. It does not mean that sins have become less attractive to that old nature of ours. But it does mean that the Spirit of God can oper-ate through the new, divine nature and bring us, who have been deliv-ered from sin, into willing submission to Jesus Christ, so that He becomes the One who rules and controls us, to produce His righteous-ness in us.

A common misconception today is that Christians are to put them-selves to death. The problem is, an individual can experience death only once. The secret of the Christian life is not repeated self-crucifixion, put-ting self to death again and again and again in order to be delivered from bondage to sin. Rather, God's secret is found in Romans 6:11, where we have already seen that we are to consider it a fact that we are dead to sin and alive to God through Jesus Christ our Lord.

When we were joined to Jesus Christ in His death, it was once for all. Paul did not write in Galatians 2:20, "I crucify myself again and again and again, so that I might be free." He says, "I have been crucified with Christ." And the effects of that crucifixion continue on and on and on. God is asking you to stand off and look at yourself as one who has died, and to deem yourself as one over whom sin's authority has been broken. When Christ died, you died; when Christ was resurrected, you were res-urrected; and now you have been set free to walk in newness of life—resurrection life under control of the Spirit of God.

This is a fact from the Bible; and like any fact, it is to be accepted and believed. That fact of Scripture is that the believer was set free from sin's power when Christ died just as truly as a wife is set free from a hus-band when the husband dies. The fact is not changed by your acceptance or rejection of it, your belief or unbelief, your knowledge of the fact or your ignorance of it. God says you are crucified, and in God's sight you are a crucified person. God is not asking you to add to the value of Christ's death by "crucifying yourself" again and again. God is asking you to accept His judgment on the sin nature and to reckon the fact to be true that you were joined to Christ in His death because God says it is true. He is also asking you to accept the truth that death with Christ has broken sin's power over you so that you have been liberated to walk in the newness of life. Such acceptance will change our whole attitude toward the sin nature within us.

As believers, if we sin, we do so not because we are obligated to sin, but because we choose to sin. Christ set us free—but it is still possible to become entangled again in bondage to sin. We may voluntarily submit to sin's enticements and walk in sinful practices. If we do, it is certainly not because our liberation is incomplete; it is because we do not consider ourselves as those over whom sin no longer has a rightful authority. We choose to submit to a deposed commanding officer. And when we choose sin, we become the servants of sin.

It would be helpful for any child of God upon waking in the morning to repeat Galatians 2:20 and say to himself, "I do not have to serve sin today because I have been set free." We need to remind ourselves constantly that God has liberated us, and then walk in righteousness and true holiness by the power of the Spirit of God.

I do not know of any doctrine that is more comforting or more helpful to the Christian than this biblical doctrine of co-crucifixion with Christ. You see, God is not asking us to break the power of sin. God is not asking us to abstain from sin by will power, by resolution, or by sheer determination. God is telling us what He has already accomplished. He is telling us that He has set us free, and that this freedom is ours by faith. Just as we come into a personal, intimate relationship with Jesus Christ by faith, so by faith we come into victory. We experience an enjoyment of this freedom by faith, considering that what God says is true, considering that we have been crucified with Christ. Consequently, sin's power over us has been broken, and we can walk in newness of life.

Notes

1. As we have already seen, the issue in our lives is not whether or not we will be enslaved; it is *to whom* we will be enslaved. We need to look only as far as the collective voice of those who advocate a total lack of moral restraint to see that the groups who claim to be most free are the most enslaved to their passions. And, as we see in the broken lives this brand of freedom produces, sin is most cruel to its most loyal subjects.

2. Whether obtained through purchase, debt, or military conquest, slaves in the ancient Near East were slaves for life (unless their masters chose to set them free). Only death could remove the obligation to serve one's master and put an end to a life of servitude. That is exactly what our identification with Christ's death does for us! We aren't required to serve sin any longer. But what a tragedy it is when, having been set free, we go knocking on our old taskmaster's door!

3. Notice how carefully Paul bases Christian experience on sound knowledge. Romans 10:17 tells us, "Faith comes by hearing, and hearing by the word of God." We cannot expect to grow in our Christian experience if we are not growing in our knowledge of God's Word. Why not make personal Bible study part of your *daily* routine?

4. Even in the midst of a spiritual explanation, the Bible assumes the lifelong permanence of marriage. Though our culture has cheapened and degraded the meaning of marriage, we should be careful to hold it in the same high esteem God's Word gives it.

5. Christians who minister effectively to young people know the value of drawing a clear distinction between obeying rules and knowing Christ personally. While rules are a necessary standard in families, schools, and other settings, they do not break sin's control over us. Teenagers who vow to be good or to try harder without coming to know Christ personally are headed for a great disappointment. On the other hand, the message that Christ can do for them what they can never do for themselves can be the best news a teenager has ever heard.

6. We all have days when we don't feel like sin's power over us has been broken. Illness, fatigue, personal difficulties, career pressure, and a host of other factors can create feelings quite different from what God's Word tells us is true. And if we follow those feelings, defeat is not far off. These are the times when we should read again the passages that emphasize our liberation from sin's power; talk to God and thank Him that we have died with Christ and been raised with Him; and then operate on the basis of fact rather than feeling.

7. Do you have a plan for beginning each day with a quiet time or time alone with God, however brief? Christian bookstores offer a great variety of devotional guides to help believers in this area; or you may choose to follow your own pattern for personal devotions. Whatever form you might choose, start now (if you haven't already) and strive for consistency.

Questions

1. In your own words, explain why it was necessary that we be identified with Christ in His crucifixion. Does this accomplish something we cannot do on our own? If so, what?

2. In light of Romans 6:6–7, how might a Christian face a particular temptation, compared to a non-Christian facing the same temptation? Would both experience temptation? On what basis might they respond differently?

3. Compare Romans 6:4–7 with Galatians 5:16–18. What is the difference between trying to be good and walking in newness of life?

4. According to Philippians 3:7–11, what are some of the benefits that follow our identification with Christ in His crucifixion?

5. What light does Galatians 2:20 shed on the idea that we should crucify ourselves repeatedly in order to please God?

6. Can you think of any areas of your life in which you are repeatedly subject to sin's power? How might the truths discussed in this chapter make a difference in these areas?

CHAPTER 13

RESURRECTED WITH CHRIST

Romans 6:11–23

Anyone who, by faith, accepts Jesus Christ as personal Savior is identified with Jesus Christ in all that He has accomplished. That person is joined to Christ in His death, in His burial, and in His resurrection. We believers have been joined with Christ in resurrection that we might walk in newness of life. Ephesians 1:19–20 illustrates this great theme when Paul prays for the saints that they might know "what is the exceeding greatness of His power toward us who believe, according to the working of His mighty power which He worked in Christ when He raised Him from the dead . . . ." Ephesians 2:5–6 also affirms this truth: "Even when we were dead in trespasses, [God] made us alive together with Christ . . . and raised us up together, and made us sit together in the heavenly places in Christ Jesus."

The Fact of Co-resurrection

The apostle Paul recognized the fact of his resurrection with Christ when he revealed the great desire of his heart in Philippians 3:10–11: "That I may know Him and the power of His resurrection, and the fellowship of His sufferings, being conformed to His death, if, by any means, I may attain to the resurrection from the dead." The desire of Paul's heart is not that some day he might be brought to physical resurrection, but rather that the resurrection life of Jesus Christ, in which he has become a partaker by identification with Christ, might evidence itself through him day by day.

Colossians 3:1 also refers to our identification with Christ in His death, burial, and resurrection: "If then you were raised with Christ [and you have been], seek those things which are above, where Christ is, sitting at the right hand of God." All of the commands and injunctions of the third chapter of Colossians are based on the assumption that believers have been identified with Jesus Christ not only in His death and burial but also in His resurrection.

Perhaps the most important New Testament passage dealing with our resurrection with Christ is in Romans 6. In Romans 6:3 Paul states the fact that we who were identified as living members of Christ's body by being baptized into Jesus Christ by the Holy Spirit were also baptized into His death. As we have already seen, we experienced co-crucifixion with Christ. Next, Paul writes in verses 4–5, "We were buried with Him through baptism into death, that just as Christ was raised from the dead by the glory of the Father, even so we also should walk in newness of life. For if we have been united together in the likeness of His death, certainly we also shall be in the likeness of His resurrection." Once again this is not primarily emphasizing the physical resurrection of the body, as important as that teaching is in the Bible. Instead, Paul's thought is the newness of life that will be made evident in the child of God because he has experienced co-crucifixion and co-resurrection with Christ. Because we have died with Christ, we have been set free from obligation to obey the old man (6:6). He that has died (6:7) has been freed from mandatory control by the sin nature. The next concern, then, is that those who have died with Christ should live for God.

Paul develops this thought by using the life of Christ as an illustration. He says, ". . . Christ having been raised from the dead, dies no more. Death no longer has dominion over Him. For the death that He died, He died to sin once for all; but the life that He lives, He lives to God" (Romans 6:9–10). Death could not claim the Lord Jesus Christ as it claims all humanity because of sin. Jesus Christ alone among men was separate from sinners—holy, harmless, and undefiled. He died not because death had a right to lay hold of Him, but because by an act of His will He submitted to death and dismissed His soul from His body. Jesus submitted to death to redeem us who were spiritually dead, and make us alive in Him. Then on the third day He emerged triumphant over physical death by His resurrection from the grave. After His resurrection, death had no more dominion over Him and could not again reach out its cold hand and hold Him in its power. Death had gripped Him for the three days He was in the tomb; but when Christ came forth from the grave, He was delivered from death's power. After the resurrection, Christ was not subject to anything death could do to Him.

The Response of Faith

Because we have been identified with Christ in His resurrection, we are expected to walk in newness of life—to live a new kind of life, the kind of life that need not submit to sin's control. But in order to live this kind of life, we must exercise faith. For this reason Paul, after presenting the great fact of the Christian's identification with Christ, calls on believers to consider themselves "to be dead indeed to sin, but alive to God in Christ Jesus our Lord" (Romans 6:11). The word translated "reckon" or "consider" in verse 11 literally means "to count a thing to be true." So Paul says, "In light of the fact that I have presented to you, I call upon you to count it to be true that you yourselves have died to sin's dominion, that you have been made alive to God because you have experienced a co-resurrection with Jesus Christ our Lord." The fact: you died and rose again. The faith: your response to the fact God declares to be true.

The Power of the Holy Spirit

In Romans 8 we discover the force by which this fact operates in a believer's life: "What the law could not do in that it was weak through the flesh, God did by sending His own Son in the likeness of sinful flesh, on account of sin: He condemned sin in the flesh, that the righteous requirement of the law might be fulfilled in us who do not walk according to the flesh but according to the Spirit" (Romans 8:3–4). The force by which the resurrection life of Jesus Christ is manifested in the life of the child of God is the Holy Spirit. The fact: you died and were resurrected with Christ. The faith: you count this fact to be true! The force: you permit the Holy Spirit to live His life through you. The resurrection life of Jesus Christ is lived by the Spirit's power in your life— moment by moment and step by step.

Galatians 5:16 offers the injunction, "Walk in the Spirit, and you shall not fulfill the lust of the flesh." This could be translated more literally, "You be constantly walking by means of the Spirit, and you will not fulfill the lusts of the flesh." We need to remind ourselves again and again that we cannot by ourselves walk in newness of life. We have been redeemed; we have been given new natures; we have new minds so we can know the truth of God; we have new hearts so we can know the love of God; and we have new wills so we can now obey God. But of ourselves we have no power to put into operation that life that has been implanted by the miracle of new birth.

However, as we continually walk in the power of the Spirit of God, the resurrection life that is ours will become evident in our lives. Our attitude should be that of Philippians 4:13—"I can do all things through Christ who strengthens me." Notice this verse does not say, "I can do all things because I have been born into God's family." Rather, it is "through Christ who strengthens me." The Holy Spirit indwelling the child of God reproduces the life of Jesus Christ in that believer, and Christ manifests His life through that Christian. The idea that we have in ourselves the wisdom, the strength, or the power to live the life of

Christ day after day, simply because we have been born into God's family, has brought about the downfall of many of God's children. We must depend on the fact that we have been crucified and resurrected with Christ, and then we must permit the Holy Spirit to live the resurrection life of Christ through us.

How can the Holy Spirit live His life through me? What is the key to understanding what it means for the Holy Spirit to live the resurrection life of Christ through me? Again we return to Romans 6 for our answer. Romans 6:13 reads, "Do not present your members as instruments of unrighteousness to sin, but present yourselves to God as being alive from the dead, and your members as instruments of righteousness to God." Again, in verse 16, "Do you not know that to whom you present yourselves slaves to obey, you are the one's slaves whom you obey, whether of sin to death, or of obedience to righteousness?" And in verse 19 we read, "Just as you presented your members as slaves of uncleanness, and of lawlessness leading to more lawlessness, so now present your members as slaves of righteousness for holiness."

Again and again the Bible emphasizes the principle of *yielding*, or *presenting*. By using this terminology the apostle shows how the Holy Spirit can live the life of Christ through the child of God. While walking by the Spirit has to do with divine enablement and supernatural empowerment, yielding to the Spirit has to do with the Spirit's direction or control over us. Apart from this act of yielding to the Spirit's control, the believer will experience no manifestation of Christ's resurrection life.

The Sacrifice of Self

The Bible reveals the secret of permitting the Spirit to do His work of conforming us to the Lord Jesus Christ when it says, "Yield yourselves to God," or "Present yourselves to God."

Several passages in the New Testament can illustrate this word. Let's look at just three of them. First, the word *present* is used in 2 Corinthians 11:2 of the presentation of a bride to the bridegroom at a marriage ceremony. Paul writes, "For I have betrothed you to one husband, that I may *present* you as a chaste virgin to Christ" (italics added). In New Testament times, the father of a bride would take the hand of his daughter and would put her hand into the hand of the bridegroom. By that act the bride was *presented* to the bridegroom, and she became his possession, fulfilling the marriage contract. Using the same word in Romans 6, Paul is emphasizing that just as there can be no lawful marriage apart from the consent of the wills of the two parties involved, so there will be no manifestation of the resurrection life of Christ apart from the Christian's consent to present himself to the Spirit's control.

Second, this word is used in Colossians 1:22, which tells us that Christ purposes "in the body of His flesh through death, to *present* you holy, and blameless, and irreproachable in His sight" (italics added). The Lord Jesus Christ will offer believers as a gift to the Father. We have become the Father's possession. We have been brought into an intimate relationship with the Father, and His home will become our dwelling place. This passage uses the word *present* to show that we have been put at the Father's disposal by this act of the Son. In like manner, we are to present ourselves to the Father, place ourselves at His disposal, so that the Spirit may manifest the life of Christ in and through us. This is the meaning of "present yourselves" in Romans 6.

The third passage is Romans 12:1, where Paul writes, "I beseech you therefore, brethren, by the mercies of God, that you present your bodies a living sacrifice, holy, acceptable to God, which is your reasonable service." The word *present* in Romans 12 is the same word used in Romans 6. Paul's climactic exhortation is to "present your bodies a living sacrifice."

In the Old Testament, every sacrifice was bound with a cord to the altar, as we read in Psalm 118:27: "God is the LORD, and He has given us light; Bind the sacrifice with cords to the horns of the altar." An animal offered as a sacrifice was not a voluntary, or a willing, sacrifice. Any animal brought to that scene of death could smell death in the spilled blood, and out of fear would run away if it were not bound to the altar. It was not until the Lord Jesus Christ came as "the Lamb of God that takes away the sin of the world" (John 1:29) that the world knew anything about a voluntary, or willing, sacrifice. Twice in Hebrews 10 (verses 7 and 9) Christ said, "I have come to do Your will, O God." Jesus Christ was a willing sacrifice. His blood had value before God above all the blood on Jewish altars because His blood was a voluntary sacrifice.

In Romans 12:1, then, God is asking His children for willing, or voluntary, sacrifices. God is not asking for a sacrifice of blood, for the blood of Christ was sufficient to cover every need. But God is asking for a willing sacrifice, the sacrifice of ourselves. So Paul exhorts believers, in view of all the mercies of God, that they present their bodies a willing sacrifice to Him. This is our logical service to God in view of what He has done for us through Jesus Christ.

While the Old Testament tells us nothing of a voluntary sacrifice, it does tell us about a living sacrifice. The beasts that were sacrificed to God on Israel's altars were dead sacrifices; but on the altar on Mount Moriah, where Abraham offered his son, Isaac, we see a living sacrifice. In perfect obedience to God, Abraham went on a long journey to the appointed place of sacrifice. He made his way up Mount Moriah and built an altar there. There he consecrated his son to God. And when, in obedience to the command of God, Abraham was about to offer Isaac as a dying sacrifice, the hand of God stayed the hand of Abraham, and Isaac stepped down off that altar to live as one who had been sacrificed to God. Isaac was sacrificed not when the knife touched his heart, but when he was put on that altar by his father in obedience to God's command. And when Isaac stepped down off that altar, he was one who had been sacrificed to God and lived.

God is asking His child to make himself a living sacrifice—one who is presented, one who is yielded to God. Apart from such a presentation, there will be no continuous manifestation of the resurrection life of Christ in the believer.

The presentation referred to in Romans 12:1 is viewed as a once-and-for-all presentation, as indicated by the tense of the Greek verb. So we might render the verse this way: "I beseech you, brethren, in view of the mercies of God, that you *once and for all* present your bodies, a living sacrifice, holy, acceptable unto God, which is your reasonable service." God is calling upon us who know Him to come face-to-face with our responsibility to Him, and to register this once-and-for-all decision: "Father, right now, I am presenting myself as a sacrifice to You." When we present ourselves to God, we at that moment take on the designation, or the character, of one who has been sacrificed. From that point on, we need not sacrifice ourselves again and again. We need only continually reaffirm the fact of our once-for-all presentation as sacrifices to God.

It may well be that you are stumbling and falling in your Christian life because you have never given yourself, or presented yourself, to God by an act of your will. God the Holy Spirit cannot continuously empower you to righteousness and true holiness, cannot manifest the resurrection life of Christ in you, until you have first of all yielded, presented, submitted yourself to God. But when you—recognizing your responsibility and loving the God who has placed that responsibility on you—by an act of your will present yourself to Him, then you too become one who has been sacrificed and yet lives.

The Christian life begins when we accept Jesus Christ as personal Savior. We begin living the Christian life when we present ourselves as sacrifices to God so that we may continually be walking by the power of the Holy Spirit. Is this something you have done?

Notes

1. At least once each year during the Easter season, we focus on Christ's resurrection. We consider the great power of God in raising Him from the dead; the victory over sin His resurrection effected; and the awesome proof of His

identity as the Son of God. But how often do we think of those same factors in relation to the resurrection life Christ wants us to experience today? Because we have been raised with Christ, we have the potential to experience God's power, God's victory, and God's proof of our identity as His children as we allow Christ to live His life through us in the power of the Holy Spirit. Not just once a year, but every day!

2. Understanding that everyone who has trusted Christ has become a living member of His universal body should cause us to view our Christian brothers and sisters with tremendous understanding and respect. That is not to say that we will always agree on everything. But it is to say that we should always look first to Him, and our accountability to Him, any time we interact with other members of the body.

3. Considering ourselves to be dead to sin but alive to God is not mere positive thinking or psychological trickery. It is a rational response to a fact that is based on an historical event, documented by eyewitnesses, and verified by the supernatural testimony of God Himself. It is not blind faith, but factual faith—personal trust in reliable information that will change our lives!

4. The power of the Holy Spirit is quite different from the nebulous Force of new-age beliefs. The Holy Spirit is not an impersonal, ethereal energy that we somehow mystically pursue. He is the personal presence of Christ in our lives, living the resurrection life in us and through us in His supernatural power as we yield ourselves to His control.

5. We need to be cautious about the way our self-help culture has permeated even some Christian teaching. By the time we listen to everyone telling us how to make our marriages work, raise our children, manage our finances, tame our teenagers, further our careers, and solve all our personal problems, we might think that God expects us to achieve righteousness through our own efforts. The Bible, however, tells us that personal righteousness and the abundant life begin with complete, total dependence on Jesus Christ, recognizing that only He can do for us that which we cannot do for ourselves. Certainly, we have a responsibility to apply His Word to the various areas of our lives. But unless we depend on the Holy Spirit's power in our lives, and trust Him to live His life through us, we will get nowhere.

6. Obeying a "Yield" sign in traffic is not too difficult when the oncoming vehicle is a huge truck! Maybe we should consider our power compared to God's power when we are faced with the temptation to not "Yield" to Him. Clearly, it's no contest!

7. One of the most moving episodes in the legendary saga of the Alamo is the point at which all the men defending the Alamo presented themselves for

defense of the fort, even though it meant certain death. If we can recognize the courage and character behind soldiers presenting themselves to a human commander, surely we can see the value of presenting our own lives to a heavenly Commander who has already guaranteed victory! Have you made this kind of personal commitment to Christ?

8. The episode of Abraham and Isaac reminds us that total dedication to God requires that we hold nothing back in our hearts. Although God did not require Isaac's life, Abraham was willing to offer it, believing that God would raise Isaac from the dead if necessary in order to fulfill His promise. Is there anything in your life keeping you from total dedication to God? Is there anything you are holding back in your heart, or anything you are not willing to let go of in order to lay hold of Him? Like Abraham, you can trust God to do what is right and what is necessary with what you give Him—when you give Him everything.

Questions

1. Read Philippians 1:19–21. What did Christ's resurrection accomplish in relation to Satan's power and purposes? Does this mean the Enemy is no longer active in the world? What does it mean to individual believers?

2. What do you think it means to "reckon yourselves to be dead indeed to sin, but alive to God in Christ Jesus our Lord" (Romans 6:11)? What difference does this make? Why?

3. In light of Galatians 5:16 and Ephesians 5:18, define what it means to walk "according to the Spirit" as mentioned in Romans 8:3–4.

4. Can you name specific areas of your life that can be described only by Philippians 4:13?

5. What kinds of things do you think could keep a Christian from yielding his or her life to Christ? How would you advise someone facing these kinds of obstacles?

6. How would you describe your personal response to Romans 12:1? What will be the outworking of this type of commitment, as revealed in verse 2?

CHAPTER 14

FILLED WITH THE SPIRIT

Ephesians 5:18

While I was serving a pastorate in the northwestern corner of Pennsylvania, my brother came to visit me in the early spring of the year. While he was there, twelve inches of new snow fell on top of the deep snow already on the ground. Then the time came for him to go to a neighboring town to take a train back to Philadelphia. Because of the road conditions we allowed extra time to get to the station. We were proceeding cautiously when, with no warning at all, the car skidded, turned around, and landed in a deep snowbank on the opposite side of the road, pointed in the wrong direction. We were prepared for such emergencies and never traveled without a shovel and a bucket of sand in the trunk of the car. We began to dig away the snow, but found that it was deeper than we had anticipated. As we were working frantically, a car came along. The driver saw the predicament we were in, courteously stopped, rolled down his window, and called out, "Do you need any help?"

"No thank you," I said. "We'll make it ourselves." I will never forget the look my brother gave me! Even though I shouted after the car as it drove away that we did indeed need help, it was too late. I was too independent for my own good! And there was nothing left to do but to dig through six feet of snow and try to clear the wheels.

When help is offered, we often would rather do without it than admit to ourselves that we need to depend on someone else. The apostle Paul was facing just such a situation with the Ephesian believers to whom he wrote, "Do not be drunk with wine, in which is dissipation; but be filled with the Spirit" (Ephesians 5:18). Earlier in his letter, Paul had outlined requirements for God's children which no one unaided by the Holy Spirit can possibly fulfill. No person, by his own efforts, can bring his whole life into conformity to Jesus Christ. No person by himself can be a living epistle to proclaim Jesus Christ, to be read and known by all men. Yet when God offers help in the fulfillment of the requirements He has set out for us, with arrogant self-confidence we look to Him and say, "No thank you; we can make it ourselves."

In the commandment given to us in Ephesians 5:18, God is offering us His assistance, His power, to fulfill His requirements. Therefore we want to focus on three things: the meaning of being filled with the Spirit, the means by which we are filled with the Spirit, and the results of being filled with the Spirit.

The Meaning of Being Filled

To discover what it means to be filled with the Holy Spirit, we need to look in the Bible at some references to something being filled.

Several biblical words are translated from the original language into the one English word *filled*. But the essential thought behind all of these words is that of filling up a container by putting something into it. An empty glass into which water is poured is said to be *filled* with water. Of course, technically the glass was not empty to start with. Unless it existed in a vacuum, the glass was filled with air until the water was poured into it. When the water was poured in, it drove out what had previously been filling it and filled it with something new. Thus when the Bible speaks of a person being filled with the Spirit, it is speaking of the Spirit supplanting that which was once within the person, and taking over the life that is filled with the Spirit of God.

To illustrate this concept, let's look first at Luke 5:26. Following Christ's miracle of healing the paralytic, "they were all amazed, and they glorified God and were filled with fear, saying, 'We have seen strange things today!' " The people were *filled* with fear. They were accustomed to seeing paralytics—but never before had they seen one instantly cured of his paralysis. As they witnessed that divine power, their complacency and doubt were removed and were replaced by fear.

In Luke 6:11 we read that following Christ's miracle of healing the man with a withered hand, the Pharisees were "filled with rage, and discussed with one another what they might do to Jesus." Christ had presented Himself publicly as Messiah, Savior, and King. The religious leaders were perfectly complacent in their own religion—looking for salvation through observing traditions, trusting in their own works. But when Jesus displayed the power of God in their midst, their self-righteousness was shamed and their self-satisfaction gave way to rage. They were filled with anger, and they began plotting to do away with Jesus.

The word *filled* is also used in Acts 2:4, where we read that the men in the Upper Room were all *filled* with the Holy Spirit. The same thought conveyed in the previous passages is intended here. The filling of these men with something new supplanted that which previously filled them. They had possessed natural power before; but now that natural power was supplanted by a new supernatural power as they were filled with the Holy Spirit.

If the men in Luke 5 had continued to be filled with indifference, they would never have been filled with fear. If the Pharisees in Luke 6 had continued to be filled with self-satisfaction, they never would have been filled with rage. And logically, if the disciples in the Upper Room had continued to be filled with their own abilities, strengths, wisdom, and power, they would not have been filled with the Holy Spirit. Being filled with one thing prevents being filled with another. Thus there is a common trait in all three of these passages: filling includes the idea of filling up something by first removing what was there. Then, that which is filled is possessed or controlled by the new thing that fills it.

A second word translated *filled* in the New Testament contains this basic idea of filling up or taking possession, but it also seems to add the thought that anything that fills an object motivates or moves that person to take a certain course of action. The emphasis here is not simply on the act of filling, but on the result of being filled. Acts 6:5 reads, "The saying pleased the whole multitude. And they chose Stephen, a man full of faith . . . ." Stephen was filled up with faith, and his faith evidenced itself in good works before the congregation, so that they knew that he was controlled by faith. We also read in Acts 5:3 that when Ananias brought in the purchase price of his field and laid it at the disciples' feet, Peter said, "Ananias, why has Satan filled your heart to lie to the Holy Spirit . . . ?" The filling by Satan produced deceit, deception, and fraud. Because Ananias was filled with Satan, he was moved to a certain kind of action. Again, in John 16:6, after Jesus told the disciples about His approaching death, He said, "Because I have said these things to you, sorrow has filled your heart." The disciples were so filled with sorrow, it dominated them and they considered themselves orphans. That is why Christ promised in John 14:18, "I will not leave you orphans." And finally, we read in Acts 4:31 that "when they had prayed, the place where they were assembled together was shaken; and they were all filled with the Holy Spirit, and they spoke the word of God with boldness."

When we put together these two ideas from the original text to form our concept of *filling*, we understand that filling involves that which comes into our lives, expels that which was there, and so fills our lives that we are possessed and controlled by that which fills us. Whether filled with rage, fear, sorrow, Satan, faith, or the Holy Spirit, the old control ends and a new person, emotion, or power dominates.

The Means of Filling

In Ephesians 5, the apostle Paul is attempting to communicate to believers that God the Holy Spirit, who came to dwell in Christians the moment they accept Christ as Savior, comes into one's life in order to possess it, own it, control it. The person who is *filled* with the Holy Spirit is not the person who is simply indwelt by the Spirit; it is the individual who is controlled, or led, by the Spirit of God. The person who is filled with the Holy Spirit is under the control of the Spirit so that his life is ordered by the Spirit of God.

In three separate passages God's Word offers a contrast between drunkenness and the filling of the Holy Spirit. Taking a closer look at these will help us understand Paul's teaching in Ephesians 5.

First, in Luke 1:15 an angel announces the birth of John the Baptizer, who was to come as the forerunner of Messiah, in fulfillment of Malachi's prophecy. Concerning John and the power in his ministry the angel said, "For he will be great in the sight of the Lord, and shall drink neither wine nor strong drink. He will also be filled with the Holy Spirit, even from his mother's womb." John would not be controlled by wine or strong drink. Instead, he would be controlled by the Holy Spirit of God, even from the moment of conception. We learn from this angelic announcement that two different powers or forces may control a person. A person may be controlled by alcohol, or a person may be controlled by the Holy Spirit of God. Both will produce a new kind of behavior, a kind of behavior far different from that which is normal. John's power, of course, was not the power of alcohol. It was the power of the Holy Spirit.

Next, in Acts 2 we read about the Holy Spirit's coming into this world to take up residence in the church, when believers were first filled with the Holy Spirit (Acts 2:4). There was something in the ministry and the message of the apostles that was not natural, something that demanded an explanation. If a person comes with a supernatural message and a supernatural power, that person should be believed and his message received. However, if a person comes claiming to be God's messenger, yet is empowered by someone or something other than God, that person should be rejected and his message scorned.

On the Day of Pentecost, Peter stood up to deliver a message to Israel, the nation that had rejected Christ and had said, "We will not have this man to rule over us." Peter's message is summarized in verse 36: "Let all the house of Israel know assuredly that God has made this Jesus, whom you crucified, both Lord and Christ [Messiah]." Now, if Peter preached a divine message by the power of the Holy Spirit, his message was to be believed and the people who heard it were responsible to act on it. However, the religious leaders questioned Peter's authority by reaching the conclusion that he was drunk. They recognized that they were seeing and hearing a man who was controlled by a power outside of himself. Verses 12–13 read, "They were all amazed and perplexed, saying to one another, 'Whatever could this mean?' Others mocking said, 'They are full of new wine.' " In the biblical language, it is clear that this insult went even deeper, inferring that the apostles were like little babies who could get drunk on grape juice!

However, Peter refuted their words by pointing out that it was only the third hour of the day—about 9 a.m. (verse 15). Since it was a holy day, no law-abiding Jew would touch alcoholic beverages from sundown the evening before until sundown that night. So it was impossible—since they were law-abiding Jews—to explain their actions as the effects of wine. So Peter said, "These are not drunk [not controlled by alcoholic spirits], as you suppose . . . but this is what was spoken by the prophet Joel . . . ." Joel had prophesied that the Holy Spirit of God would take up residence in people and would control people and use them for God's glory (Joel 2:28). Thus we find that Peter was contrasting control by alcoholic beverages with control by the Holy Spirit.

Then, in Ephesians 5:18 we find this same contrast when Paul gives the prohibition, "Do not be drunk with wine, in which is dissipation; but be filled with the Spirit." Why should the disgusting spectacle of drunkenness be mentioned in the same breath with the glorious experience of being controlled and moved by the Holy Spirit of God? Because both experiences completely transform a person. Whether one is under the control of alcohol or under the control of the Spirit of God, one's conduct will be entirely different from what it was before. When alcohol takes control, a person will be unable to walk the same, talk the same, think the same. Why? Because alcohol controls and transforms people by removing their inhibitions, along with their good sense.

What the Bible shows us in stark contrast to alcohol's control is that when we are under the control of God's Spirit, our lives are so altered that where we once were unable to conform to God's standards of righteousness in our own strength, through the Spirit's power we live a new quality of life. The Holy Spirit can conform us to Jesus Christ in our daily walk. The Holy Spirit can cause us to be witnesses for Jesus Christ, and cause timid lips to speak the gospel with boldness and authority. We are utterly transformed by the Spirit of God who fills, or controls, us. God's ideal for His child is to have His child so controlled, so possessed by the Spirit of God that Christ's life is manifested through us by the Holy Spirit's power.

The Results of Filling

It goes without argument that as God's children, we are living in a degenerate world. We are tempted daily to accept standards that do not conform to the standards of the Bible. We are surrounded by practices that are contrary to the teaching of Scripture; we are despised by the unregenerate around us because the Lord Jesus Christ is despised; and we are persecuted because Jesus Christ was rejected and persecuted. Yet the difficulties we face today do not remove our obligation to the holiness, righteousness, and godliness imposed on us by a holy and righteous God.

The economic future of the world is uncertain. No one can predict what will happen. The world political situation is such that experts are grasping for some solution. Religiously, the world is in equal turmoil. Those who voice allegiance to Christ seem to be diminishing in number, while unbelief and apostasy seem to be increasing at every turn. How are Christians to stand up under the religious, political, economic, and social pressures put on us? God has provided His children with One upon whom we can rely and who will sustain us through every trial and pressure.

In the Upper Room, our Lord told His disciples that it was necessary for Him to go away. In view of this, He promised, "I will pray the Father, and He will give you another Helper, that He may abide with you forever" (John 14:16). The word translated *Helper* literally means "one called alongside to help." We can illustrate the meaning of this word by saying that the Holy Spirit has come to be a crutch. While a crutch is a sign of its user's weakness, it also is his strength. The child of God is like a disabled person who has no power to stand alone, or to walk as he should. Therefore he needs a crutch upon which he can lean and depend. God has given us that One upon whom we can depend—the Holy Spirit.

Even so, that illustration doesn't entirely satisfy the Spirit's ministry to believers, because a crutch is an *external* support. God the Holy Spirit has come to dwell within us to be an *internal* support, as we read in 2 Corinthians 3:5, "Not that we are sufficient of ourselves to think of anything as being from ourselves, but our sufficiency is from God." In this same epistle God said to the apostle Paul, "My grace is sufficient for you, for My strength is made perfect in weakness" (2 Corinthians 12:9). What was to be the source of Paul's sufficiency? On what was he to lean? The grace of God! He was to be sustained and empowered by the Holy Spirit. This is the same reason many of us, in times of testing, discouragement, trial, defeat, or need have gone to Philippians 4:13 and echoed the words, "I can do all things through Christ who strengthens me." God promised divine help. His grace, His power, His strength all are made available to the child of God, when the child of God is walking by means of the Spirit of God. The Holy Spirit can sustain us in every experience of life.

Even though God has given believers the One who can sustain and uphold us, far too many do not avail themselves of the Helper God has provided. We naturally expect unbelievers to turn to something outside of themselves for support, since they do not have the indwelling, empowering ministry of the Holy Spirit. The unregenerate have many props and crutches on which they depend. Of course, all those things are finite, temporary, and utterly inadequate. What a tragedy it is, then, when the child of God abandons the Helper and trusts in self or those things upon which the world depends.

One support too many unsaved people depend on is alcohol. An alcoholic is not an alcoholic because of the amount of alcohol he consumes; he is an alcoholic because he depends on, trusts in, and relies on alcohol to see him through experiences that are too much for him. The same is true of people who must reach for a cigarette any time they are under stress. The same can be true—and often is true—of those who absolutely must have a cup of coffee, sweets, or food as a crutch whenever they face stress, strain, or pressure. Grossly overfed Christians are a silent testimony that they may be depending on something other than the Spirit for comfort. Because they do not know how to depend on the power of God that is available through the Spirit-filled life, other believers may run to some diversion—the newspaper, a magazine, television—when they suddenly face strain or pressure.

The question we should ask ourselves concerning anything that may be a crutch in our lives is, "Why do I use these things? Am I expecting them to do for me what the Holy Spirit should be doing? Am I asking them to do what only God the Holy Spirit can do?" If these things are true in your experience, it would be good to begin building a rubbish pile right now. When things are used as substitutes for the blessed experience of being filled with the Spirit of God, they need to be thrown out of our lives. Only then can we cast all our dependence on the Holy Spirit. We must remember that when we trust the world's false supports, we may get some temporary relief, but we will not at the same time enjoy the help of the divine Comforter.

Do not be drunk with wine—do not depend on the world's supports—but be filled with the Spirit.

Notes

1. It is a trick of our pride to believe we are sufficient in ourselves to live a victorious Christian life. Like a lost motorist who refuses to stop and ask for directions, we may blunder around for years before we are willing to admit that we cannot do the impossible. But why should we even attempt the impossible when all God asks of us is that we let Him live His life in us and through us? And how difficult is it to go to God on our knees and admit to Him that apart from His power, apart from His enablement, we cannot live a life that glorifies Christ? In 2 Corinthians 12:9 Paul wrote, "He said to me, 'My grace is sufficient for you, for My strength is made perfect in weakness.' Therefore most gladly I will rather boast in my infirmities, that the power of Christ may rest upon me." Power in our Christian lives begins when we recognize our own weakness and our need for His power.

2. Luke 6:11 shows us that we should not be surprised at all when the world is enraged by Christians' good works. Let's not be misled to think that if we simply live a good Christian life, the world system will be content to leave us alone and non-Christians will be drawn to faith in Christ. Those who would oppose Jesus Christ to His face will be just as outraged at our good deeds; and those whose hearts have been prepared by the Holy Spirit still need to hear the good news of the gospel in order to trust Him as Savior. A dynamic Christian walk will include both—walking the walk *and* talking the talk.

3. What kinds of things fill your life right now? If not the power of the Holy Spirit, perhaps it is one or more of the many distractions we face every day, diversions like job stress, career climbing, absorbing relationships, moral compromise, or simply day-to-day busyness. Being filled with the Holy Spirit does not mean we add one more thing to our busy lives; it means we allow Him to take absolute control of all those things that are now controlling us. We allow Him to take the place of those inferior, finite things that will otherwise fill our lives and dominate us.

4. Remember—the Holy Spirit is *in* our lives from the moment we trust Christ. Being *filled* with the Holy Spirit is a matter of our lives being *controlled* by Him who already indwells us.

5. Isn't it interesting that our mass-media culture bombards us constantly with the commercial messages of alcohol—painting a picture of lives made happy, joyful, and fulfilled because the subjects are drinking a particular brand of beer? It sounds ludicrous, and yet it is extremely effective. The question is, do we really understand that the Spirit-filled, Spirit-led life is the only life that will provide us with true joy and fulfillment?

6. One Bible teacher puts it this way: "What in your life can be explained only in terms of the supernatural?" Yielding control of your life to God's Spirit will produce a supernatural quality of life. If we take the parallel of Ephesians 5:18 literally, the control of God's Spirit will permeate our lives as completely as alcohol permeates a drunk person's behavior.

7. History has shown us that as religious oppression and persecution increase in a country, the number of people who profess Christ goes down—but the level of commitment within their ranks turns sharply upward! Why? Because living a steadfast Christian life in the face of ridicule, public disapproval, and even government intimidation requires power outside ourselves, specifically, the power of the Holy Spirit. Do you want to go the distance, no matter what the circumstances? Yield your life to Him and expect great things!

8. Have you ever attempted to rid your life of a habit or dependency, only to be defeated just as you thought you were making headway? As we have learned, the best way to empty a glass of air is to fill it with something else; likewise, the best way to empty our lives of those things that hold us back spiritually is to fill our lives with the controlling power of God's Spirit. His power to cleanse, restore, and heal is far greater than ours can ever be.

Questions

1. Compare Ephesians 5:18 to Romans 8:9. Is it possible to be a Christian and not have the Holy Spirit dwelling in you? How would you describe the difference between the *indwelling* of the Holy Spirit and the *filling* of the Holy Spirit?

2. How do the descriptions of "fear" in Luke 5:26 and "rage" in Luke 6:11 help us understand the meaning of "filled with the Spirit" in Ephesians 5:18? What other things might fill a person? How might these affect their actions?

3. In Acts 4:31, what was the immediate result of the filling of the Holy Spirit? Do you think this result will be evident in those today who are filled with the Holy Spirit? In what ways, specifically?

4. In light of the previous question, what does Acts 1:8 tell us about the purpose of the indwelling and filling ministry of the Holy Spirit? Who spoke these words? To whom do you think they apply?

5. Read Ephesians 5:18–21. What will be some visible results as believers are filled with the Holy Spirit?

6. Relate 2 Corinthians 3:5, 12:9 and Philippians 4:13 to what you have learned about being filled with the Spirit. How might these become realities in your life?

CHAPTER 15

YIELDING TO THE SPIRIT

Romans 6:11–23

While I was a seminary student, our president—Dr. Lewis Sperry Chafer—came into class one morning with a twinkle in his eye. He had just returned from an extended trip, and said that at the close of one meeting, an individual came up to him and said, "Oh, Dr. Chafer, I have just received the baptism of the Holy Spirit. Tell me, have you ever had the second blessing?"

Dr. Chafer replied, "Yes, I have. In fact, I have had the third."

The person looked at him rather surprised and said, "I've heard of a second blessing, but I've never heard of a third. What is that?"

Dr. Chafer said, "Well, come to think of it, I guess I have had the three-thoι sandth blessing instead of just the third." The questioner gave Dr. Chafer a look that showed that she thought he was beside himself. Then Dr. Chafer used the occasion to explain to that believer the difference between the baptizing of the Holy Spirit and the filling of the Holy Spirit.

In Ephesians 5:18 we are commanded, "Be filled with the Spirit." But exactly how are we filled with the Holy Spirit?

Baptism and Filling

There is a difference between being baptized by the Spirit and being filled with the Spirit. First Corinthians 12:13 tells us, "For by one Spirit we were all baptized into one body—whether Jews or Greeks, whether slaves or free—and have all been made to drink into one Spirit." The baptizing work of the Spirit of God is the divine act by which a believer in Christ is joined as a living member to the body of which Jesus Christ is the head. This is entirely different from the command of Ephesians 5:18, "Be filled with the Spirit." To recognize the difference between the baptizing work of the Holy Spirit and the filling of the Spirit in the believer's life, we can look at several contrasts.

First, 1 Corinthians 12:13 shows us that the baptizing work of the Holy Spirit takes place once and for all. It is not repetitive. It takes place the moment a person accepts Jesus Christ as personal Savior. In contrast to this, the filling of the Spirit is continuous and can be an often repeated experience for the child of God.

Second, if you know Jesus Christ as Savior, the baptizing work of the Holy Spirit has already taken place in your life. It is a past act or event that initiated you into God's family. The filling of the Holy Spirit, on the other hand, is a present command to believers concerning their daily walk and experience.

Third, every child of God already has experienced the baptizing work of the Holy Spirit and need not seek some subsequent experience or "second blessing." Paul said to his fellow believers in Corinth, "By one Spirit we were all baptized into one body" (1 Corinthians 12:13). There is no such thing as a believer who has not been baptized by the Holy Spirit, for all who accept Christ are joined or identified (baptized) into the body of Christ. But the filling of the Spirit is true only for those believers who respond to the command of Ephesians 5:18. If all believers were filled from the moment of spiritual birth, it would be unnecessary for Paul to command any to be filled. Again, we see that the baptizing work of the Spirit concerns our initial union with Christ, while the filling of the Spirit concerns our daily practice and our experience of Christ living His life through us.

Finally, we can search the Scriptures and find that the Bible never commands any believer to be baptized with the Spirit. In contrast, believers clearly are commanded to be filled with the Spirit. Again we see a difference between what the Holy Spirit does to bring us into union with Christ, and what our daily experience with the Spirit should be.

With these contrasts in mind, we can see why Dr. Chafer felt it was necessary to show that it would be impossible for any believer to have a second baptism. On the authority of God's Word we can declare that if you have accepted Christ as Savior, you are already blessed "with every spiritual blessing in the heavenly places in Christ" (Ephesians 1:3), though our realization of glorified bodies awaits our resurrection with Him. No other gifts have been withheld. So, if you have never entered into the blessings God has already promised and provided for you the moment you believed and were baptized by the Spirit into Christ's body, you indeed need to know the joy of being continuously filled and controlled by the Spirit of God.

Preliminary Considerations

To fully understand the command to be filled with the Spirit, we need to notice several things.

First, the grammatical construction is important. The verb, *be filled,* is an imperative, a command—not a plea—issued to all Christians. We aren't to debate whether we should be filled. It's not something we can take or leave. God has given us this command because it is His purpose that every child of His should be controlled by the Holy Spirit.

Second, the verb is in the present tense, indicating that it expresses an action going on and on. It is difficult to translate this literally into English, but what the command, "Be filled with the Spirit," is saying is, "You believers be constantly being filled with the Spirit." This may be rough English—but it is good theology. As we have seen, being filled with the Spirit is not a once-and-for-all action; rather, it should be a daily, hourly, moment-by-moment experience in which we are consciously under the control and authority of the Holy Spirit.

Third, the Greek verb *be filled* is in the passive voice, meaning that someone else is to do the filling *to* us. We aren't told to fill ourselves; instead, we are to allow the Holy Spirit—who indwells us—to possess and control us continuously. Notice that we do not need to get more of the Holy Spirit; rather we need to let the Holy Spirit have all of us. We aren't commanded to seek more of the Holy Spirit than we received at the moment of spiritual birth. We are commanded to permit the Holy Spirit to preside over every aspect of our lives and personalities.

An Act of Faith

How can we who have been born into God's family and have been baptized into the body of Christ experience the filling of the Holy Spirit and be brought under the Spirit's moment-by-moment control? We find the answer to this question in something the Lord Jesus said when He was in Jerusalem for the Feast of Tabernacles, as recorded in John 7:37–39: "On the last day, that great day of the feast, Jesus stood and cried out, saying, 'If anyone thirsts, let him come to Me and drink. He who believes in Me, as the Scripture has said, out of his heart will flow rivers of living water.' But this He spoke concerning the Spirit, whom those believing in Him would receive; for the Holy Spirit was not yet given, because Jesus was not yet glorified."

This invitation indicates how a child of God may be filled with the Spirit. It begins with a desire, or thirst. Jesus said, "If anyone thirsts. . . ." Apart from thirst a person will not drink; and no person will ever be controlled by the Holy Spirit who does not desire to be controlled, to have every area of life brought under the Spirit's authority. What a tragedy that so many Christians are satisfied with so little! They are content with their present experience, content with the knowledge they have, content with past victories. They have no desire to be conformed to the image of

Christ, to evidence God's righteousness in their lives on a daily basis. In their complacency they never lift a voice to cry to God for anything beyond that which they already have.

Consider the spiritual thirst of Moses, David, and the apostle Paul. Moses, after he had been on the mountain with God, prayed, "Show me now Your way, that I may know You" (Exodus 33:13). David cried out, "As the deer pants for the water brooks, so my soul pants for You, O God" (Psalm 42:1). Paul revealed his thirst for God in Philippians 3:10 when he wrote that he counted all things as loss "that I may know Him . . . ." Jesus Himself said, "Blessed are those who hunger and thirst for righteousness, for they shall be filled" (Matthew 5:6).

As long as we are satisfied with the blessings we have enjoyed in the past, as long as we are satisfied with the kind of lives we are living now, we will not thirst for God's control over our lives through the Holy Spirit, nor for the Spirit's empowerment to a new life and new evidences of God's righteousness in our daily lives. Therefore we need to abandon our satisfaction and complacency with our present state of growth in Christ. We need to say, "Lord, I cannot attain Your goal and purpose for me as Your child. But I want to turn my life over to the Holy Spirit and let Him empower me so that Christ's holiness might be manifested through me." We *must* have a desire for what God wants to give us.

When we respond to our Lord's invitation—"If anyone thirsts, let him come to Me"—we admit our own defeat by coming. Too often, however, we let our stubborn pride hinder the Spirit's control over us, because we are independent by nature. Christ said we will never be brought under the control of the Spirit of God until we come to the end of ourselves; until we give up our struggling, our trying, our hoping, and our promising; until we admit defeat and come to Him.

Why are people so reluctant to come to Jesus Christ when He offers them forgiveness of sins, eternal life, and a position as children and heirs of the living God? It is because of pride. We say, in effect, "It's an insult to my morality, an insult to my intellect, and an insult to my religion." Thus because of stubbornness people will choose not to receive God's gift of eternal life. But for those who have trusted Christ for salvation and have received God's gift of eternal life, why do we not come to Him and avail ourselves of the provision God has made in the Person of the Holy Spirit? Again, it is because of pride and stubbornness. We don't want to admit to ourselves or to God or to anyone else that we can't live the Christian life. So we keep struggling, keep trying, and keep failing. With grim determination we say, "I can, I can, I can. Well, I didn't, but I'll try,

I'll try, I'll try." And we refuse to confess our inability and come to Him to quench our thirst for holiness and spirituality.

Notice, too, that a person must not only come to Him, but a person must also drink. "Let him come to Me and drink," Christ said. This is the act of appropriating, or claiming by faith, what God has provided. Remember Paul's statement in Ephesians 5:18—"Do not be drunk with wine, in which is dissipation; but be filled with the Spirit." A bottle of liquor may be set in front of a person, but he will not get drunk by staring at the bottle or even by handling it. He will not become intoxicated until he takes the bottle, opens it, and drinks enough of the liquor that it takes over control of all his faculties and senses. In the same way, no one ever becomes controlled by the Spirit of God simply by being around other Christians who are, or by being at church every time the doors are open, or by attending a Christian school, or even by working for a church or Christian organization. No one is ever controlled by the Holy Spirit apart from the conscious act of submitting to the Spirit's domination and control. Active belief, or faith, appropriates all God has provided.

God's Method of Control

In Romans, Paul tells us a great deal about the method by which we are filled, or controlled, by the Holy Spirit. Romans 6:11 asks us to believe a fact, to consider something to be true. In that passage, the fact is our relationship to Christ's death and resurrection. But the same principle holds true in regard to being controlled, or filled, by the Holy Spirit. We need to acknowledge certain facts. When you were born into God's family you received everlasting life, you were forgiven of your sin and guilt, and you were joined to the body of which Christ is head. Also, the moment you trusted Christ, God the Holy Spirit took up residence in your body and made it His temple. These are facts to be believed. On the basis of these facts, a response is demanded of the Christian. This response comes to us in the verb translated "yield" or "present."

Romans 6:12–13 admonishes us, "Do not let sin reign in your mortal body, that you should obey it in its lusts. And do not present your members as instruments of unrighteousness to sin, but present yourselves to God." The word *present* is the same word used in Romans 12:1, where Paul writes, "I beseech you therefore, brethren, by the mercies of God, that you present your bodies a living sacrifice . . . ." It is a word which means "to turn yourself over to another; to submit yourself to another." We are to present ourselves, yield ourselves, to God. For, as we read in Romans 6:16, "Do you not know that to whom you present yourselves slaves to obey, you are that one's slaves whom you obey . . . ?"

It was my privilege many times during my twenty-eight years as a pastor to officiate at wedding ceremonies. The time would come in the ceremony where I would ask the groom, "Will you have this woman to be your wife?" His reply was, "I will." Then I would address the bride: "Will you have this man to be your husband?" to which she would reply, "I will." Only then could I respond by saying, "I pronounce you man and wife." I did not marry them. They were married when by the consent of their wills they entered into that married state before God and witnesses. The consent of the will was absolutely essential. So it is with the filling of the Spirit. It is only when we consent, as an act of the will, to be controlled by the Spirit that we are filled with the Spirit.

Notes

1. Assurance of salvation may seem like old news to the person who has known Christ for many years, but uncertainty of eternal security in Christ can be a source of genuine anxiety for new believers. However, 1 Corinthians 12:13 assures us with absolute certainty that we have been baptized into Christ—that is, at the moment we trust Christ as Savior, we are completely identified with Him. That means that in order to reject us when we sin, God would have to reject His own dear Son with whom we have been identified. In other words, our immediate identification with Christ is absolute, irreversible, and eternal.

2. Although we may be accustomed to receiving and obeying orders from employers, teachers, military commanders, government agencies, or others in authority over us, we rarely hear about commands—*imperatives*—that God issues to His children. Do we take His authority in our lives as seriously as all those on a human plane? Are we as eager to please Him by obeying His commands?

3. In the language of the New Testament, the voice (active, middle, passive) of a verb was very significant. That is why it is so helpful to know that the command to "be filled" with God's Spirit is *passive*; that it is God's responsibility, not ours. It is not our place to conjure up some kind of emotional experience or ecstatic display. God's Word tells us that we simply yield ourselves to His control, and then He manifests the life of Christ in us. It is His work, not ours.

4. The newspaper occasionally carries stories of people who for years have possessed valuable treasures (art, coins, baseball cards, etc.) without knowing their value. Of course, once the owners realize the value of these things, they do what they can to cash in on them. Imagine, then, hearing about someone in poverty who possesses something of great value, something that is worth enough to ensure one's financial security for a lifetime, but does nothing to appropriate its value. Naturally, we would think he or she is being extremely

foolish. Yet that is the way many Christians are living their lives. They possess the Holy Spirit within them; but they are doing nothing to appropriate the spiritual wealth He offers. Is that any less foolish?

5. If you are like most people, when something major breaks in your house, you reach for the phone to call a plumber, a roofer, a mechanic, an electrician, or whoever might be needed to make repairs. When we encounter something beyond our ability, we willingly call someone who is duly qualified rather than making things worse by trying to fix it ourselves (or sometimes we call *after* we make things worse). In the same way, if we understand from God's Word all that the Christian life is supposed to be, we can see that it is well beyond our capabilities to live it. We can only make things worse by trying to do it ourselves. That's why God has given us the option of turning it over to the Holy Spirit, who is the only One qualified to live the life of Christ through us.

6. Anyone who has regularly attended a gym or fitness center knows there are always a few people who seem to believe they can become stronger through "osmosis." They come to the gym, mill around the equipment, visit with people who are working out, dress correctly, know the terminology, and even pay their dues to be there. But they don't get any stronger, because they're not actually exercising. Likewise, no matter how much you participate in the Christian environment, you must exercise your will in submitting to the Spirit's control over your life in order to experience a victorious, Spirit-filled life.

7. The more we think of our bodies as the temple of the Holy Spirit, the more we will eliminate from our lives those activities that are unacceptable as temple activities. Is there anything in your life that you should not bring into the temple of the Holy Spirit? If so, wouldn't your life be better off without it?

Questions

1. Compare Matthew 5:6 with John 7:37–39. What seems to be the logical conclusion we can draw from these two verses?

2. What kinds of things do you think would keep a person from yielding his or her life to the Holy Spirit's control? Which of these can provide an adequate substitute for the Spirit-filled life? What was Paul's opinion of anything that would stand between Him and a Christ-filled life (see Philippians 3:10)?

3. What choice or decision is evident in Romans 6:12–13? Do you think this is a once-for-all decision, or one that can be made repeatedly?

4. According to Romans 12:1, whose responsibility is it to offer a living sacrifice? According to Ephesians 5:18, whose responsibility is it to produce the filling of the Holy Spirit?

5. Read Romans 6:16. What kinds of sins produce an obvious enslavement—physical, mental, or emotional—in people's lives? What is the only thing that can set people free from this type of enslavement?

6. If it is the Spirit's responsibility to control us (Ephesians 5:18), what part do we play in the process of being filled with the Spirit? What element of human personality (heart, mind, or will) is most evident in this?

CHAPTER 16

LIBERTY IN THE CHRISTIAN LIFE

Romans 14:1–3

The book of Romans presents glorious truths concerning the believer's freedom from the condemnation of sin and liberty to walk in newness of life in Christ. It also presents the great fact of Christ's righteousness imputed, or credited, to us; and it explains the outworking of that righteousness in our lives through the power of the Holy Spirit.

There had never been a declaration of independence or a proclamation of liberty like the one made by Paul as a messenger of God's grace. His pronouncement was made to those Jews who had been in bondage to the Law and to those Gentiles who had been in bondage to the licentious practices of heathenism. To the Jews, he proclaimed liberty from the Mosaic code, which for countless generations had controlled every aspect of Israel's life, and he announced that things formerly forbidden by the law of Moses now are lawful. To the Gentiles, who had practiced lawlessness and knew nothing of the restraints of the Law, the apostle likewise brought a message of liberty—that God had cleansed all things and had made all things acceptable to Himself.

This is the message the apostle wrote about to the Christians at Rome as, in chapter 14, he introduced the problem of doubtful things. When we mention doubtful things, we recognize immediately that we are not dealing with things that clearly are sinful in themselves, for anything that is intrinsically sinful is already forbidden to the child of God. However, doubtful things may be put to sinful uses. Therefore Romans 14 does not deal with things that are inherently worldly, but with things that may be used for worldly ends. It does not deal with those things that are carnal (fleshly) in themselves, but with those things that can be corrupted to a carnal use.

Every generation of believers has had to face decisions about doubtful things. In dealing with the believers at Rome, Paul made no attempt to draw up a list of things that were acceptable and things that were not. But he did lay down certain principles that are timeless and that—if properly applied to Christian conduct—will settle questions about doubtful things.

In Romans 14–15, we come to Paul's discussion of questionable things, as he lays down certain principles to guide God's children. Obviously, today—just as in Paul's day—Christians face temptations and enticements which, if practiced, will jeopardize their spiritual growth and Christian testimony. If Paul had specifically addressed the doubtful practices of his day, today we might assume that those portions of the Bible do not apply to us because those problems no longer exist. Instead, however, the apostle Paul set forth timeless principles concerning doubtful or questionable practices, so that any Christian living in any culture might discern the fitness or unfitness of any habit, practice, or area of personal conduct.

The first of these principles, found in Romans 14:1–13, is the principle of freedom in Christ.

The Mosaic Law

When God called Abraham out of Ur of the Chaldees, He separated a man to Himself. It was God's purpose to raise up a great nation from him, so He set apart Abraham and his descendants through the promise He gave to Abraham in Genesis 12:1–9. Later, when God brought that set-apart nation out of Egyptian bondage and instituted the Mosaic Law, God said, "You have seen what I did to the Egyptians, and how I bore you on eagles' wings and brought you to Myself. Now therefore, if you will indeed obey My voice and keep My covenant, then you shall be a special treasure to Me above all people; for all the earth is Mine. And you shall be to Me a kingdom of priests and a holy nation" (Exodus 19:4–6). God—who had set apart Abraham and Abraham's descendants (Israel) as a special treasure—intended that the children of Israel should be a kingdom of priests and a holy, set-apart, nation.

Now, in order that Israel should have this peculiar characteristic of a kingdom of priests and a holy nation, God gave instructions to Moses: " 'These are the words which you shall speak to the children of Israel.' So Moses came and called for the elders of the people, and laid before them all these words which the LORD commanded him" (Exodus 19:6–7). The law which the Lord then gave to Moses, which Moses in turn gave to the children of Israel so that they might be a kingdom of priests and a holy nation, was designed to govern their entire lives.

In order that Israel should be a witness to the glory and holiness of God before all the other nations on earth, God gave laws that governed every aspect of life. The calendar of the year's events, with all the holy days and Sabbaths, was carefully set before the people. Keeping the Sabbath day was a religious law that set Israel apart from every other national entity. In addition to religious laws, God prescribed dietary laws for Israel. God did not call certain animals unclean because they were unfit for human consumption, nor did He call other animals clean because they were more nourishing. Rather, God established a division between clean and unclean so that as Israel ate only those things that were deemed clean and refrained from eating unclean foods, they would be a unique, distinctive, set-apart nation.

God's laws governed the kitchen of the Jewish home, dictating what foods could be put together and what could not. There were laws concerning the Jewish wardrobe, telling the children of Israel what they could and couldn't wear. God's laws detailed which fabrics could be combined in clothing and which could not. And, in fact, the Mosaic law governed every area of Jewish life, from marriage to military service, from parenthood to priestly sacrifices. All these were designed to set apart Israel as a unique people and a holy nation. It is important to understand that these laws were not given to redeem a people; they were given to an already redeemed people. They were not an end in themselves; rather, God's laws were His means to the end of providing the world with a witness to His grace, goodness, and holiness.

But as the centuries passed, the Mosaic Law became a burden to the Jews. The Pharisees were so conscious of a person's responsibility to God's Law that they had tried to codify and systematize all of the laws within the Law of Moses, adding many regulations of their own. By the time of Christ's ministry, they had arrived at 248 positive and 365 negative commandments. They claimed that these were the sum total of the Law, and taught the people that it was every Jew's obligation to keep these commandments.

Freedom From the Law

As we read the record of Christ's life and ministry, we discover that He anticipated the cancellation of the Law. The Law of Moses was for the Jewish nation—but the nation, through its religious leaders, officially rejected Jesus as God's Messiah. At that point, Israel ceased to be a unique people set apart by God as His witness to the rest of the world. Thus the laws that were designed to set Israel apart as a witness to God's plan of salvation no longer served that purpose. The tearing of the veil in the temple at the time of Christ's crucifixion (Matthew 27:51) was God's sign that the Mosaic law was being terminated as the code which should regulate the life of God's people. Hebrews 8:13 states it this way:

"In that He says, 'A new covenant,' He has made the first [the Mosaic law] obsolete.' Now what is becoming obsolete and growing old is ready to vanish away." The writer of Hebrews had in mind the Mosaic law when he referred to that which was "becoming obsolete and growing old," and further predicts the destruction of Jerusalem and the temple (in 70 A.D.) as that which is "ready to vanish."

Thus we see that Israel, which for countless generations had been under a law that governed every aspect of its people's lives, rejected Messiah and lost its position as a separated, holy nation, set apart as God's unique witness to the world. At that point, the Law which regulated them and set them apart was annulled.

We see in Acts 10 that this fact was revealed to Peter, when "Peter went up on the housetop to pray, about the sixth hour. Then he became very hungry and wanted to eat; but while they made ready, he fell into a trance and saw heaven opened and an object like a great sheet bound at the four corners, descending to him and let down to the earth. In it were all kinds of four-footed animals of the earth, wild beasts, creeping things, and birds of the air. And a voice came to him, 'Rise, Peter; kill and eat' " (Acts 10:9–13). As Peter looked into the sheet let down from heaven, he saw that it was filled with animals forbidden as food by the law of Moses. He recoiled in horror at the prospect of breaking the Law. When God said, "Kill and eat," Peter replied, "Not so, Lord! For I have never eaten anything common or unclean" (10:14). Then came a great revelation from God. He said to Peter, " 'What God has cleansed you must not call common.' This was done three times. And the object was taken up into heaven again" (10:15–16).

God revealed to Peter that the distinction between clean and unclean, between common and sacred, had been obliterated because He had done away with the Mosaic law. This setting aside of the Mosaic law showed that uncleanness was not in the animal itself, but rather was in the divine regulations against eating those things God deemed unclean. Once God took away the Law, there was no longer a distinction between clean and unclean.

We can well imagine how difficult it was for Peter to accept this revelation. Peter later shared this message with Cornelius' household and with the apostles and Christian brethren. But when we look in Galatians, we discover that while Peter knew intellectually that God had broken down the wall of division between clean and unclean (and between Jew and Gentile), it was difficult for him to act on the basis of that knowledge. In Galatians 2:11, Paul wrote about his contact with Peter in Antioch, "When Peter had come to Antioch, I withstood him to his face, because he was to be blamed." Why did Paul oppose Peter in this face-to-face encounter? Because, as we read in verse 12, "Before certain men came from James, he [Peter] would eat with the Gentiles; but when they came, he withdrew and separated himself, fearing those who were of the circumcision."

Peter had been practicing what God revealed to him on the rooftop. He had been eating with Gentiles (who formerly were considered unclean). But when Jews from Jerusalem came to Antioch, Peter separated himself from the Gentile believers because he was afraid of what the Jews would think. He denied the liberty God had given him (and all believers), and he re-built a barrier between himself and his Gentile brothers in Christ. He effectively put himself back under the Mosaic law, observing distinctions that had been canceled by the death of Christ. Not only did this affect Peter, but "the rest of the Jews also played the hypocrite with him, so that even Barnabas was carried away by their hypocrisy" (2:13). Other Hebrew believers followed him in his defection from the truth that all things were now clean. Therefore, because Peter had denied the gospel's liberty from the Law, Paul strongly rebuked him.

When we come to Romans, we find this same basic problem confronting the believers in Rome. While the Roman church was primarily a Gentile church, there were a number of Jews in the assembly. The Jews had a background entirely different from that of the Gentiles. The Gentiles were likely to look at the Jews and ask, "Why do they observe those odd customs?" Likewise, the Jewish believers might look askance at the Gentile believers and ask, "How can they eat those awful, unclean things?" Therefore Paul needed to write to this group of believers and outline certain principles in the area of doubtful, or questionable, practices so that they would not be divided.

The first and foremost principle Paul taught was the principle of freedom from the restrictions of the Mosaic law, since God has done away with the Law as His method of separating a holy people to Himself. Today—no less than in Paul's day—God is concerned about a separate, set-apart people for Himself. It is God's intention that you and I should be part of a unique, holy, separate kingdom of priests. But His method of setting apart that holy nation is not to institute a new set of laws as a substitute for the Law of Moses. Rather, He conforms us to the image of Christ through the power of the Holy Spirit, that we should be His conspicuous and distinct people, to His glory.

Freedom in Christ

The principles found in Romans 14, laid down by Paul to guide the Christians of his day, continue to serve the same purpose today—once we understand them. Romans 14:1–2 begins, "Receive one who is weak in the faith, but not to disputes over doubtful things. For one believes he may eat all things, but he who is weak eats only vegetables."

Paul recognized that there was a danger that some believers might set up a list of rules or requirements in the area of doubtful things, and then make those requirements a test of fellowship. Therefore he told them to "receive any brother, even though he is weak in the faith. But do not receive him for the purpose of becoming entangled in a debate about doubtful things." He recognized that in any group of believers there will be two types of people—those who are weak in the faith, and those who are strong. In the case of the Romans, the weak brother is the one who did not have faith to believe that God had indeed made all things clean and acceptable. The strong brother, on the other hand, was the brother who accepted God's revelation and believed that all things were allowable for him because God had set aside the law that delineated between clean and unclean. The weak brother could not accept the revelation; the strong brother believed it and acted on it.

When Peter first received the revelation of Acts 10, told the brethren of the revelation, and then sat down to eat with Gentiles, he was showing himself to be a strong brother. But later, when he adjusted his behavior because of the Jews who came from James, he could not accept the fact that his fellowship with Gentiles had God's blessing, and he became a weak brother. Based on these passages, we must be extremely careful about our definition of who is a strong believer and who is weak. It is directly related to the question of faith—trust—in the revelation God has made.

When Paul presented the principle of freedom in Christ, he pointed out three things. First, believers, whether weak or strong, must refrain from judging one another. This does not mean that Christians should not recognize sin for what it is, according to God's clear revelation. Rather, when moving into the gray area of doubtful or questionable things, the weak Christian must refrain from judging the strong Christian who has accepted God's revelation that all things are clean. Likewise, the strong Christian must abstain from judging the weak Christian who cannot exercise the faith to believe that he may eat anything. The danger of judging or despising (literally, *looking down one's nose at*) a fellow believer faces both the strong and the weak, and either can fall into that trap. Therefore Paul said, "Let not him who eats despise him who does not eat, and let not him who does not eat judge him who eats . . ." (Romans 14:3).

Why are both courses of action forbidden? Because God has received both the strong brother and the weak brother because of their faith in Christ. Basically, it did not matter to God whether they ate the previously unclean food or did not eat it. Eating cannot bring a person to God, and refraining from eating cannot set someone apart to God.

The second thing Paul pointed out about the principle of freedom in Christ is found in Romans 14:4–9. Both the weak and the strong must recognize that Jesus Christ is Lord. The title "Lord" implies the right to command someone. And the correct response to a lord is obedience. What this passage points out, then, is that God has not appointed the stronger brother as a commander over the weaker brother; nor has He appointed the weaker brother as a "lord" over the stronger. God has not set aside His rights over both.

So Paul wrote, "Who are you to judge another's servant? To his own master he stands or falls" (14:4). Paul was saying, "It is none of my business what your master permits you to do. If your master permits you to do something that my master does not permit me to do, it does not give me the right to condemn you because you do what your master lets you do. Just as soon as you step into the role of a judge to condemn another's servant, you are assuming the authority of his lord. No one has the right to do that."

Then Paul gave an illustration. He said, "One person esteems one day above another; another esteems every day alike" (14:5). He was referring to the observance of the Sabbath under Jewish law. The Gentiles had never observed a sabbath; the Jews were required to observe every Sabbath. Many Jews, once saved, could not break the habit of observing the Sabbath day, so they continued to observe Sabbath as a day set apart to the Lord. Other saved Jews suddenly felt free to do many things they had never dared do before they trusted Christ. So Paul wrote, "He who observes the day, observes it to the Lord" (14:6). This explains why Paul could frequently attend Jewish services on the Sabbath day, and why many Jewish believers, in the early days of church history, continued to observe Jewish ritual and ceremony. They were observing it to the Lord.

So, in regard to doubtful things, Paul emphasized that it is the Lord who determines for each of His servants what He wants that servant to do. Then Paul concluded this portion of this thought by saying, "For this end Christ died and rose and lived again, that He might be Lord of both the dead and the living."

The third thing Paul points out about the principle of freedom in Christ is that the Lord does have the right to judge. In Romans 14:10–12 we read, "Why do you judge your brother? Or why do you show contempt for your brother? For we shall all stand before the judgment seat of

Christ. For it is written, 'As I live, says the LORD, every knee shall bow to Me, and every tongue shall confess to God.' So then each of us shall give an account of himself to God." No believer shall be examined or asked to give an account of himself to another believer. Each individual is answerable to the Lord, his Master, and has the responsibility of conducting his life to please the Lord who has called him. When a Christian lives to please others, those others become his judges, and Christ is deposed from His rightful place as sovereign Lord of his life. "Therefore," concludes verse 13, "let us not judge one another anymore."

Once again, this passage is not a discussion about known, indisputable, confirmed sin in the life of a believer. No Christian has a right to think it is a matter of no consequence to God if he or she commits sin. Sin never has God's endorsement. Those things which are expressly forbidden in Scripture and are classified as sin are as much sin in the life of the believer as they are in the life of the unbeliever. Further, believers are urged to "test the spirits" (1 John 4:1) and to be spiritually discerning enough of sin in other believers' lives to "restore such a one" in a spirit of gentleness. Those who use the injunction "do not judge" to ignore other believers' exhortations about known sin in their lives are either ignorant of God's Word or in rebellion against Him. This passage, on the other hand, is discussing those practices that in themselves are not sinful; those that, whether we do them or don't do them, are a matter of indifference to God.

The dangers that faced the church in Paul's day also face the church today. The first danger is that any assembly of believers may become so divided over inconsequential questions that they produce disunity in the family of God. The second danger is that Jesus Christ will be set aside from His place as head and that others will begin to control the lives of members of His body. The third danger is that a person or a group will set up a list of do's and don'ts that substitute for the Law of Moses as a law governing the Christian life. But anytime Christians put themselves back under law—whether it is the Law of Moses or a self-imposed law— and when they obey that law thinking that's how they will please God, they have become as legalistic as the Pharisees of Christ's day. A Christian does not become a legalist by conforming to the standards of Christ's holiness; a Christian becomes a legalist by submitting to law as a means of producing righteousness in daily life. That is why Paul was so concerned that believers should not set up laws for themselves, thinking that by conforming to rules and codes of conduct they will please God.

God has removed the Law of Moses as that which sets a people aside for Him. He now is concerned that His people be a holy, set-apart people as the righteousness of Christ is reproduced in God's children through the power of the Holy Spirit. The Christian life is not a lawless life; it is a disciplined life, a life controlled by the Spirit of God. It is not regimented by law—neither the Law of Moses nor self-imposed legalism. It is a life under the law of Christ as revealed in His Word.

Notes

1. The first test of decisions we face about doubtful things is whether we are sincerely seeking answers for our own Christian conduct, or whether we simply disapprove of another's conduct because it conflicts with our own views. As we will see, it is the weaker brother who is pulled into sin by another's behavior concerning doubtful areas that do not contradict Scripture. By the same token, a sincere believer seeks answers to questions concerning his or her own conduct.

2. The calling to be "a kingdom of priests and a holy nation" has been extended to the church of Jesus Christ because we have become partakers with Israel of God's promises. This means that we are indeed a part of something even greater than our individual salvation, that we are identified with all those God has set apart to be distinctly different from the world. This assumes that we will *want* to be different, set apart, and distinct. Without this desire, we will continue to be subject to the world around us, and spiritually defeated. With it, we are free to become what He wants us to be.

3. As we can see in Israel's history, it is a short trip from principles given in God's grace to laws enforced according to human self-righteousness. It is a quirk of the fallen human heart that we want to make God's sound precepts just slightly more restrictive in order to make sure no one steps across the line, or to show ourselves to be extra holy. One author has described these one-step-removed laws as "fences." Whereas God established certain restrictions, the Pharisees built fences around these with added restrictions. When Jesus offended the religious leaders during His earthly ministry, He did not violate God's Law. But He trampled the Pharisee's fences at nearly every turn.

4. When we understand that the Law was annulled when the veil of the temple was torn from top to bottom (Mark 15:38), we might logically ask, "Then of what value is the Old Testament Law?" Paul wrote in 1 Timothy 1:8, "We know that the law is good if one uses it lawfully." God gave the Law to fulfill two functions: (1) a *regulatory* function, regulating life of God's people, Israel, in their role as a unique and set-apart nation; and (2) a *revelatory* function, revealing a holy God to sinful mankind. While the regulatory aspect of the Law ceased with Christ's death, the revelatory aspect of the Law continues today. We study the Law and the rest of the Old Testament in order to discover what it reveals to us about God, and to live according to that knowledge. That is using the Law lawfully.

5. Although we normally think of *hypocrisy* as talking righteously while acting unrighteously, notice that the Word of God also applies that term to adding our own standards of righteousness beyond that which God requires. It is hypocritical because with our mouths we are acknowledging God's grace and the liberty of His Word, but with our actions we are denying both.

6. Even those of us who consider ourselves free from legalism in the Christian life may be subjecting ourselves or others to a false standard of righteousness under the misnomer of "biblical principles." The process is simple: we take a biblical command, add to it a broader interpretation and call it a "principle," then extend the divine prohibition to everything that might fall under that "biblical principle." For example, God clearly forbids idol worship. The broad principle is that God forbids anything and everything that has ever been associated with idol worship. The legalistic application is that if we do anything in our lives that has ever been associated with idolatry, we are guilty of sin. This is popularly applied to the secular observance of Halloween, meaning that any Christians who participate in observing any festivities on that day are in sin. But if that is a valid "law," then it would have to apply equally to other pagan-tainted holidays, like Easter and Christmas. Likewise, it would have to apply to pagan-based customs, like wedding rings, birthday candles, Christmas trees, even neckties. We would also have to extend it to the names of the months and the days of the week, since they are pagan-based as well. And so on. If we take this to its logical extreme, we could spend our entire lives just arguing about the hundreds of so-called biblical principles we have added to God's Word. But, as we will see in Paul's discussion of meat sacrificed to idols, there is a better way. And it involves a valid principle built on a sound interpretation of God's Word.

7. Always keep in mind that doubtful things do not include those things clearly forbidden by the Word of God. This discussion assumes a believer's willing obedience to the Bible's clear instructions concerning sin.

8. How many times have we fallen into the trap of criticizing a fellow believer for behavior that fell into the area of doubtful things? In these situations, we were in the wrong—not the person who is exercising his or her Christian liberty!

9. The other side of this coin is that no believer will be asked by the Lord to give an account of *someone else's* life. Since it is our own lives that will be called to account before the judgment seat of Christ, shouldn't we be most concerned with our own obedience to Him rather than others' behavior?

10. Unfortunately, issues of liberty and legalism almost always affect the life and vibrancy of a local assembly. Rather than being a lighthouse in the midst of darkness, a local church becomes a hotbed of controversy over inconse-

quential issues. One of the greatest things we can do to support the life of our local churches is to avoid needless controversies over questions of optional Christian conduct.

Questions

1. How many areas of "doubtful things" can you list from your own experience? How do you know for sure these are doubtful things?

2. What did Peter's vision in Acts 10:9–13 reveal about his relationship to the Mosaic law? What do we learn from Galatians 2:11–13 about Peter's struggle with this? Do you think Christians today struggle with their freedom in Christ? If so, how?

3. According to Romans 14:1, what should be our attitude toward believers who do not exercise their freedom in Christ? Should we look for opportunities to debate them about those issues? Why or why not?

4. Although many Christians consider those who are more restrictive in their behavior as stronger than those who don't, what terminology does the Bible use in Romans 14:1–2? How should the two respond to each other, according to 14:3?

5. Does Romans 14:13 teach that we should not recognize sin in the lives of other believers? If not, what does it mean?

6. In light of Romans 14:13, what is one of the dangers a Christian faces in exercising his or her Christian freedom in the presence of a weaker Christian? To whom does that makes us accountable (see 14:10)?

CHAPTER 17

GIVING NO OFFENSE

Romans 14:13b–23

In the previous chapter we considered the basic principle of freedom in Christ. The Mosaic law has been abolished, for by the death of Christ the rule of law was broken. The New Testament put a new standard before believers. No longer was the Jew's standard conformity to the Law, but conformity to Christ. For Gentiles, rather than being molded to the world, they were to be molded to the image of Christ. As consequence of this new freedom, believers must refrain from judging one another in relation to doubtful things. Each individual is responsible to the Lord, and the Lord will direct each of His children in what He permits them to do. It is exclusively the Lord's right to judge, and He will judge each believer's conduct in a day of reckoning set aside for believers. Therefore, no Christian has the right to sit in judgment on that which the Lord permits another believer to do.

The Weaker Brother

Next we need to consider the second principle presented in Romans 14. The first principle is the basic truth of our freedom and liberty in Christ. When we by faith accept the fact that God has broken down the distinction between that which is unclean and that which is clean, we honor God with our faith. But as you may already have noticed, the doctrine of liberty might be misinterpreted or misapplied to give the Christian license to do whatever he or she wants. Someone might adopt the attitude, "Since God has declared all things clean, and all things that were formerly forbidden now are acceptable to God, it makes no difference what I do. I can do anything I want." Others may teach that in order to prove that we are not legalistic Christians, we should engage in all those things that were formerly forbidden, since restricting our liberty puts us back under law.

However, continuing to read Paul's instructions in Romans shows us that there is a second principle, given to prevent us from turning our liberty in Christ into license and lawlessness, and it takes precedence over the first principle of liberty. Simply stated, that principle is *give no offense*. In Romans 14:13–21, we are clearly instructed that believers should refrain from those things that might cause another believer to stumble.

In developing this second great principle, Paul first said that believers should "resolve this, not to put a stumbling block or a cause to fall in our brother's way" (Romans 14:13). In verse 21 he wrote, "It is good neither to eat meat nor drink wine nor do anything by which your brother stumbles or is offended or is made weak." Notice that he used three expressions to describe what might happen to a weak brother as a result of our actions: a believer might be caused to stumble, to be offended, or to be made weak. In the apostle's mind, there were distinctions among these three.

First, a Christian stumbles when he patterns his life after another believer but does not have faith to accept the fact that God gives him liberty to do that thing the other Christian is doing. When one does this, he falls into sin, because "whatever is not of faith is sin" (14:23). Thus God's Word tells us that it is good for Christians to abstain from exercising their liberty in such a way that it causes a fellow believer who patterns his life after ours to fall into that which is sin for him because he cannot accept God's declaration that all things are clean or acceptable.

Next, it is good for a Christian to abstain from doing anything that causes another believer to be offended. What does it mean to offend another believer? We offend a brother or sister in Christ when we permit him or her to see us exercise liberty which we have, but which he or she does not have, thus jeopardizing our testimony before that fellow believer. The difference between causing someone to stumble and causing them to be offended may be stated like this: if, when we exercise liberty, another believer does what we do, but without the faith we have, then he stumbles into sin. On the other hand, if a fellow believer sees us doing that thing and is caused to question or set aside our Christian testimony because of it, then we have offended that brother or sister in Christ. In the second instance, we have not led someone into sin; but we have caused that one to question our Christian life and testimony.

Third, this passage tells us that it is good for a Christian to abstain from doing anything by which a fellow Christian is made weak. This believer is viewed as being in spiritual childhood or spiritual immaturity. He has not learned the truths of freedom in Christ, but he is studying the

Word of God. He is reaching out to lay hold of the revelation God has made. But if he sees another believer doing what he does not have the liberty to do and is offended by it, he may be driven backward in his spiritual progress.

As an illustration, suppose one of those new Jewish believers saw an older Jewish believer sitting down to eat some meat that was specifically forbidden by the Law of Moses. The older believer had learned the lesson of Peter's vision in Acts 10 and could sit down to a roast pork dinner and enjoy it tremendously. The younger believer, however, has not yet matured to the point of receiving the truth of Peter's vision, and is so offended by the sight of a Jewish person eating pork that he wants nothing to do with Christian liberty. He is driven back from the truth of liberty and wants to put himself back under the Law to protect himself against the seemingly repulsive behavior of the older Christian. He was made weaker because he was offended by the stronger Christian's liberty.

The Responsibility of the Stronger Christian

In covering these three areas, the Bible places a tremendous responsibility on believers to whom the Spirit of God has brought the truth of liberty in the gospel.

First, we must so guard our conduct that a weaker brother or sister does not follow our pattern of life and fall into sin. We must so live our lives that a weaker believer is not given cause to discount our testimony. We must so conduct ourselves that a less mature believer is not turned from the truth of God's Word by those things our liberty in Christ permits us. These requirements are very stringent, and they are inflexible. Clearly, there is no rationale a stronger Christian can use to justify causing a weaker believer to stumble, to be offended, or to be weakened in Christian growth.

Second, we must realize that things in themselves do not defile us. Romans 14:14 says, "I know and am convinced by the Lord Jesus that there is nothing unclean of itself; but to him who considers anything to be unclean, to him it is unclean." The key thought here is the phrase, "there is nothing unclean of itself." In the previous chapter, we saw that God once made a distinction between clean and unclean animals, not because there was anything harmful or unhealthy in the unclean animal, but because He wanted the people governed by those laws to be a unique people, set apart to God. God prescribed certain garment materials, not because a combination of fibers rendered a person unclean, but because He wanted to make a distinction between those who were set apart to God and those who weren't.

But if a Christian can't accept this fact of revelation, that "there is nothing unclean of itself," and continues to believe that certain things or certain practices are unclean, then to him or her they are. The defilement is not in the thing itself, but in the child of God's attitude toward it. This area constitutes the distinction between the strong Christian and the weak Christian. The strong believer does by faith in God's declaration accept that all things are clean and acceptable. But the weak believer cannot bring himself to believe God's declaration and accept, for example, that lamb is no better in God's sight than pork. It is the weak Christian's attitude that makes pork continue to be unclean for him or her.

Paul's point in this passage is that the child of God who has become strong in the faith cannot argue that since God has made all things clean he can go ahead and eat anything he wants. Not at all. The strong brother must take into consideration the attitude of the weak brother. The strong brother has no right to say, "My poor weak brother can't believe that he can eat pork; but I know that pork is clean, therefore I'll go ahead and eat it." Rather, the strong brother must say, "I know my weak brother can't accept the fact that he can eat pork. To him it is unclean. Therefore, I will not eat the pork lest I lead my brother to stumble by doing as I do, or offend my brother by nullifying my testimony, or cause him to turn from the whole truth of liberty because of his weakened state."

Third, verses 15–20 point out that the strong believer who recognizes that all things are clean is responsible to *relinquish his own rights* for the good of the weak brother. This is difficult, for there is a stubbornness in every one of us that leads us to say, "I know my rights, and nobody is going to take them from me." This attitude is a manifestation of the old nature, which exerts itself forcefully in matters of Christian liberty and freedom. It reasons, "I know that God permits me to do these things. I don't care what my weaker brother says. It's his fault if he can't grow up."

But the Bible teaches us that stronger Christians have a responsibility to waive their rights in order to avoid offending, weakening, or tripping up other believers. "If your brother [that is, a believer who does not have faith to believe that all meats are clean] is grieved because of your food [because you eat it], you are no longer walking in love" (14:15). If you practice your liberty in front of a weaker believer who has not grown to the point of accepting his or her own liberty in Christ, you sin against love, because your liberty may lead that person into sin. If you do not relinquish your rights, then you sin, because you wound the conscience of the weaker believer. The conclusion of verse 15 admonishes,

"Do not destroy with your food the one for whom Christ died." This clearly does not refer to the loss of the weaker Christian's soul, but rather to the prevention of spiritual growth in his or her life.

This is the same as making another Christian weak, rather than strengthening him (14:21). "Do not let your good be spoken of as evil," says verse 16. The "good" in this verse is the liberty the stronger brother has. Why permit your liberty to be denounced? The kingdom of God is not merely meat and drink. Meat is not the essence of the life God has given us. God has not saved us so that we can eat and drink what we want. Personal liberty is not the essence and end of salvation. The essence of salvation is righteousness and peace and joy in the Holy Spirit.

Some of the saved Jews of Paul's day could not see anything beyond a slice of ham in their salvation. They viewed salvation as giving them the right to eat the things that were formerly forbidden, the right to wear what they couldn't wear before, the right to marry whom they could not marry before. To such people Paul said, "Is that all your salvation means to you? Haven't you grasped the fact that the gospel of Christ is concerned with righteousness and peace and joy in the Holy Spirit?"

In contrast, verse 18 reveals, "He who serves Christ in these things is acceptable to God and approved by men." The Christian who serves the higher good of Jesus Christ and the care of His children still is acceptable to God, and is approved by people as well.

Goals in View

In verse 19, we find the application of this principle in two goals for believers: "Let us pursue the things which make for peace and the things by which one may edify another."

The first goal is to "pursue the things which make for peace." The union of Jews and Gentiles into one body and into one fellowship of believers in Paul's day created tremendous practical problems for those who so recently had been saved out of Judaism and Gentile hedonism. The Gentile would look at the Jew, who still retained some of the old attitudes toward certain meats, and would turn up his nose and say, "Why don't you go ahead and eat it? Even Peter said it is clean."

Meanwhile, the Jews would sit across the table and look at those converted Gentiles and say, "How can they do it? How can they eat that stuff?" There was division and friction in the body of believers because some Gentiles were insisting on their right to eat things some Jews considered detestable. Paul said that in the area of doubtful things, every believer's goal should be to pursue the things which make for peace. The Gentile in that assembly, if he followed this injunction, would say, "If my

Jewish brother can't yet accept the fact that certain meats are clean, then when I eat with him, I won't eat anything but lamb. That won't cause him to stumble, to be offended, or to be made weak."

The Jew, on the other hand, would say, "It is hard for me to give up this custom, but if it is going to promote the unity of believers, I won't insist that we continue a kosher diet when we are together." He might also say, "At home we will have nothing but kosher food, but when we are together as believers, we will eat what is set before us, asking no questions, for conscience' sake." This, too, would be pursuing those things that make for peace in the body of Christ.

The second goal was to "pursue the things . . . by which one may edify another" (14:19). The Jew was to eat, and the Gentile was to refrain from eating, with a view to building up the faith of the other. If a body of believers from such heterogeneous backgrounds came together, determined to conduct themselves in a way that would promote peace and edify fellow believers, how different that fellowship dinner would be! Surrendering rights for the good of the brethren would produce peace and unity, and would build them in their faith.

Romans 14 deals with a situation that was prevalent in Paul's day, but the same principle is extremely applicable for us today. Doubtful things are things which do not fall into the category of sin. They are doubtful because Scripture does not specifically forbid them. If the Bible explicitly forbids them, they are completely removed from the category of doubtful things.

By faith we accept the fact that God no longer distinguishes between clean and unclean, between acceptable and unacceptable. By faith we lay hold of our liberty in Christ, and we stand in that liberty and will not permit anyone to bring us into bondage to any law that forbids what God permits. But we do not have to practice that liberty in order to possess that liberty. A second, higher principle supplants the practice of liberty.

We consider our fellow believer's good and so order our lives that we do not lead that person into sin or cause him to stumble as he patterns his life after ours. We make it our goal to refrain from jeopardizing our Christian testimony by doing anything that will prevent a weaker believer from going on to maturity. Why? Because surrendering our right to practice liberty does not put us under law. Rather, it patterns our lives after the Lord Jesus Christ, who surrendered His rights that we might have salvation.

Notes

1. The principle of giving no offense becomes especially difficult in our "culture of victimhood," as some have called it. It seems that nearly everyone is

looking for a point of offense in everything around them, then demanding that their "rights" be observed in one way or another. The big difference in Scripture, however, is that the basic principle is one of giving up our own rights rather than demanding that others give up theirs. It is other-centered, rather than self-centered. We look for ways to voluntarily do what's best for the weaker Christian rather than forcing someone else to do what's best for us. This in itself moves the issue from a point of law to a point of grace. It is God asking us to willfully do what's best, not human law forcing us to do what is popular or politically correct.

2. Inevitably we will encounter immature Christians who are more interested in controlling others' behavior than in cultivating their own spiritual growth. What do we do, then, when others tell us what we should or should not do based on the fact it "offends" them? First and foremost, we must consider whether they have a valid complaint in light of Romans 14:13–21. Are we causing them to sin? Are we hindering a genuine desire for spiritual growth? Are we causing them to disregard our Christian testimony? If so, we need to be willing to voluntarily adjust our behavior for their good. On the other hand, if that person is meddling in others' lives with no real concern for spiritual growth or maturity, rather than defending ourselves we probably should concentrate on ministering to that person's real spiritual need, which is to understand and apply the principles of spiritual growth and the Spirit-filled life. In short, we might look on the confrontation as an opportunity to minister to someone who needs to grow spiritually.

3. Throughout Scripture, wherever we find a privilege we will also find a corresponding responsibility. In this case, the privilege is our freedom in Christ; the corresponding responsibility is to consider the welfare of the weaker Christian.

4. In plain terms, verse 15 is telling us that it is selfish and silly of us to consider a matter of meat (or any other temporal enjoyment) more important than Christ's death for that weaker Christian. If Jesus willingly endured the crucifixion for every Christian, then surely we can willingly forego some small liberty for the weaker believer!

5. One other aspect of our Christian liberty we should consider is how our behavior might affect those outside the family of faith. Will exercising your Christian liberty actually turn someone away from the gospel rather than attracting him or her to it? Just as a foreign ambassador weighs every action by how he or she is representing his or her country, so we—as ambassadors for Christ—should weight our actions by how we represent Him.

6. Unity and edification—these are the values within the body of Christ that the Bible considers more important than personal rights. Do we consider

them so important that we consider them first, before the right to prove our liberty in Christ?

Questions

1. What two attitudes are contrasted in Romans 14:13b? What do you think is meant by the command to "resolve this"?

2. Rephrase Romans 14:21 in your own words. What do you think it means to cause another believer to be "offended"? To be made "weak"?

3. Throughout Romans 14:13–21, do you think the weaker Christian shares the stronger believer's desire for spiritual growth and maturity? Why or why not? What is the stronger Christian's attitude concerning the weaker brother's growth?

4. What other problems might be created by Christians disagreeing about matters of conduct in doubtful things? What effect might these have on a local assembly of believers?

5. What do you think the word *destroy* means in Romans 14:15? How does this relate to the issue of doubtful things?

6. In the area of doubtful things, what does God request of the more mature believer? Is this something you feel you can accept and apply? Why or why not?

CHAPTER 18

A GOOD CONSCIENCE BEFORE GOD

Romans 14:22–15:3

There are many areas in the Christian life in which we are called on to make a decision concerning doubtful things. The Bible provides us with clear principles by which Christians may determine what is right and what is wrong in the area of doubtful things. The first principle, as we have seen in Romans 14, is the principle that God has nullified the distinction between what the Mosaic law said was clean and what was unclean. The second principle is that no Christian should use that liberty to cause a fellow Christian to stumble into sin.

Now, in Romans 14:22–15:3, Paul applies these principles and gives some practical exhortations. His line of thinking in this passage is that there are two types of Christians—weak and strong. The strong Christian has sufficient faith to accept God's declaration that things previously unclean now are clean, while the weak believer cannot accept that revelation. Paul recognized that no congregation would be entirely made up of strong believers or of weak believers. If any local body was all weak or all strong, there would be no conflict within the body. But because in every fellowship there will always be some who are strong and some who are weak, it was necessary to lay down certain guidelines lest the weakness of one group or the strength of the other cause division and destroy unity. That is why Paul wrote that the weaker should not judge the stronger for eating, nor should the stronger judge the weaker for not eating.

The Danger of Liberty

The apostle Paul then goes on to give further injunctions which lay down a third principle in the matter of doubtful things. This third principle may be summarized by saying that both the weak and the strong must have a good conscience before God in their manner of life in regard to doubtful things.

Romans 14:22 presents a question and then gives a mandate to the stronger believer: "Do you have faith? Have it to yourself before God." The faith referred to here is not saving faith in the Lord Jesus Christ, nor is it the faith to walk before men. The faith in Paul's mind in this verse is that particular aspect of faith we have already discussed: the faith to accept God's revelation that restrictions have been removed from the things previously forbidden by the Law, and that these things may now be used as unto the Lord. This verse is saying, "Do you have faith to accept the revelation God gave through Peter that He has cleansed all things and made them acceptable? If your answer is 'yes,' then have that faith to yourself before God."

Today, as in the first century, there is a popular misconception that says that any limitation placed upon one's liberty—whether by another Christian or by the individual himself—puts one under the Law and imposes a legal system upon the believer. As a result, some Christians erroneously believe that if a believer knows he has the liberty to do these things, he *must* do them to prove his liberty. The rationale behind this is that if a Christian knows he is free to do these things but does not do them, then he is a legalist, is in bondage to the Law, and does not enjoy the liberty that is his in Christ.

This passage was written to correct that misinterpretation and to affirm that a Christian's liberty is primarily a matter of one's attitude in private, not one's conduct before an assembly of believers. The message is, "Have this faith to yourself before God that the things previously forbidden are now acceptable. You are free as soon as you recognize the liberty that is yours. It is not necessary for you to flaunt your liberty before others in order to be delivered from legalism or bondage to the law."

Paul recognized that the greatest danger in a local body of believers was *not* that the weak would refrain from eating. The greatest danger that confronted the assembly in Paul's day—just as in our day—was that the strong believers would insist on exercising their liberty to show everyone that they had been delivered from the law. So he advised, "I want to warn you stronger believers, lest you cause your weaker brethren to become offended (and thus lose your testimony before them), or cause your weaker brethren to stumble and fall into sin because they do not have the same faith you have."

Again, we should all take note: The greatest danger to the unity of the assembly is stronger believers insisting on exercising their rights!

After addressing this word of caution to both the strong and the weak, Paul wrote in verse 22, "Happy is he who does not condemn himself in what he approves." This applies to the strong Christian who could rightly congratulate himself if he so ordered his conduct that the weaker believer did not become offended by his conduct or stumble into sin. If I, as a stronger brother, exercised my liberty and then noted that you, as a weaker brother, followed me and defiled your conscience, then my conscience would be burdened because I did not walk carefully before you in love. If I cause you offense or grief, it condemns my heart. By contrast, I am happy—blessed—if I surrender my liberty and do not do something that is well within my liberty but would be detrimental to you.

But this principle applies equally to weaker believers, for it says to them, "You will be blessed if you do not stand condemned because you patterned your life after the stronger Christian when you did not have the stronger Christian's faith." This is the way this principle might work: If I am the weak brother and you are the strong Christian, and I see you eating something that I do not have faith to believe is acceptable, and I eat it because you are eating it, then I stand self-condemned and would be disheartened. I, as a weak brother, will be happier if I do not pattern my liberty after your liberty, without your faith.

The principle, then, clearly is that each Christian ought to conduct himself so as to have a good conscience before God in the matter of doubtful things.

Verse 23 explains why a weaker brother who patterns his liberty after a stronger brother, without the stronger brother's faith, falls into sin. It says, "He who doubts is condemned if he eats . . . ." The word *condemned* here does not mean "condemned to eternal punishment." This brother has not lost his salvation. Rather, that brother stands self-condemned, reprimanded by his own conscience, "because he does not eat from faith."

Then Paul adds the important words, "For whatever is not from faith is sin." Notice that this statement is delivered to the weaker believers. They have been born into the family of God and enjoy fellowship with God. But Paul says to them, "If you pattern your conduct by the conduct of another believer, without that believer's faith, you will fall into sin. That which is allowable for the strong Christian is not allowable for you as a weak Christian—not because it is wrong, but because you eat doubting God's declaration that it is acceptable." And anything a believer does, convinced beforehand that it is sin, is in fact sin, because "whatever is not from faith is sin."

The Sacrifice of Liberty

The matter of a good conscience will eliminate certain practices for us because of the possible effects on a weak Christian who might say,

"Because you did it, I am going to do it." Paul had very little to say to weaker believers, because the greatest danger to the assembly was not the weaker Christians' weakness, but the stronger Christians' insistence on exercising their liberty. Therefore he tells the stronger believers how they should act toward the weaker brethren. "We then who are strong ought to bear with the scruples [weaknesses] of the weak, and not to please ourselves." We should be more concerned about weaker believers than we are about ourselves and our liberty. Our natural reaction would be to ignore the weaker brethren or despise them for their weaknesses. Instead, we should "bear with"—literally, assume or carry ourselves—the weaknesses of the weak.

No strong Christian has any right to exercise a liberty which a fellow believer in his assembly does not have the faith to accept for himself. Even if you are the strongest Christian among the strong in your assembly, you are to impose on yourself the same restrictions that the weak conscience of the weakest brother imposes on himself. This is difficult! It is excruciatingly difficult to follow the principle that we should voluntarily put limitations on our liberty according to the conscience of the weakest believer in our midst. It means that for the sake of a weaker Christian we will have to sacrifice something we know we have perfect liberty to practice. But this is the crux of the whole problem of doubtful things. We believe we have the right to do certain things. We know from God's Word that God has no objection to our doing them. But we voluntarily surrender our rights on the basis of not pleasing ourselves, but instead assuming the burdens of the weaker believers among us.

Romans 15:2 tells us clearly why we should impose such limitations on our own liberty. It says, "Let each of us please his neighbor for his good, leading to edification." The strong Christian should give up what he knows God permits him to do because he is concerned about his weaker brother's spiritual welfare. The ultimate goal in seeking the weaker Christian's good is that believer's edification, his building up in faith, the strengthening of his walk with Christ. This is why Paul asked the stronger brother to surrender the use of his liberty until the weak brother could be taught the truth and could accept the strong brother's faith as his own. This surrendering of one's liberty is seen as temporary, with a view to the weaker brother joining the stronger in Christian liberty.

So then, when a stronger believer gives up his or her liberty for the sake of a weaker believer, it actually begins a work of teaching, edifying, and instructing in the Word of God with the goal of building the weaker believer in knowledge and faith.

Self-Scrutiny

The principle this passage of Romans sets before us is intensely valuable in the life of any group of believers. This principle is meant to bring our lives under the closest scrutiny—not scrutiny by another believer, but by ourselves. Stronger Christians must consider the effect of their behavior on weaker believers in the congregation. We must ask ourselves questions like, "Will this jeopardize my testimony?" or, "Will this lead an immature believer into sin if he sees me do it and then does it himself?"

Too many Christians today mistakenly believe that the greatest virtue in the Christian life is proving that they have liberty. But according to God's Word, that is not the greatest virtue. The greatest virtue is to enjoy your liberty, and set aside that liberty for the benefit of a weaker brother or sister in Christ. We voluntarily, even eagerly, give up our rightful liberty for the weaker believer's good, with the objective of building him up, bringing him out of babyhood and into maturity in Christ.

Paul wrote in Romans 14:7, "None of us lives to himself, and no one dies to himself." Our every word and action has an effect on someone. Before we exercise our liberty in Christ, we need to impose on ourselves the weakness of the weakest believer around us, with a view to his good and edification. The Lord Jesus, of course, is the perfect example of this. He did not insist on His own rights, but surrendered His liberties for the good of those He came to save. May the mind of Christ so control us in the area of doubtful things that we will consider the weaker members of God's family with the goal of their edification.

Notes

1. Sometimes it is difficult for us to simply *accept* another believer's position in Christ, whether they are strong or weak. Though we appear to surrender our rights on the outside, we may harbor deep resentment and bitterness inside. This can lead to even more damage than would have been caused by a difference of opinion over the doubtful practice. Let's make sure that when we surrender our rights externally, it includes submission to the Lord internally (see Hebrews 12:15).

2. Have you ever felt the urge to prove your Christian liberty right under the nose of someone who has criticized or condemned you for it? That's pride speaking—trying to get you to violate God's principle of considering the weaker believer first. Don't give in!

3. This matter of conscience is more than the old motto to let your conscience be your guide. For the Christian, one's conscience is to be governed at all times by the Word of God (2 Timothy 3:16–17), conformity to Jesus Christ

(Romans 8:29), and the control of the Holy Spirit (Ephesians 5:18). The more we walk in submission to Him, the more our consciences will reflect His character and concerns rather than ours, and will be reliable guides for us.

4. Unless we believe that something is permissible, we must reason, "God may not allow this—but I'll do it anyway." At that point we have expressed a willingness to disobey God, which is sin. This attitude, in turn, can easily lead to disobeying those things we *know* to be unacceptable to Him.

5. One reason it is so difficult to surrender our rights for another's good is that we fail to see our lives in terms of eternity. That is, we are thinking in terms of the here and now, of life on this earth as the ultimate experience. Anything we miss out on here is an irretrievable loss. But what of eternity? How can anything in this life compare with what is ahead of us? And how can any brief enjoyment in this life be better than receiving Christ's approval both now and in the future?

6. This shows us that we can view the surrender of personal liberty as a ministry in itself. And as for the power to do it willingly, remember that Philippians 4:13 tells us, "I can do all things through Christ who strengthens me."

7. We may scoff at the way the tabloids and gossip columns keep tabs on some ce ebrities' every move, but we might also ask ourselves, "How would I fare ur der the same kind of scrutiny?" If you are known as a believer among y(o)ur unbelieving co-workers, family members, friends, fellow students, or neighbors, is your life consistent with your reputation? Do you harbor any secret sins that would jeopardize your testimony (not to mention retard your spiritual growth)? And is your walk with Christ of the quality a younger Christian can emulate and imitate?

Questions

1. Write out Romans 14:20a, leaving a blank where the word *food* appears. What other things might be put into that blank? Are there areas of your life you would not be willing to give up for the sake of a weaker brother or sister in Christ? Would this verse apply to those?

2. Read Romans 14:21. How would a stronger Christian "condemn himself"? How would we avoid this mistake? What will be the result if we do avoid it?

3. Compare Galatians 5:13–14 with Romans 14:20–23. What thoughts does Galatians 5 add to this discussion of Christian liberty? What does it confirm?

4. Using a specific example (real or hypothetical), explain how a stronger Christian might cause a weaker believer to stumble or fall into sin. Explain how a

Christian's testimony might be compromised by an inappropriate exercise of Christian liberty.

5. How might Philippians 2:5–8 relate to the things Paul had to say about Christian liberty?

6. What are some specific things a stronger Christian might choose to give up for the sake of a weaker believer? Does that mean no Christian should practice them at any time? Why or why not?

CHAPTER 19

DO ALL THINGS TO THE GLORY OF GOD

Romans 15:1–7

As we have seen, Paul was intensely concerned about the possibility of division in a body of believers over matters of Christian conduct in the area of doubtful things. To avoid this kind of division and to preserve unity, he laid down certain principles to guide God's children in their decisions concerning doubtful things.

The first principle is that there is freedom, or liberty, for the Christian. The second principle is that no believer, even though free from the Law, has any right to do anything that would cause a weaker believer to be offended or to sin. The third principle—which applies equally to the stronger believer and the weaker believer—is that both must be satisfied in conscience concerning their own actions.

That brings us to a fourth and final principle, which takes precedence over all the others. It is the principle that everything we do is done to the glory of God. This principle is summarized in Romans 15:6: "That you may with one mind and one mouth glorify the God and Father of our Lord Jesus Christ."

Again, this principle applies equally to both the strong Christian and the weak Christian. If the strong brother exercises his liberty and eats meat, he is to eat to the glory of God. If the weak brother, for conscience' sake, refuses to eat meat, his refusal should be to the glory of God. If the two brothers, differing as they do in the interpretation of what is lawful or unlawful, do all things to the glory of God, they will not be judging one another, nor will they offend and be offended.

Pleasing Another

Romans 15:2 tells us that everyone is to please his neighbor for his good, with the goal of his edification. This asks strong believers to voluntarily surrender the *exercise* of their liberty. This does not ask them to give up their liberty, or to disavow their liberty. When the stronger believer imposes on himself the weakness of the weaker Christian, it does not mean the stronger becomes weaker. It does not mean he denies his faith that God has made all things clean and acceptable. But it does mean he lays aside the exercise of his liberty to please his fellow believer, for that fellow believer's benefit, until the weaker believer can be built up in faith.

Basically, the problem that arises is one of selfishness. Often a stronger Christian selfishly wants to exercise Christian liberty, while a weaker Christian selfishly refuses to give the stronger believer the right to do that. Both are selfish. Each wants to insist that the other conform to his way of thinking. To these Paul was saying, "If you are to glorify God together, then you must be concerned not with yourselves, not with what pleases you, but with that which will be for the other's good." His point is, "Set aside your own selfish desire, your insistence on your own way, your proof of your liberty, and be concerned instead with your neighbor's good. Impose limitations on yourself in order to bring him to the place where he can exercise the same liberty you enjoy." With a view to glorifying God, let each one try to please his neighbor instead of pleasing himself.

Promoting Liberty

The principle of doing all to the glory of God concerns not only seeking to please one's fellow believer instead of one's self, it also concerns promoting the unity of the assembly. "May the God of patience and comfort grant you to be like-minded toward one another, according to Christ Jesus, that you may with one mind and one mouth glorify the God and Father of our Lord Jesus Christ" (Romans 15:5–6).

What does Paul mean when he prays that God may grant believers to be like-minded toward one another? He is not inferring that after a period of time all believers will come to the same settled convictions concerning doubtful things so that there is no division. The goal of the assembly is not to impose one set of standards on every believer. Rather, the goal for them is to be like-minded toward one another according to Christ Jesus. What Paul is emphasizing goes back to the first principle expressed in Romans 14. To be like-minded means that the weaker believer will not condemn or discount the testimony of the stronger brother because of what God permits him to do. To be like-minded does not mean ultimately reaching the same conclusion on all things, but rather acknowledging that the Master may allow one servant to do one thing and another servant to do another thing. It means agreeing that whatever God allows you to do is none of my business, and what the Master allows me to do is not your responsibility, either.

In the closing chapter of John's gospel, Peter asked Jesus, "Lord, what about this man?" The Lord replied, in effect, "That is none of your business. You be concerned with My will for you. You have enough to do discharging My will for you without worrying about My will for him." The same principle applies to matters within the body of Christ. With a view to the glory of God, there should be unity of minds but not necessarily conformity of decision about these doubtful things.

Romans 14–15 deals with problems that resulted from integration—an integration far more difficult and volatile than anything we have faced in our culture. It was the integration of Jew and Gentile, who had been separate and often at enmity with one another for many hundreds of years. But in presenting certain principles to guide them in their new oneness, the apostle Paul was concerned not just with the oneness of two groups that had previously been separate. His highest goal was that all things should be done to bring praise, honor, and glory to the name of the Lord Jesus Christ.

In some situations unity is achieved at the expense of sound doctrine; in others unity is achieved at the expense of sound practice. But the New Testament concept of unity is never achieved by denying the faith. It is never unity at the expense of condoning sin in the life of the assembly. It is always a unity based on the Word of God and the person of Jesus Christ, a unity that arises out of a meeting of minds because believers in the assembly have the mind of Christ.

As believers, we can do no better than to do all things to the glory of God. Any pattern of conduct can be tested by this principle. Can I do this for the glory of God? If I practice this thing, will God be honored? If this is a part of my life, will I attract others to Jesus Christ, or will I repel them from the gospel? We must realize that frequently the world has a far higher standard of behavior for the Christian than do Christians for themselves. Many things that we would allow in the name of liberty, the unregenerate person would not tolerate and would consider entirely out of harmony with a Christian's testimony. In living the Christian life, we have a responsibility not only to fellow believers, but also to the world that watches us more critically and is more ready than anyone to point a finger of accusation at us.

Therefore God's Word admonishes us to do everything, whether in word or in deed, to the glory of God.

Notes

1. Once again we see the importance God places on Christian unity—the one mind and one mouth with which we are to glorify Him. Obviously, this does not mean that all Christians will agree on everything all the time. But it does

mean that in the same way a military unit possesses a distinct oneness under a single commander, we will possess a distinct oneness as His body.

2. Most elementary school teachers agree that the most difficult aspect of teaching first graders is not what's done in the classroom, but what happens in the schoolyard. A hallmark of immaturity is an inherent selfishness that demands, "I want everything *my* way!" Spiritual immaturity is quite similar. Giving in to the needs of another indicates real spiritual progress.

3. One writer points out that when Jesus said that we would each bear fruit, He did not intend that we become an army of fruit inspectors! How much more might the church of Jesus Christ accomplish if we paid as much attention to our own walks with Christ as we do to others'. The next time you are tempted to judge another believer's behavior in an area the Bible does not specifically address, read Romans 14:14–23 and ask yourself, "Is there an area of my own spiritual growth I can concentrate on instead?"

4. Notice that God's idea of unity is genuine unity under His standards for salvation—not unity for the sake of unity alone. That is the difference between Babel and the church!

5. Unity based on a sound interpretation of the Bible requires that we know what we believe, and why we believe it. The Christian who plays down the importance of studying and knowing the foundational doctrines of the faith is setting himself up to be deceived by a cheap imitation.

6. What a test for determining whether an attitude or action is worthy of our time and energy! We can ask ourselves, "Does this glorify Christ?" and almost immediately know whether or not it belongs in our lives.

Questions

1. What do you think it means for believers to be of "one mind"? Of "one mouth"?

2. What does it mean to "glorify God"? Be specific in your answer(s).

3. Do you think God is glorified by a group of believers that is unified, even if some of them clearly disagree with what the Bible teaches? Why or why not?

4. In light of Romans 15:5, what aspects of the Spirit's ministry in our lives will move us toward becoming like-minded?

5. Do you believe a Christian has a duty to fulfill Christian unity by remaining in an assembly that denies basic tenets of the faith? What Scriptures can you use to support your answer?

6. What does it mean for us to be "like-minded toward one another, according to Christ Jesus"? How does John 15:9–12 relate to this?

CHAPTER 20

HOW FAR CAN A CHRISTIAN GO?

1 Corinthians 8:1–13

The church in Rome was threatened by division over the conflict between Jews and Gentiles due to different social, cultural, and religious background. This conflict made it necessary for Paul to lay down certain principles to guide both groups in their Christian conduct. These principles were intended to guide them in the area of doubtful things so that one believer should not judge another; so that there should be no division in the assembly; so that a weaker Christian should not be offended or caused to stumble; so that there should be no loss of testimony for the stronger Christian; and so that God would be glorified through the lives of all believers.

But when we come to Paul's letter to the Corinthians, we find that he was facing a slightly different situation. A conflict had arisen in the church at Corinth, too. But it was not a conflict between Jews and Gentiles, for virtually all the people in the Corinthian church had been brought to Christ out of the same social, cultural, and religious background. This assembly, which was made up of Gentiles who had come to Christ out of a background of pagan hedonism, faced a problem concerning doubtful things and questionable practices among them. This concern about doubtful things outside the realm of old Jewish practices caused Paul to state the same principles we have already looked at in Romans. But because of the makeup of the church at Corinth, we now will see how the principles Paul applied to the saved Jews and Gentiles in Rome are equally relevant in a setting of Christians who have been saved out of a similar hedonistic background. This is especially fitting for our culture today.

The city of Corinth was a center of heathen paganism and the site of great temples built to Greek gods and goddesses. Many of the false gods of Corinth were worshiped by the offering of meat sacrifices. An animal's flesh would be taken to the temple, presented to a priest, and then

---

placed by a priest onto the altar. It remained in the temple for only a short time, then was taken to the local marketplace and offered for sale. Temple meat, in fact, was sold at a lower price than other meats. Therefore a Christian homemaker who shopped the marketplace would notice a significant difference in the prices of what appeared to be identical portions of meat. If she asked why one piece of meat was more expensive than the other, the butcher would tell her that the more expensive piece of meat had come directly from the slaughtering pens, while the other had come from an idol temple.

Suppose, then, that two believers—Mrs. A and Mrs. B—went together to the market. Mrs. A would reason, "Money is short at our house. I don't see any reason why I shouldn't buy that bargain piece of meat, because I know an idol is nothing. An idol could not feast on that meat even though it was on the altar. The idol has not changed the meat nor destroyed its value as food. Therefore I can buy it and serve it to my family."

However, when confronted with the same situation, Mrs. B would reason, "I used to be a worshiper of that god. Many times I brought meat into that temple and gave it to the priest, who offered it to that idol. I will not, under any circumstances, touch meat that has been in an idol temple, because it reminds me of my past life and my past idolatry. I'll have nothing to do with it." And so she would buy the more expensive portion of meat so that she would not defile her conscience by eating meat that had been offered to idols.

So far there had been no conflict between the two, for each had a good basis for doing what she did. Mrs. A was exercising the liberty given to her in Christ. Mrs. B was zealous to have a good conscience before God and to not give offense to anyone. Conflict arose, however, when Mrs. A and Mrs. B began to judge each other. Mrs. A would accuse Mrs. B of needless extravagance in paying the higher price; or she would question Mrs. B's narrow conscience and spiritual immaturity because her conscience was so easily defiled. Mrs. B, on the other hand, would accuse Mrs. A of trafficking with idols and neglecting to maintain separation from that out of which they had been saved. Soon the conflict between the two would erupt into an open conflict in the Christian congregation and sides would be taken. One group would accuse the other of a lack of spiritual maturity, while the other group would accuse the first of a lack of separation from the world. Thus the assembly would become deeply divided.

In writing to the polarized believers at Corinth, Paul applied the same principles he set forth for the believing Jews and Gentiles at Rome.

This alone shows us that these same principles are relevant and applicable to any society, to any culture, in any age. We don't need a different set of principles today, because these are universally acceptable.

Principles of Conduct

In 1 Corinthians 8:1, Paul began by stating the principle of liberty in Christ: "Concerning things offered to idols: We know that we all have knowledge." Knowledge, as he explained in this passage, is the knowledge that an idol is nothing. By buying meat offered to idols, a believer is not approving the false religious system carried on in the temple. So he writes, "Concerning the eating of things offered to idols, we know that an idol is nothing in the world, and that there is no other God but one. . . . yet for us there is only one God, the Father, of whom are all things, and we for Him . . ." (8:4, 6).

The knowledge these believers had gave them the liberty to eat meat offered to idols. Paul knew well that putting meat in an idol temple could not contaminate it so that it could not be used by a believer. To use it or not use it was strictly a matter of conscience. Because they knew that an idol is nothing, and knew that there is but one God, it made no difference whether that meat stayed overnight on an idol altar, or whether it stayed overnight in the butcher's shop. Thus Paul affirmed the principle of freedom in Christ.

But verses 1–2 warn that knowledge can be a dangerous thing: "Knowledge puffs up, but love edifies. And if anyone thinks that he knows anything, he knows nothing yet as he ought to know." A believer's knowledge of his freedom should not be the exclusive determining factor in his Christian conduct. Knowing we *can* do something does not mean we *should* do it. Because God has declared all things clean, we will not permit anyone to take away our freedom, to impose law on us, or to put us under a legal system. But we are not under obligation to *exercise* our freedom.

There is a second principle that takes priority over the first, as indicated by verses 7 and 9: "There is not in everyone that knowledge; for some, with consciousness of the idol, until now eat it as a thing offered to an idol; and their conscience, being weak, is defiled . . . . But beware lest somehow this liberty of yours become a stumbling block to those who are weak." This second principle, which Paul also affirmed in Romans 14, was the principle that no believer should use his liberty to cause a weaker brother to stumble or be offended. Though some of the believers at Corinth had a working knowledge of their liberty, Paul recognized that not all had the same working knowledge (1 Corinthians 8:7), which Paul equates with the faith to believe that something is acceptable. Therefore he gave the warning that those with that knowledge should be careful lest their liberty should cause weaker believers to stumble.

The danger involved in causing a weaker Christian to stumble is clearly outlined in verses 10–11: "If anyone sees you who have knowledge eating in an idol's temple [that is, he sees you using the idol's meat, and as a result concludes that you are joining yourself to the idol], will not the conscience of him who is weak be emboldened to eat those things offered to idols? And because of your knowledge shall the weak brother perish, for whom Christ died?" The scenario here is that the weaker Christian concludes that if the stronger believer can eat meat from an idol temple, so can he. So he eats idol-offered meat, but his conscience is defiled. The result is that the weaker Christian may perish. This word does not mean that the weak Christian loses his salvation. Remember that in Romans 15 Paul wrote that we were to consider the weaker brother with a view to his good, his edification, his spiritual growth. The thought is the same here. A believer who patterns his life after the stronger Christian but without the stronger Christian's faith, so defiles his conscience that there can be no development, no progress, no growth, no edification in the doctrine of grace.

Verse 12 adds another crucial thought: "When you thus sin against the brethren [by insisting on using your liberty and exercising your rights, no matter what it does to the weaker brethren], and wound their weak conscience, you sin against Christ." Take note: "You sin against Christ." The believer who insists, "I *can*, therefore I *will*," and does not assume the conscience of the weaker believer, is guilty of sinning against Christ.

So, then, the second principle is that no believer has the right to exercise his God-given liberty if it means he is going to cause his brother to stumble, for if he causes his brother to stumble, he not only is sinning against that believer, he is sinning against Christ.

The third principle is found in verse 13, and then is illustrated in chapter 9 of 1 Corinthians. The principle is that of surrendering our rights, or surrendering the exercise of our liberty, for the good and the edification of another believer. Paul wrote, "If food makes my brother stumble, I will never again eat meat, lest I make my brother stumble." Here the apostle is going well beyond what would be expected or demanded in this situation. If the weaker believer would be offended because Paul ate idol meat, the simple remedy would be for Paul to eat the other kind of meat. But he said, "If my brother saw me eat idol-offered meat and it caused him to be offended, I would give up all meat, because I might eat non-idol meat and the weaker brother might think I was eating idol meat. Therefore I would gladly go beyond what would be expected of me, because my greatest desire is to avoid sinning against Christ by causing the weaker brother to come to a spiritual standstill." This indeed is surrendering one's rights for the good of the brethren.

Surrendering Rights

Paul next cites some examples of rights he surrendered for the good of the brethren. In chapter 9 he affirms the fact that he is an apostle. Because he is an apostle he knows he has certain rights and liberties, as shown by his question in verse 4: "Do we have no right to eat and drink?" The answer would be, "Yes, you do have the right to eat and drink." He asks in verse 5, "Do we have no right to take along a believing wife, as do also the other apostles, the brothers of the Lord, and Cephas?" Again the answer would be "Yes, you do have that right." He further asks in verse 13 whether he has the right to be supported by the churches, which again would be answered in the affirmative.

But what was Paul's response to all this? "For though I am free from all men, I have made myself a servant to all, that I might win the more" (9:19). He did not say, "I demand that the weaker brethren recognize that I am an apostle and have certain rights and liberties." No—he put himself into the servant class and submitted to the conscience of the weaker believer. "To the Jews I became as a Jew, that I might win Jews; to those who are under the law, as under the law, that I might win those who are under the law; to those who are without law, as without law (not being without law toward God, but under law toward Christ), that I might win those who are without law; to the weak I became as weak, that I might win the weak. I have become all things to all men, that I might by all means save some. Now this I do for the gospel's sake" (1 Corinthians 9:20–23).

Thus Paul gives his own personal testimony about how these principles affected his life. In effect, he said, "I gave up meat and lived on vegetables that I might not give offense. I did without the companionship of a wife. I labored making tents when it was the church's obligation to contribute to my needs. I imposed on myself the conscience of the weak brother and gave up those things I personally would have enjoyed. I even observed days and months of the old Jewish calendar that I might win those that are under the law." Why? "For the gospel's sake."

So how would Paul have summarized his teaching concerning the problem of whether the believing household in Corinth should eat idol-offered meat? He would have advised something like this: "First of all, it doesn't matter to God. Second, you must be satisfied in your own conscience about which meat God wants you to buy and eat. If God gives you liberty to buy meat that is cheaper because it has been offered to idols, eat it and enjoy it. If God won't let you, then don't buy idol-offered meat. Each believer must have a clear conscience before God in this matter. Third, be extremely careful that you do not cause another believer to stumble by the use of your liberty; for if you do, you sin against Christ. It is far better to give up the use of your liberty than it is to cause a brother to come to a spiritual standstill."

Dangers to Avoid

These principles are extremely relevant to situations we face today. Most of us aren't bothered about whether we should or shouldn't eat ham, as were the Christians in Rome. Likewise, most of us aren't bothered about whether we should buy meat sacrificed to idols, as were the Christians in Corinth. But there are other issues that cause problems and divide believers today. What should we do about these issues, and how do these principles apply?

In different parts of the country Christian groups have different standards concerning what is right and what is wrong. If we tried to draw up a list of so-called doubtful things, it would vary tremendously according to locale. Some doubtful things have been debated for some time, while others have faded in seeming importance. Doubtful things fit into many different categories. Some fit into the social realm, while others fall into the category of amusements or entertainment. Still others are classified as personal pleasures or habits.

How do we make personal decisions about these issues? First, we must determine if the issue we face is indeed one of those doubtful things. Is this really a questionable issue, or is it already forbidden by the Word of God? Is there something inherent in it that would clearly violate the Word? If so, then it is instantly removed from the area of doubtful things.

Some Christians try to avoid this question by equating a legalistic code with Scripture and imposing it on believers. They will say that a person cannot be a believer and do certain things (whatever the list might include). But a legalistic code contradicts the individual liberty we have in Christ and nullifies the believer's conscience in these matters. To say that a person cannot be a Christian and do certain things is to impose a legalistic system that is not taught in the Word of God. Further, to say that a person cannot be a Christian and do certain things is to make salvation depend on works rather than on the grace of God. Certainly, it may be right for a Christian organization to impose some restrictions for the sake of its testimony. But to avoid the question of doubtful things by imposing legalistic standards is wrong.

Second, we must determine if exercising our liberty in any particular doubtful thing will cause us to lose our testimony or cause a fellow believer to sin. If God gives me the liberty to do something, I have perfect liberty to do it. I *could* do it—but that does not mean I *should* do it. As we have seen, it would be better for me to forego that which might be enjoyable or relaxing, rather than to prevent a fellow Christian from growing in grace and in the knowledge of our Lord and Savior.

It is a misconception to think that giving up certain liberties is an evidence of spirituality. I do not grow more spiritual by foregoing my liberty; but I do show concern for my testimony and for my fellow believer. Dr. Homer Hammontree used to say that there is a city with two million inhabitants, none of whom drink, smoke, dance, or play cards. But not one of them has a bit of spiritual life. He was referring to the Greenwood Hills Cemetery in New York City. Refraining from certain things is not synonymous with spirituality. To be spiritual is to be controlled by the Holy Spirit. Spirituality will certainly produce a different kind of life, and will remove offensive things from the Christian's life. But we cannot equate spirituality with observing certain prohibitions in the area of doubtful things.

A believer should exercise liberty to the extent that his testimony is not jeopardized and fellow believers are not led into sin. One of the greatest dangers believers face today is the danger of losing their testimony before the world by being so much like the world that they have nothing to offer it. We will never attract unbelievers to Jesus Christ by being like the world. If all we have to offer is what the world already has, no one will see a need for it. The only way we can attract people to Jesus Christ is by having something they don't have, thus creating an appetite in them for what God can give them. That appetite is created not when we are just like the world, but when we are distinctly different from it.

Peter did not hesitate to call us a *peculiar*, or set-apart, people. Some Christians don't want to be considered peculiar, to be different. But God is asking us to stand apart, to surrender our practice of some of the liberties He has given us in order to attract people to Jesus Christ. The question is not, "Can a believer do this?" The question is, "Can I give this up for the gospel's sake to maintain my testimony before other believers, and before the world?" Will we dare to be different by refusing to conform to the world, no matter what our rights?

Notes

1. The situation facing the Corinthian church is very similar to what we face today—knowing Christ in the midst of rampant hedonism. We need to remember that many, if not most, people who come to Christ and join our fellowship today will be coming out of a background devoid of biblical influence. Therefore we need to leave room for Christian growth rather than expecting some kind of instant maturity in our fellow believers. That means applying selfless sensitivity as we encourage spiritual progress in our Christian brothers and sisters.

2. Another aspect of eating meat sacrificed to idols would have been the possibility that someone who had been saved out of idol worship might have mistakenly concluded that if a mature Christian could eat meat from that idol's temple, then it must be okay to mix worship of Christ with worship of that idol. That would be similar today to a newly saved drug user being misled by a believer's freedom to listen to drug-culture music; or a newly saved, recovering alcoholic being misled by a believer's freedom to drink wine; or a newly saved former gang member being misled by a young believer's freedom to wear gang-related clothing. We must be sensitive to the effects our liberty might have on the weakest, spiritually youngest believers around us.

3. The explosion of a two-person debate about meat into a church-wide conflict might seem ludicrous to someone who has not seen churches polarized by issues just as small. But many of us have seen churches erupt into conflict over things like carpet, musical instruments, youth concerts, softball teams, even coffee pots! Our trouble begins when one or both sides decide that God takes a firm stand on the issue. That means the opposition doesn't just have a differing opinion—they are opposing God! God's instructions concerning doubtful things—those things which are inconsequential except in regard to one's individual influence on weaker believers—should show us how we might handle conflicts over other, even less significant, issues.

4. One of the big problems with Christian activism—boycotting and protesting against any business that supports un-Christian values—is that it's virtually impossible to keep up with all the political and economic connections that unite the world system. Well-intentioned Christian activists must know which corporations own which businesses that support which causes in order to bring negative pressure to bear against them. Or must they? Obviously, God had no qualms about a believing homemaker buying meat sacrificed to a pagan idol, because her heart was pure in doing it. In fact, for all we know she might have used that meat for an evangelistic dinner, or a prayer feast, or a church meal. But even if she simply fed it to her family, she was not at fault before God—unless she caused a weaker fellow-believer to stumble. The lesson is this: God is most concerned about unity of the body, because unity is

necessary in order for the church to fulfill its *real* mission of ongoing aggressive evangelism.

5. Some Christians mistake the statement "knowledge puffs up" as a divine escape clause from serious Bible study. However, the indictment here is not against knowledge, but against knowledge applied without love. Let us never lose sight of God's many admonitions that the child of God thoroughly know the Scriptures (see 2 Timothy 2:15; 3:16–17; Hebrews 4:12).

6. Anyone who has ever watched wildlife documentaries on television knows that there are many types of animal communities in which the responsibilities of rearing young are shared among all members. What an ideal picture this is of the way in which all believers in a fellowship should be concerned with the growth and well-being of the spiritually young among them. While we all rejoice at a person's decision for Christ, we should remain just as enthusiastic about his or her continued progress in spiritual growth, helping make our local fellowship a spiritual incubator.

7. We see the biblical standard of surrendering our own rights rather than demanding rights at the expense of others. Is this our attitude even toward those who are spiritually immature, uninformed, and unreasonable?

8. Notice that Paul's entire motivation in making personal sacrifices was the advance of the gospel. What sacrifices are we making each day to ensure that the gospel goes out to unbelievers?

9. A particularly frustrating trait of legalism is that it becomes an entirely closed, cyclical system. That is, the list of legalistic requirements that guarantee salvation (or sanctification) almost always precludes questioning the list of legalistic requirements itself. "If you don't follow these requirements," legalism asserts, "you are not really a Christian. And if you question these requirements, you are not really a Christian." Salvation and sanctification are by grace, through faith—not by intimidation.

10. If giving up an area of liberty becomes a point of pride for the person doing it, it has become sin rather than sacrifice. Don't lose sight of the real purpose, which is the edification other believers.

11. One Bible teacher regularly encourages his young audiences to not ask, "Can I do this? but rather, "As an ambassador of Jesus Christ in the world, why *should* I do this?"

Questions

1. Based on the information in this chapter, in what ways is our modern culture similar to the one found at Corinth? In what ways is it different? What kinds

of things in our culture might correspond to the practice of idol worship in Corinth?

2. Based on 1 Corinthians 8:1–3, how would you describe the discussions that were taking place in the church at Corinth? What element apparently was missing? How does this compare with church conflicts you have seen in the past?

3. Based on the information in this chapter, what was Mrs. B's beef against Mrs. A? How might Mrs. A have responded? Can you draw a parallel to a similar situation that might occur today?

4. If exercising our liberty causes a weaker believer to stumble, what else has taken place, according to 1 Corinthians 8:12?

5. Read 1 Corinthians 9:19. What was Paul's attitude toward those who might find fault with him even when he had done nothing wrong? What was his motivation?

6. Can you think of any areas of Christian liberty believers today might give up in order to ensure that a weaker believer would not be caused to stumble? What will happen if we try to turn these into absolute rules of conduct? What should be our attitudes toward these and other areas of doubtful things?

CHAPTER 21

THE GOAL OF THE CHRISTIAN

John 17:1–10

What is the goal in the Christian life? When Paul dealt with doubtful things, he concluded by saying that we should do all things to the honor and glory of God. If we eat, let us eat not to demonstrate our liberty, but to glorify God. If we refrain from eating, let us do it not for our own glory in surrendering our liberty, but for the glory of God. One bumper sticker that always catches my attention is the one that says, "Don't follow me. I'm lost." Because many Christians have no clear goal in view, it is impossible for them to accomplish anything in the Christian life. Because we are so vague in our thinking about what constitutes Christian living, we have to confess that we are lost and do not know where we are going. But if we really want to glorify God, we must first understand how God is glorified.

To the Glory of God

John 17 gives us an indication of what it means to glorify God. We recognize that God is a God of infinite glory, and that it is impossible to add anything to the infinite glory He already possesses. In what sense, then, can we glorify God? In His conversation with the Father just before going to the cross, Jesus said, "I have glorified You on the earth. I have finished the work which You have given Me to do" (John 17:4). Jesus Christ glorified the Father because, in perfect obedience to the will of the Father, He completed the work the Father had given Him to do. What was that work? We find the answer in verses 6 and 8, where Jesus said, "I have manifested Your name to the men whom You have given Me out of the world. . . . I have given to them the words which You have given Me."

The Lord Jesus Christ was sent into the world to reveal the Father to humanity. He glorified the Father when He revealed the Father to humanity. Having revealed the Father to humanity, He could say to the

Father, "I have glorified You on the earth. I have finished the work which You have given Me to do." John 1:18 tells us that "the only begotten Son, who is in the bosom of the Father, He has declared [or revealed] Him." Jesus Christ came into the world so that the world, which was ignorant of God, might have a revelation of God. And when Jesus Christ revealed God to humanity, He glorified the Father. When people received the revelation Christ gave, and responded to that revelation by honoring, worshiping, obeying, and adoring the One who was revealed, they glorified God. Further, those who received the revelation were then called on to manifest the glory of God to the world just as Jesus Christ had glorified the Father on earth. So when the apostle Paul wrote, "You were bought at a price; therefore glorify God" (1 Corinthians 6:20), he was saying, You who have received Christ are responsible to reveal the Father to those who are in ignorance and darkness.

How does God work in the Christian to glorify Himself? First, the child of God glorifies God through the very fact that he has received Christ as his personal Savior. His salvation in itself glorifies God. Three times in Ephesians 1 the apostle Paul emphasizes the fact that our salvation brings glory to God. In Ephesians 1:6 we see that all the Father has done has been planned to be to the praise of the glory of His grace. In verse 12 we discover that all the Son did was done with this in view: that we should be to the praise of His glory. And verse 14 states that all the Holy Spirit accomplishes in and through the child of God is to the praise of His glory. So we see that salvation by grace, which has been offered to us by the Father through the Son, and accomplished by the Holy Spirit, brings glory to God.

Romans 9:23 emphasizes the same truth when Paul states that God's purpose is to "make known the riches of His glory on the vessels of mercy, which He had prepared beforehand for glory." This emphasizes that God has chosen us for salvation, that we should be *vessels,* or instruments, through which God would make known the riches of His glory.

God is glorified because He saves sinners. God did not select the good, the kind, the nice, the upright, and the righteous, and save them because of what they were. God saves sinners, those who deserve nothing. And by reaching down in grace, mercy, and love to redeem sinners, He brings glory to Himself.

First Timothy 1:16 again emphasizes the glory God receives by saving sinners when it says, "For this reason I obtained mercy, that in me first Jesus Christ might show all longsuffering, as a pattern to those who are going to believe on Him for everlasting life." The salvation given to Saul of Tarsus displayed God's patience with a stubborn rebel—seeking him, finding him, and bringing him to Himself. We see, then, that the salvation provided for us is a salvation that glorifies God.

Second, we glorify God through a daily life lived in conformity to the image of Jesus Christ. The privilege of our salvation places upon us a responsibility to walk worthy of the Lord, so that through our transformed lives God is revealed and glorified. First Thessalonians 2:12 emphasizes "that you would have a walk worthy of God who calls you into His own kingdom and glory." Again, 1 Corinthians 10:31 encourages us, "Whether you eat or drink, or whatever you do, do all to the glory of God." God's desire for believers is that they will so conduct themselves in their daily lives that they will bring glory to God.

Third, we discover that God will be glorified throughout the unending ages of eternity as He brings His children into glory. Colossians 3:4 emphasizes, "When Christ, who is our life appears, then you also will appear with Him in glory." The phrase *in glory* does not describe *where* we shall be, but rather *how* we shall be. It might be paraphrased, "When Christ shall appear, then you also will appear with Him, as glorious ones." Paul focuses his attention on the outcome of our salvation, and that is conformity to Christ in glory.

This same truth is presented in Hebrews 2:9–10, where we read, "We see Jesus, who was made a little lower than the angels, for the suffering of death crowned with glory and honor, that He, by the grace of God, might taste death for everyone. For it was fitting for Him, for whom *are* all things and by whom *are* all things, in bringing many sons to glory, to make the author of their salvation perfect through sufferings" (italics added). Jesus Christ offered Himself as a sacrifice and died to bring many into glory. He was resurrected to be the first fruits of a great harvest of glorified ones who shall be transformed into His likeness, so that through the ages of eternity we should bring glory to the Father.

When we take all these passages together, we find that the believer glorifies God through the salvation he has received by grace, through the new life that he lives, and through being one in whom God's promise will be fulfilled that "when He is revealed, we shall be like Him, for we shall see Him as He is" (1 John 3:2). Therefore the paramount goal for the Christian is the goal of bringing glory to the Father.

In the Likeness of Christ

The question will logically arise, "How can a redeemed sinner glorify God?" In Galatians 2:20 Paul writes, "I have been crucified with Christ; it is no longer I who live, but Christ lives in me; and the *life* which I now live in the flesh I live by faith in the Son of God, who loved me and gave Himself for me" (italics added). Christ lives in me! We Christians, in and of ourselves, cannot glorify God. But as Jesus Christ lives His life in us and through us as children of God, He can do through us what He did when He walked here on the earth. And it is just as much Christ's purpose to glorify God today as it was then.

Therefore, if we are to glorify God, we must reproduce the likeness of Jesus Christ. First Peter 2:21 tells us, "For to this [to this end] you were called, because Christ also suffered for us, leaving us an example, that you should follow His steps." Peter goes on to show the submission that characterized the Lord Jesus Christ, emphasizing that as the Christian submits to the Lord in his or her daily experience, Christ will manifest His life through that person to the glory of the Father.

This theme appears also throughout Paul's writings. For example, we read in 2 Corinthians 3:18, "We all, with unveiled face, beholding as in a mirror the glory of the Lord, are being transformed into the same image from glory to glory, just as by the Spirit of the Lord." Why is the Lord Jesus Christ revealed to us? That we might be changed, or transfigured, into His image. We cannot, with these natural eyes, look on His glorious face. Yet the glorified, risen, ascended Christ is revealed to us through the Bible, which is like a mirror reflecting His glory. And as we look at the One who is revealed in its pages, God intends to conform us to that image, so that the Son might glorify the Father through us.

We read in 2 Corinthians 4:11, "We who live are always delivered to death for Jesus' sake, that the life of Jesus also may be manifested in our mortal flesh." Think of it! Jesus Christ so transforms the Christian that His life is evidenced through the believer's mortal body, with the objective that God is glorified. "All things are for your sakes, that grace, having spread through the many, may cause thanksgiving to abound to the glory of God" (2 Corinthians 4:15). God's purpose is that the life of Jesus Christ be made so evident in our mortal bodies that glory might be directed to God.

In 1 John 2:6 the apostle John wrote, "He who says he abides in Him ought himself also to walk just as He walked." When God seeks to glorify Himself through us, He does so by revealing Jesus Christ in and through our lives; and as Christ lives His life through us, God is revealed to the world around us, bringing glory to Him.

This brings one more question to mind: "Since God's goal for my life is that I should glorify Him, and since God can be glorified only as the life of Christ is reproduced in my body, how can I manifest Christ as I live day by day?" That question is answered by our relationship to the Holy Spirit. In our own power, we cannot reproduce or display the life of Christ, for we are not Jesus Christ. We do not have His perfection. We do not have His holiness. We do not have His wisdom and knowledge of the Father. We live in unredeemed bodies with a sinful nature, in the midst of an unredeemed world. How can we glorify God by manifesting the life of Christ?

We can reproduce the life of the Lord Jesus Christ only by the power of the Holy Spirit of God. Paul repeatedly emphasized this theme as he wrote about the Christian life. He said in Romans 8:5–13, "Those who live according to the flesh set their minds on the things of the flesh, but those who live according to the Spirit, the things of the Spirit. For to be carnally minded is death, but to be spiritually minded is life and peace. Because the carnal mind is enmity against God; for it is not subject to the law of God, nor indeed can be. So then, those who are in the flesh cannot please God. But you are not in the flesh but in the Spirit, if indeed the Spirit of God dwells in you. Now if anyone does not have the Spirit of Christ, he is not His. And if Christ is in you, the body is dead because of sin, but the Spirit is life because of righteousness. But if the Spirit of Him who raised Jesus from the dead dwells in you, He who raised Christ from the dead will also give life to your mortal bodies through His Spirit who dwells in you. Therefore, brethren, we are debtors—not to the flesh, to live according to the flesh. For if you live according to the flesh you will die; but if by the Spirit you put to death the deeds of the body, you will live."

This tells us that if we manifest our nature, we reveal the flesh: what is dead, that which cannot bring glory to God. But if the Spirit of God takes charge of our mortal bodies, He will reproduce the life of Jesus Christ in us and use our mortal bodies as His instruments to reveal Christ and glorify the Father.

Ephesians 1:19–20 emphasizes that we Christians should know "what is the exceeding greatness of His power toward us who believe, according to the working of His mighty power which He worked in Christ when He raised Him from the dead and seated Him at His right hand in the heavenly places." And if we compare this passage with Romans 8:11, we will discover that the Holy Spirit who raised Jesus Christ from the dead is that same power that works within us to empower our mortal bodies to do God's will. That is why Ephesians 5:18 admonishes us, "Do not be drunk with wine, in which is dissipation; but be filled with the Spirit." As we are controlled by the Holy Spirit, the Spirit will reproduce Christ's life in us, and God will be glorified. Galatians 5:16 summarizes this concept as well as any one verse: "I say then: Walk in the Spirit, and you shall not fulfill the lust of the flesh."

The apostle Paul revealed his own spiritual secret in Philippians 3:10, where he said that it was the great desire of his heart to know

Christ and to know the power of His resurrection. A paraphrase of his statement could read, "I want to know Him. Then I want to know in my experience the power that brought Jesus Christ to resurrection." Paul's great goal was to know Him so that he might be like Him; and then to be so related to the Holy Spirit that the power that brought forth Jesus Christ from the grave might be the power operating in his life. Then all those around him would see Jesus Christ; and seeing Christ, some would come to know the Father and He would be glorified.

In Colossians 1:11 Paul prayed that believers might be "strengthened with all might, according to His glorious power, for all patience and long-suffering with joy." What this stresses is that when God's power through the Holy Spirit operates in us, God will be glorified because the Spirit will produce the patience, longsuffering, and joy of Christ in us.

People today are motivated by many different goals. They want security; they want happiness; they want material prosperity; they want ideological power; they want political influence; they want reputations. All of these things satisfy the flesh, but they do not fulfill God's purpose for each of us, because God's purpose for each person is that His life might be reproduced in us, bringing glory to God. The greatest goal in the Christian life is not enjoyment of salvation. It is not learning the truths of Scripture, Christianizing a nation, or even teaching and preaching the Word of God. The greatest goal for the Christian is to live out Jesus Christ before the world so that people may know the Father. God is glorified through a transformation of our lives that enables Him to use us to reveal Himself to the world around us. And as people around us respond to what they see of Christ in us, God will be glorified and people will come to know Him.

Jesus Christ could say, "I have finished the work which You have given Me to do" (John 17:4). May God the Holy Spirit so possess and control us, and so reproduce Jesus Christ within us, that we can say at the close of each day, "I have finished the work which You have given Me to do today. The Holy Spirit has reproduced the life of Christ in this mortal body, to Your glory."

Notes

1. Have we been influenced by our modern North American standards to believe that the goal of the Christian life is to live comfortably and successfully? If so, that might explain why the Christian church in some of the most oppressed, impoverished countries in the world are doing so much more than we are in terms of evangelism and discipleship. Perhaps our entertaining worship services, comfortable Christian circles, self-help spiritual teachings, and infatuation with self-esteem are not the answers we once thought they were.

2. Preparing and giving one's personal testimony is one of the most worth-while—and most natural—exercises a Christian can pursue. Not only is it easy to prepare (because, after all, it is your own experience), it is also a powerful and effective means of evangelism as God draws people to Himself through the conversion experience of others. If you can't give your personal testimony at a moment's notice, ask your pastor or Sunday school teacher to help you prepare for all the future opportunities you will have to share it with others. Prepare it, perfect it, and make it your own!

3. How comforting it is to know that we do not have to be super saints to bring glory to God. God is glorified by saving those who need Him most—us!

4. Too often we think of the Christian life in terms of what we will get out of it, and then adjust our behavior accordingly. Scripture, on the other hand, views the Christian life in terms of how God is glorified. What daily decisions might we make differently if we measure them according to the glory they bring God, rather than the gain they bring us?

5. As any sailor knows, a lighthouse with no light shining out from inside is worthless on a dark night. It is only when the lamp is lit that the lighthouse fulfills the purpose for which it was created. Likewise, it is only as the light of Jesus Christ, living His life in us and through us, shines out from our lives that we fulfill the purpose for which we were created.

6. Do we define our Christian lives in terms of Christlikeness? According to these passages, God's desire for us is that we conform to the image of Christ, not to some other image of success, attractiveness, prestige, popularity, or whatever. Consider asking yourself at the end of each day, "How have I represented the image of Christ to the world around me today?"

7. It would be extremely presumptuous of us to think that we humans can glorify an infinite, perfect God—*if* we did not depend on the power of God's Spirit to produce Christ's righteousness in us. But because it is He who produces righteousness in us, He receives all the credit and glory for any goodness evident in our lives.

8. What is your motivation in life? If you were asked to write out your priorities according to the amount of time you devote to each one, what would top the list? Which aspect of life really receives the most time and attention? The Bible teaches that the only worthwhile priority for the Christian life is revealing Jesus Christ to the world around us so that people might come to know Him. Anything less is something far less than the best.

9. Can you name anything your great-grandparents accomplished with their lives? If you can, you are part of a small minority of people who know any-

thing at all about the life and accomplishments of relatives only three generations removed from themselves. Let's look at it another way: three generations from now, what will your great-grandchildren be able to say you accomplished with your life? What would you want them to be able to say? Measured in worldly terms, only a few people ever accomplish something truly great—a scientific breakthrough, an amassed fortune, a brilliant political career. Measured in spiritual terms, however, we can accomplish great things if we devote ourselves to finishing the work God has given us to do, that of revealing God to people, through the power of His Spirit. And that is work that lasts forever—not just a generation or two.

Questions

1. Based on John 1:8 and 17:4–6, what was the work Jesus finished? What was the result of that work (17:4)?

2. What is the command given to Christians in 1 Corinthians 16:20? Upon what is that command founded?

3. In light of the work Christ said He finished during His earthly ministry, what is the work He wants us to do in order to glorify God today? How will this glorify God?

4. What does 1 Thessalonians 2:12 reveal about what God desires for every Christian? What do you think Paul meant by the phrase, "a walk worthy of God"?

5. Read John 17:4, 6. How would Jesus have measured up as an accomplished person in the eyes of our modern society? Based on that, how might we expect the world to view our accomplishments if we live our lives for the purpose of glorifying God?

6. What kinds of things in one's life might take the place of bringing glory to God? Does this mean that we cannot glorify God and see success in other areas? Explain your answer.

CHAPTER 22

THE CHRISTIAN AND THE WORLD

Romans 12:1–2

As Christians, we face many difficulties on our journeys from earth to heaven. The first great difficulty is sin. We are tempted on every side by those things which would entice us away from becoming more like Jesus. The Bible makes it very clear that sin has no rightful place in the Christian's life. We have no right to entertain any thought, deed, or word that is contrary to the holiness of the Lord Jesus Christ. Such things are clearly forbidden by the Word of God.

The second great difficulty comes in the area of doubtful things, things that in themselves are not sinful, but which may be put to sinful uses or sinful ends. As we have seen, the Bible provides certain principles to direct us in our decisions concerning our conduct in these areas, and we should be guided by these principles in each specific circumstance.

A third tremendous difficulty is in the area of worldliness. This is the problem we want to examine more closely in this chapter. When God created the world, He created it as an instrument through which He would reveal His glory to all the intelligent beings He had created. But with Adam's rebellion against God's authority, this world—which had been designed and created to serve God's purposes—was seized by Satan to serve his purpose, to promote his goals, and to further his rebellion against God. Our present problem, then, is the problem of how a child of God can use that which Satan has commandeered to use against God. How can we use the things that are in the world without promoting the purpose and programs of our adversary, the devil?

The World System

We need to remind ourselves that when we were born, we were born *into the world*—not as merely a geographical place, but as a condition or state of being. The Bible repeatedly refers to this fallen world as a condition of existence, or a system. The world has its prince, Satan.

Jesus called Satan "the ruler of this world" (John 12:31). Paul called Satan "the prince of the power of the air" (Ephesians 2:2). Regardless of how things may appear in the visible realm, this world is ruled by an unseen administration operating under the control of Satan as its prince, or head. Paul also called Satan "the god of this age" (2 Corinthians 4:4). This world has its own false religious system which can take many different forms, but which demands of its subjects (whether they realize it or not) worship, loyalty, and submission to Satan as its god. This world is the instrument Satan uses to promote his goals, his aims, his ends, and his ambitions—which ultimately are to usurp the rightful place of Messiah the king and reign in His place (see Isaiah 14:13–14 and Ezekiel 28:14–16).

But if Satan is to accomplish his purpose of overthrowing the kingdom of God and of elevating himself to the Son's rightful place of authority over all things, he must have some means through which he operates. This organized system through which Satan operates and over which he rules is the world we know. When Satan caused the fall of man and man's world, he did so in order to take command of that sphere in which God ruled. At that point, this world ceased to be an extension of God's kingdom and became Satan's "turf"—the means through which he would accomplish his purpose. Since that time, people born into this world have been born as "worldlings," under Satan's authority (and sharing in the condemnation that abides in him). Satan is the god who controls, guides, and directs our lives. His purposes are our purposes. His standards are our standards, his ethics are our ethics, and his morality is our morality because we are in the world. Moreover, his deceptions about God deceive us completely.

This is the world system. John, in 1 John 5:19, describes this system graphically when he says, "The whole world lies under the sway of the wicked one." This terminology pictures a nurse holding a child in her bosom; John says the whole world system [cosmos] around us is cradled in the arms of the evil one. The Bible also tells us that the world system is characterized by ignorance. First Corinthians 1:21 says, "The world through wisdom did not know God." The world system into which we were born does not know the true God, but knows only the god of this world who transforms himself into an angel of light to deceive the human race. Second Peter 2:20 speaks of the defilement of this world, which is under Satan's control and serves his purposes. Further, 2 Peter 1:4 refers to "the corruption that is in the world through lust." The world as a system is marked by corruption, and those who are in the world participate in its corruption.

What's more, 1 Corinthians 11:32 tells us that the world system is set apart for God's judgment. Because the world has been seized by Satan and is now under his authority, and because our Lord Himself announced that the prince of this world is to be judged (John 12:31), the system over which he rules will come under divine judgment. God created man for Himself, with the purpose that His creatures would enjoy fellowship with Him. But because of Adam's rebellion under Satan, God's purpose could not be accomplished in the world or in the citizens of the world as a whole. Therefore the world and its citizens are under divine judgment.

The Christian's Relationship to the World

One of the glorious truths of the gospel is that the death of Christ changes the believer's relationship to the world. The death of Christ has so many consequences—both in time and in eternity—that it is impossible for us to comprehend with our limited minds all God has accomplished through that one event. Not only did Christ's death provide redemption from sin, satisfy God's righteous requirements, and reconcile the world to Him, it also makes possible a change in our relationship to the world, once we enter into a relationship with Jesus Christ. As believers we can say with Paul, "Our citizenship is in heaven" (Philippians 3:20). This emphasizes a significant benefit of Christ's death. We who were born into this world as citizens of the world system have now had our citizenship transferred. Even though physically and geographically we are on the earth, we are no longer of the world system; we have been given a new citizenship in a new kingdom ruled by a new Prince, the Lord Jesus Christ. This kingdom, or state, is not characterized by ignorance, but rather by a knowledge of the true God. It is not characterized by defilement and corruption, for we have been made clean and righteous through the death of Christ. And we who are citizens of this state have been delivered from divine judgment, because we are now identified with Christ the righteous Judge, not with the world.

Let's consider some of the things that take place in our relationship to the world at the time we accept Christ as Savior. First, in John 17 our Lord spoke of us in His prayer to the Father as no longer being of the world: "I have manifested Your name to the men whom You have given Me out of the world. They were Yours, You gave them to Me, and they have kept Your word . . . . they are not of the world, just as I am not of the world" (John 17:6, 14). To His disciples Christ said, "If you were of the world, the world would love its own. Yet because you are not of the world, but I chose you out of the world, therefore the world hates you" (John 15:19). In these passages, which are just a few of many more like them, we see that by faith in Christ we have been taken, positionally, out of the world. Our citizenship has been transferred from Satan's dark kingdom of the world to the Son's kingdom of heaven. Paul's phrase in Ephesians is that we who once were worldlings are now "in the heavenly places" (2:6). One result, then, of our relationship with Jesus Christ is that we have been taken out of the world.

Another result of Christ's death that affects the Christian's relationship to the world is found in Galatians 6:14, where Paul wrote, "God forbid that I should glory except in the cross of our Lord Jesus Christ, by whom the world has been crucified to me, and I to the world." One who has gone through crucifixion can no longer respond to the world's stimulus as before. Because he was crucified with Christ, Paul said that the world could no longer dangle its wares before his eyes to attract him. He was separated from the world as much as a man who had been executed and buried. And by using the example of crucifixion, Paul graphically showed that the world has no right to attract the Christian, just as the Christian has no right to respond to the world's enticements. The Bible says that we have died with Christ and have been buried with Him. Therefore, just as someone in the grave cannot respond to a voice from the world of the living, we have no right to respond to the voice of the world.

Next, the Lord made it clear in John 17 that we who have been taken out of the world, and who have been separated from God's judgment abiding on the world, are sent by Him into the world to be witnesses to those who are still held captive by the world system. In verse 11 Christ said, "I am no longer in the world, but these are in the world, and I come to You. Holy Father, keep through Your name those whom You have given Me, that they may be one as We are." And then in verse 18 He said, "As You sent Me into the world, I also have sent them into the world." Why was Christ sent from heaven into this world? To reveal God to a world that was ignorant of Him. Likewise, we who have been called out of the world and separated from it have been left here in its midst that we might reveal the Father to lost people.

This was the thought in Paul's mind when he wrote in Philippians 2:14–16, "Do all things without murmuring and disputing, that you may become blameless and harmless, children of God without fault in the midst of a crooked and perverse generation, among whom you shine as lights in the world, holding fast the word of life." We are to shine as lights before the unregenerate of the world so that they who are in darkness might be drawn to the Light they are seeing in us and through us. However, if we are so conformed to the world that the unsaved around us see no difference between our conduct and their own, then they will see no light at all. The only way we can hold forth the word of life is for our lives to be so separated from the world that the unsaved around us see a marked contrast. That is why a Christian is to "keep oneself unspotted from the world" (James 1:27).

In Romans 12:2 Paul wrote, "Do not be conformed to this world." The word *conformed* means literally, "to be stamped out in the mold of." A piece of metal put into a press will bear the image of the mold, and every piece that comes out of the mold will be identical. Therefore, if the child of God bears on himself, on his character, on his walk, and on his conversation the image of the world's mold, the world will write him off as just another citizen of the world system. He will attract no one to Jesus Christ. He will have no light to present to the world. Therefore the command of Scripture is, "Be not pressed into the mold of this world, but instead be transformed by the renewing of your mind." The word *transformed* literally means "transfigured." At Christ's transfiguration, the glory that was within Him shone out for those around Him to see. The light a Christian has within him is the light of Christ, given to him at the time of new birth. But if the child of God conforms to the patterns, standards, ethics, and habits of the world, that light is veiled. Therefore Paul says to each of us, "Do not be conformed to this world."

In 1 John 2:15 we find a command from John: "Do not love the world or the things in the world." Paul's command of Romans 12:2 deals with a believer's outward conduct; this verse, on the other hand, deals with allegiances of the heart and mind. This passage gives us three reasons why we should not love the world around us. First, we cannot love the world and the Father at the same time. "If anyone loves the world," wrote John, "the love of the Father is not in him." The second reason we should not love the world is found in verse 16 and deals with the essential content of the world system: "For all that is in the world—the lust of the flesh, the lust of the eyes, and the pride of life—is not of the Father but is of the world." The third reason we should not love the world is that it is transitory, temporary, and abiding under God's judgment. "And the world is passing away, and the lust of it; but he who does the will of God abides forever" (2:17). Only the person who does the will of God abides eternally. Thus the Christian's affections and allegiances should revolve around the things of God, not the things of the world.

Worldliness

It is easy to make a list of things we consider worldly and then conclude that anyone who does anything on that list is worldly, while anyone who doesn't do them is not worldly. But are we correct in saying that these things in themselves are worldly? Perhaps it is better to say that there are things that may be put to worldly uses. For example, a hypodermic needle can be an extremely beneficial thing in the hands of a physician; but in the hands of a drug addict, it becomes a harmful, wicked thing. Therefore we cannot say definitively that a hypodermic needle is a wicked thing; only that it can be put to wicked uses. Again, an automobile cannot be considered a worldly, negative thing when it is used to rush an injured person to the doctor; but if it is used as the get-away car in a crime, then it becomes something harmful and negative.

So it is the use of a thing that determines whether it is worldly or not worldly in the life of a Christian. A stereo or a television is not in itself a worldly instrument, but it can be put to a worldly use, or used to promote the purposes and programs of Satan. On the other hand, it might be used to promote that for which Christ came, to bring a knowledge of God to those who are in darkness. The same could be said of a nice car, a comfortable house, a large salary, and so on. It is impossible, then, to sit down and make a list of things that in themselves are worldly.

Christians must continually sit in judgment upon our own use of the things that are in the world—for worldliness is not concerned principally with our acts, but with our attitudes that control our acts. It is entirely possible that you could refrain from doing something in order to be acceptable to the Christians around you, and yet wish with all your heart that you were doing that very thing. That desire is what constitutes worldliness in your life. You are conforming to the world in your thoughts. Therefore, in considering any matter of personal conduct, or in questioning what is right for you as a child of God, you must go beyond the thing itself and determine your attitude toward it. Each of us must examine our thoughts, our goals, our aims, and our ambitions in light of the Word of God.

In writing to the Corinthian church, Paul made it clear that the solution to this problem is not in prohibiting certain things. First Corinthians 7:31 speaks of "those who use this world as not misusing it." The Bible's principle is this: use the things of the world, but do not abuse them. The Word of God does not tell us to withdraw from the world. That is certainly the easier way; but it is not God's way. Rather, we are to use those things the world has devised, but use them to serve God's goals and ends, not Satan's.

God's purpose to conform us to Christ is not achieved when we withdraw into a monastic-like existence. As God conforms us to Christ, He permits us to use the world's innovations; but we use them in submission and service to the Lord Jesus Christ. If we use the most modern means of communication—radio, television, computers—to advance the gospel of Jesus Christ, we are using without abusing. If we use the world's means of transportation to speed our work and ministry, we are using without abusing. We are here as servants of Jesus Christ, with the goal of revealing His glory. How will we best do that? Not by conforming to the world, not by loving the things that are in the world, but by being conformed to Christ and loving Him with singleness of heart and purpose.

The world has its own system of goals and rewards. Many Christians so covet the rewards offered by the world that they are willing to set aside their distinctiveness as followers of Christ. They want to be like Christ—but they also want to receive what the world has to give. They are like the double-minded man James describes as being "unstable in all his ways" (James 1:8).

However, Christ has taken us out of the world and separated us from it that we might be His witnesses to it. May God give us the grace to examine our conduct, our ambitions, and our motives. May we desire that our every thought, word, and activity conform to Christ instead of conforming to the standard the world sets for its own. May we consider carefully the command, "Do not be conformed to this world."

Notes

1. We don't have to look far to see the undeclared spiritual system that permeates the various philosophies and religions of the world. As cults, sects, and "isms" spring up, nearly all allow tolerance for anything and everything—except biblical beliefs. Likewise, secular philosophies loudly advocate open-mindedness and freedom—except when it comes to voicing and living out a biblical lifestyle. For all the diversity found in the world's views on life, death, morality, and worship, they are universally blanketed with an anti-God, anti-Bible, anti-Christ sameness.

2. Understanding Satan's control and authority over the world system shows us the folly of trying to Christianize society around us. It will not happen—in fact, it cannot happen—until Messiah Himself returns to rule over all the earth. The job Christ has given us to do is to populate His future kingdom by leading people to faith in Him, which removes them from the world as its citizens. The more we do that, the more society around us may reflect the positive effects of people coming to know Christ. But control of the world system will nevertheless remain with Satan until Jesus returns in His full glory to overthrow the enemy's unrighteous rule.

3. Do you ever feel out of place as a Christian in the midst of your non-Christian coworkers, family members, friends, and other acquaintances? Good—the

Bible says you should! Once you come to know Christ, you are a citizen of His kingdom, left as His ambassador in a foreign land. While that does not mean we should be obnoxiously conspicuous, it does mean we will be distinctly different from the unsaved around us, and that we will feel that difference in our own lives.

4. What makes a mold work best is *pressure*—and the world exerts plenty of pressure on the Christian! What exerts the greatest pressure in your life to conform to the world's mold? Music? Fashion? Morality? Movies? Wealth? Popularity? Whatever the source of your personal pressure to conform to the world, the Bible teaches that the only remedy is time spent in God's Word. Are you giving yourself that chance to escape the world's pressure?

5. Notice that the three pitfalls of the world—lust of the flesh, lust of the eyes, and the pride of life—are the same areas in which Satan tempted Eve in Genesis 3. For that matter, they are mainstays of modern advertising! If we can be convinced something will feel good, look good, or add to our status, we'll buy it! Unless, that is, we are tuned into a more reliable source of information.

6. Are you sensitive to opportunities God may open up to use something worldly to tell others about Christ? How about taking the initiative to use so-called worldly items and events for godly purposes? Sports and recreation present ideal opportunities for sharing Christ with friends and family members. Perhaps God has entrusted to you a spacious house so that you might have the privilege of using it for home Bible studies. If you're a great cook or enjoy good food, perhaps that could be a bridge of common interest to help you reach someone else for Christ. Maybe you could attend to your own spiritual responsibility to your family through a trip to an amusement park or a ski trip. When we start looking for them, the possibilities are endless!

7. The idea of Christian isolationism is tempting, especially when it looks like our society has lost all traces of common sense. But in Matthew 16:18 Jesus promised that the gates of Hades would not prevail against His church; therefore, what do we have to fear from the world? Christ's promise assumes that we will be in an *offensive*, not *defensive* position in the world. The gates of Satan's kingdom are trying to withstand our assault, our offensive strategy of being used by God as He snatches citizens out of the enemy's dark kingdom and transfers them into the kingdom of His dear Son. If we are committed to and involved in that work, promised Jesus, even the very gates of Hades will not overcome us!

Questions

1. What do John 12:31, 2 Corinthians 4:4, Ephesians 2:2, and 1 John 5:19 tell us about the personality who is in authority over the world system? Does that mean that God is not in control of all things? Explain your answer.

2. What is Satan's present position, according to John 16:8–11? Does this mean he will not use the things of the world to distract and divert believers? Why or why not?

3. What does 1 John 4:4 tell us about our position as believers in a world ruled by Satan? What does this imply about our relationship to the things of the world?

4. Read 1 John 2:15–16. What methods will Satan use to tempt the child of God to love the things of the world? What attitude does God want us to have toward these things? Does this mean we must separate ourselves completely from the world? Why or why not?

5. What do you think is God's supreme example of the way He can turn around Satan's control of the world to accomplish His purpose? How does this relate to our position in the world today?

6. What sets the child of God apart from unbelievers in the world (see Philippians 3:20)? How should this affect the way we view, use, and possess the things of the world? What might prevent this from being true in our lives? How might we solve that problem?

CHAPTER 23

THE CHRISTIAN AND THE FLESH

Romans 8:1–13

Satan uses both the world and the flesh to promote his program and achieve his ends. As a result, we must be on guard continually against both worldliness and carnality (or fleshliness). In the previous chapter we saw that the Christian is being perpetually tempted to conform to the world and to accept its standards, ethics, morals, methods, and goals. In this chapter, then, we will see how Satan seeks to defeat God's purpose in Christians' lives by tempting them into carnality.

Romans 8:4 states God's purpose for the Christian: "that the righteous requirement of the law might be fulfilled in us who do not walk according to the flesh but according to the Spirit." The Mosaic law was a revelation of the demands of a righteous God. But under law humankind was unable to fulfill God's righteous demands. Therefore God's purpose to have the righteousness of the law fulfilled in us is achieved by reproducing in us Christ's life through the power of the Holy Spirit.

Definition of Carnality

God's purpose to reproduce Christ in the Christian is achieved as the believer allows himself to be controlled by the Holy Spirit. But the child of God also has the option of being controlled by the flesh. When he is controlled by the flesh, he is what the Bible calls "carnal." In contrast, when he is controlled by the Holy Spirit, he is "spiritual." In Romans 8, Paul dealt with the question of carnality before showing how God's Spirit will reproduce Christ's life in the Christian. He first showed why the carnal Christian can never live out Christ's righteousness in his life: "To be carnally minded is death, but to be spiritually minded is life and peace" (8:6).

To be *spiritually minded* is to be controlled by the Holy Spirit. To be *carnally minded* means to be controlled by the flesh. So this passage affirms that the flesh can never reproduce the righteousness of Christ in us, because to be carnally minded—controlled by the flesh—means a person is dead with regard to his or her ability to produce fruit that is pleasing to God.

The next verse in this passage shows that the carnal Christian cannot reproduce the righteousness of Christ, "because the carnal mind is enmity against God; for it is not subject to the law of God, nor indeed can be" (8:7). The carnal mind is a rebel. It is at war with God, and it will never agree with what God commands. The natural mind is a lawless mind and intuitively rebels against all that God reveals as His will. If we seek through the flesh to fulfill the righteousness of the law, we will discover that the flesh naturally turns against the commands of God, because the righteousness of God is utterly repugnant to the carnal mind.

Christ's righteousness will never be fulfilled in carnal man because "those who are in the flesh cannot please God" (8:8). This is not saying that a Christian who lives on the earth can never please God. It is saying that the one who lives under the control of the carnal mind cannot please God, because the carnal mind is marked by a latent inability to reproduce the righteousness of Christ. Suppose you planted a tree in your yard, hoping to harvest fruit from it the next season. If one day you discovered that the tree had died, you would immediately abandon all hope of ever receiving fruit from that tree, because that which is dead cannot yield fruit. This is the argument of this passage. The flesh is dead; therefore it cannot yield the righteousness of Christ in the believer's daily experience. Thus to live by the carnal mind is to be dead, unable to produce fruit in God's sight.

The term *the flesh* is also used to describe a person's natural effort, independent of God. That which is of the flesh is that which a person does of himself, without the enablement of the Holy Spirit. Galatians 3:3 emphasizes this when Paul asks, "Are you so foolish? Having begun in the Spirit, are you now being made perfect by the flesh?" What Paul is saying is, "The Spirit began a work of conforming you to Christ. Has it now become your concept that, independent of the Holy Spirit, by your own efforts, you can continue to maturity, or be conformed to Christ?" Again, in Philippians 3:3 Paul says, "We are the circumcision, who worship God in the Spirit, rejoice in Christ Jesus, and have no confidence in the flesh." In other words, Christians have no confidence in what they can do of themselves, independent of God, and apart from the enablement of the Holy Spirit.

When Paul said that the flesh cannot please God and that the flesh cannot reproduce the righteousness of Jesus Christ, he was viewing the flesh as human nature which, as a result of the Fall, is utterly incapable of conforming to the will of God, to the holiness and righteousness of God, or of reproducing the life of Jesus Christ.

We see then that the flesh is characterized by inherent weakness. In Romans 6:19 Paul writes, "I speak in human terms because of the weakness of your flesh." In Romans 8:3 he says, "What the law could not do in that it was weak through the flesh, God did by sending His own Son in the likeness of sinful flesh, on account of sin." In other words, the law was weak because it depended on the flesh, the old capacity, the old man, the old nature—which is inherently weak.

In Romans 7:5, Paul refers to the flesh as the sphere in which the unregenerate live: "When we were in the flesh, the passions of sins which were aroused by the law were at work in our members to bear fruit to death." This points to the flesh as the state in which the unsaved live, or the state in which a saved person may live when controlled by the old nature. The person who is controlled by the flesh is a vehicle through which sin operates. Paul even saw this to be true of himself, as he stated in Romans 7:14—"We know that the law is spiritual, but I am carnal, sold under sin." He was speaking of his basic constitutional makeup when he said, "I am carnal." Paul did not mean that he was living by the flesh, but rather that he possessed two capacities. We sometimes refer to these as the old nature and the new nature, or the sin nature and the new divine nature. Paul recognized that he not only had the capacity to reproduce Christ's righteousness, but that he also retained the capacity he had before he was saved, the capacity to reproduce the fruit of the sin nature within.

We need to recognize, as Paul did, that when we trusted Christ as Savior the old sin nature was not eradicated, as some mistakenly teach. It was not even purified, improved, or changed. We still live with this old nature within us.

The terms *flesh* and *the carnal mind* are used in the New Testament to refer to the vehicle through which sin operates. Some sins are physical sins. Some sins are mental sins. There are religious sins and social sins. But all sin, no matter what kind, is the product of the carnal mind, or the carnal nature. Paul referred to this in Romans 13:14 when he exhorted believers, "Put on the Lord Jesus Christ, and make no provision for the flesh, to fulfill its lusts." When we give the flesh opportunity to control our actions, our words, and our thoughts, it will conceive and bring forth sin. And so the apostle faces the fact that we possess potential for sin because we are carnal, sold under sin.

Examples of Carnality

Perhaps no passage so clearly states the product of the flesh as well as Galatians 5:19–21, which lists the works of the flesh. Just before listing the works of the flesh, Paul said, "Walk in the Spirit, and you shall not fulfill the lust of the flesh" (Galatians 5:16). This is the same truth presented in Romans 8, that the Christian may be controlled either by the Holy Spirit or by the flesh. Every action, every thought, every word, every deed is under control either of the flesh or the Holy Spirit. So then, if we let the flesh control us, what will it produce?

Paul first mentions four sensual sins: "adultery, fornication, uncleanness, and licentiousness" (5:19). Then he mentions two religious sins: "idolatry and sorcery" (5:20), showing that the flesh is not only perverted and corrupt concerning morality, but concerning God as well. Next he mentions a number of sins which reveal the basic selfishness of the flesh: "hatred, contentions, jealousies, outbursts of wrath, selfish ambitions, dissensions, heresies, envy" (5:20–21). In other words, the flesh is immensely self-centered and selfish. Finally, Paul mentions sins of a total lack of self-restraint: "murders, drunkenness, revelries, and the like" (5:21). Thus does the Bible portray the natural heart, the flesh, the carnal mind. Carnality can make itself evident in any or all of these ways.

It is not difficult at all to find within the pages of Scripture examples of the carnality Galatians 5:19–21 describes. For example, in 2 Samuel 11 we read about the adultery of David and the death of Uriah, for which David was responsible. Here we see David as a carnal man. Yielding to the lust of the flesh and controlled by the flesh, he committed the sins of adultery and murder.

Likewise, 1 Samuel 28 provides us with a record of Saul's carnality. When he was set upon by the Philistines, he sought the counsel of the witch of Endor and turned his back on God's spokesman, the prophet Samuel. Saul also displayed the carnal man's manifestations of hatred, contentions, dissensions, envy, and murders. First Samuel 18 tells of Saul's jealousy of David because of the praise that came to David as a result of his military prowess. Twice Saul tried to pin David to the wall with his spear because of the jealousy and hatred within him.

Noah's carnality is recorded in Genesis 9:20–21, where we read that Noah became drunk, so drunk that he lay naked in his tent and became involved in detestable carnality. And Scripture abounds with other examples of God's people failing miserably when they allowed themselves to be controlled by the flesh.

Some of us might feel quite complacent when we compare ourselves with David, Saul, or Noah. We conclude we aren't really carnal because we have never murdered anyone, have never been drunk, or have never committed adultery. But this is a misconception. Peter had done none of these terrible things, yet he was carnal. In Matthew 26:31 Jesus warned the disciples, "All of you will be made to stumble because of Me this night." But Peter insisted, "Even if all are made to stumble because of You, I will never be made to stumble." Jesus said to him, "Assuredly, I say to you that this night, before the rooster crows, you will deny Me three times." What was Peter's reply? "Even if I have to die with You, I will not deny You!" Peter's self-confidence was an evidence of his carnality. He was trusting his own flesh to keep him from the event Christ had predicted.

In 3 John, the apostle John wrote concerning Diotrephes, "I wrote to the church, but Diotrephes, who loves to have the preeminence among them, does not receive us" (verse 9). Diotrephes had set himself up as a teacher, but when his teaching was contradicted by John's teaching, he attempted to discredit John as an apostle and to repudiate his message. His pride and his love of high position among the brethren showed that Diotrephes was a carnal man. So we see that while on one hand carnality may manifest itself in gross sins of the flesh, it also may reveal itself through sins of the mind, which can be just as destructive to a Christian's life and testimony. In the pride, self-satisfaction, complacency, and indifference that characterize so many of us, we see a manifestation of carnality which can never glorify God, and which prevents the Holy Spirit from reproducing Christ's righteousness in our lives.

As believers, we must constantly examine our motives, ambitions, and goals to bring them into conformity to the righteousness of Christ. Otherwise, the very things God provides for our physical well-being and comfort may be perverted to expressions of carnality. For example, God has provided food to nourish and sustain our physical bodies. No one can exist for long without food. Food of itself cannot be considered carnal; yet many of us express carnality by the way we eat. When we over-indulge to the point of obesity or endangering our health, we are manifesting carnality. Again, it is right and proper that we should have a roof over our heads. But many of us need to examine our attitudes toward the home in which we live. When we covet material things for the position or status they might give us, this is carnality. The car we drive, the clothes we wear, the styles we follow may all be expressions of carnality in our lives.

Listing *things* that are carnal might make it quite easy for us to refrain from certain manifestations of carnality. But when we define carnality in terms of *attitudes*, then we must examine ourselves in everything we do, and bring every thought, desire, action, and motive under the Spirit's control. Things God provides may be legitimately used, but they also may be illegitimately used. Therefore, each of us must yield himself to the Holy Spirit in every area of life so that He might reproduce Christ's righteousness in us.

What is carnality? According to the Bible, any thought, word, or action that is generated by the flesh, motivated by the flesh, and indulges the flesh is carnality. It is not always what we *do* that marks the difference between being carnal or being spiritual; rather, it is *what* or *who* controls us in that action. The flesh produces carnality; but the Spirit produces spirituality.

Notes

1. We may wonder how it is that even fine, seemingly godly Christian leaders can succumb to adultery and immorality. Yet Romans 8:7 warns us that the fleshly mind is always "enmity against God"—literally, at war with God's plan and purpose in our lives. That means that if we give the flesh a mere toehold in our thought lives, it won't be long before it has taken command of all our thoughts and turned them against what we know about God and His will. Trying to reconcile the flesh with God in our thoughts, we will make adjustments to God's truth in order to accommodate the flesh. Once we do that, anything can happen, even to someone who has a long history of walking with Christ.

2. Young people are especially susceptible to the idea that we mature spiritually by "trying harder" to be "good Christians." While their desires to grow are very positive, it is extremely important that they understand that the mature Christian life is one of recognizing the inability of the flesh to please God, and learning to walk in the Spirit's enablement. A young Christian who repeatedly fails to see Christ's righteousness reproduced in his or her life can quickly lose heart and become bogged down in spiritual immaturity.

3. In dealing with recurring sin in our lives, we need to be especially mindful of the weakness of the flesh. Have you ever promised yourself, "I'll never do that again," only to find yourself engaged in the same sin a short time later? This is the weakness of the flesh—it simply cannot adhere to law, whether the Mosaic law or a law we make for ourselves. In contrast, learning to walk in the power of the Holy Spirit and to feed regularly upon God's Word can provide the enablement we need in order to be set free from those troublesome, recurring sins.

4. Notice that the opposite of fulfilling the desires of the flesh is to "walk in the Spirit." The word *walk* shows us that this is a daily, moment-by-moment pro-

cess, not some kind of instant experience that ensures perpetual holiness. Walking in the Spirit is a steady, ongoing, lifelong pursuit for the mature Christian.

5. How interesting that the New Testament word for "sorcery" is *pharmakeia*, from which we get our English word *pharmacy*. Obviously, drug addiction is among the works of the flesh; but this is as true for adults addicted to prescription or over-the-counter drugs as it is for teenagers hooked on crack. If you are a Christian with a drug dependency problem (including alcohol), seek professional help from your pastor and your doctor. Don't let this area of the flesh hold you back from experiencing all Christ has to offer.

6. If your spiritual shortcomings were documented in Scripture, what kind of reading would it make? We can all be thankful God has not chronicled our failures in Scripture, but we should remember that we will one day stand before Jesus Christ for an evaluation of our lives as Christians—not to determine salvation, but to determine reward. Do we live each day with this accountability in mind?

7. None of us is exempt from the flesh's tug on our attitudes. Do we insist on special status at work or in our social groups? Are we eager in our hearts for others to notice the kind of cars we drive or the house in which we live? Is our annual income or job title something we like to work into conversations with friends or family? Do we long to show off a special skill or ability around others? Are we eager to impress fellow believers with our Bible knowledge, Christian service, or position in His work? While these may not seem like big issues because "everyone's doing it," they are generated by the flesh and can short-circuit our spiritual lives and provide a toehold for further carnality. "Let this mind be in you," admonishes Philippians 2:5, "which was also in Christ Jesus. . . ."

Questions

1. What do you think it means to be carnally minded (Romans 8:6)? Is this something that is possible for a believer?

2. Explain Romans 8:8. How does this apply to a Christian? What are some attitudes or actions that might be evidence of being in the flesh?

3. What situation is described in Galatians 3:3? What does it mean to be made perfect? If we can't be made perfect by the flesh, how are we made perfect?

4. Explain Paul's command in Romans 13:14. How do we put on the Lord Jesus Christ?

5. Which of the works of the flesh listed in Galatians 5:19–21 do you think are most evident in the culture around us? What negative effects might these have on you as a Christian? How might you counteract those effects?

6. Will yielding to the Spirit's control rather than to control by the flesh always result in a drastic change of lifestyle? Why or why not? What might be the result(s)?

CHAPTER 24

THE WHOLE ARMOR OF GOD

Ephesians 6:10–24

When we read the last chapter of Ephesians, we find that the epistle that began in the heavenlies concludes on the battlefield. In the first chapter, Paul directed our attention to our glorious position in the heavenlies in Christ. In the second and third chapters, he traced the glorious union of Jew and Gentile in one body, through the work of the Holy Spirit. In the fourth and fifth chapters, he described the walk of believers in unity. Then, as he brought the letter to a close, he found it necessary to give a warning to those who had received these truths, for a life lived in Christian unity and love will be lived on hostile ground. Paul wanted all those who had accepted these truths to be ready for battle. God's children are not just servants, they are soldiers. They must be equipped for the life they are called to live, and prepared for the warfare they are called to fight.

Paul knew from his personal experiences that there were many enemies of the faith in Ephesus. For example, when he wrote from Ephesus to the church at Corinth, he said, "I will tarry in Ephesus until Pentecost. For a great and effective door has opened to me, and there are many adversaries" (1 Corinthians 16:8–9). We can read for ourselves in Acts 19:23–41 an extensive account of the adversaries in Ephesus. Ephesus was given over to a nearly unanimous worship of the goddess Diana. Much of the population profited from employment in the temple or in arts and crafts associated with the worship of Diana. So when Paul came into the city to declare that there is one true, living God, and that people can approach Him only through Jesus Christ, the Ephesians rose up to put him to death because he had belittled Diana. It was only out of the Ephesians' fear of higher government authorities that Paul and his companions were delivered from physical death in the arena at Ephesus.

Paul's adversaries were visible, human, and persistent. Their movements could be traced and their plans could be thwarted. But Paul also recognized that he had a greater adversary, an unseen adversary, an adversary who carries on his war in the spiritual realm. This is the kind of warfare for which Paul wanted all believers to prepare. So after he described the warfare in which all Christians are engaged (Ephesians 6:10–13), he described in detail the armor God has provided so that the child of God might be victorious in his conflict with the evil one.

Strengthened in the Lord

The Christian's strength is mentioned in verse 10 where Paul writes, "Finally, my brethren, be strong in the Lord and in the power of His might." The word translated *be strong* does not mean we are to strengthen ourselves, flex our muscles, and exercise ourselves until we have become model warriors. Instead, the grammatical construction here shows that we who are set apart to spiritual battle are to receive strength from someone else. This can be translated, "Finally, my brethren, be strengthened in the Lord." We are not to battle in our own strength, but in the strength given to us by the Lord Jesus Christ.

The phrase *in the Lord* shows us where this strengthening takes place. In fighting a human battle, strength often is evaluated in terms of manpower, that is, how many soldiers a commander can muster. Or it might be determined by military might, what weapons a commander has at his disposal. Or it might even be determined by the abilities of the commander himself. But here Paul is showing us that as the Christian enters into conflict, he has no strength, no weapons, and no wisdom or expertise except in the Lord. If a soldier loses confidence in his commander, he becomes fearful of the battle's outcome. He will not press forward in the fight if he does not believe his commander has the ability to lead him to victory. Therefore we should direct our thoughts to the Lord, in whom we can have complete confidence as the One who will strengthen us for our daily conflict. We are to be strengthened in the Lord and in the power of His might.

In his opening prayer for the Ephesian believers, Paul prayed that they might know "what is the exceeding greatness of His power toward us who believe, according to the working of His mighty power which He worked in Christ when He raised Him from the dead and seated Him at His right hand in the heavenly places" (Ephesians 1:19–20). He expressed His desire for believers to know the greatness of the power which saved them. When God saves a person, He brings into effect the same power that raised Jesus Christ from physical death, elevated Him to glory, and seated Him at the right hand of the Father. The power that brought Christ out of the tomb after He bore our sins on the cross is the same power that operates to bring us into spiritual life and salvation. This is also the same power mentioned in Ephesians 6:10 as "the power of His might." That awesome, incomparable power is available to each one of us as we are strengthened in the Lord by relying on Him.

Wearing Full Armor

In verse 11 Paul gives a command: "Put on the whole armor of God, that you may be able to stand against the wiles of the devil." When Paul wrote this to the Ephesians, he was a Roman prisoner. Perhaps the soldier assigned to guard him was standing nearby even as he wrote. If so, seeing that soldier would have guided Paul as he described the armament God has provided for His children. He did not describe a soldier in a toga, which was worn by an inactive soldier. Instead, he described someone who was wearing all the military equipment provided by a Roman commander for those who served under his command. This fully equipped soldier presented a perfect object lesson: Christians have not been called to ease, leisure, or the life of inactive soldiers. They have been called to wear the full armor of God, that they may be able to contend against the devil and his spiritual hosts of wickedness.

The verb *put on* in the original text means "put on once and for all." In commanding these believers to assume this garb once and for all, Paul is revealing to us that we should consider ourselves engaged in unceasing warfare. We are not engaged in a brief skirmish, or even an occasional campaign, after which we can retire to a life of ease. This passage tells us we are to put on the full armor of God and never take it off as long as we are in the flesh. The battle we face is continuous, unceasing, and relentless because of the nature of our adversary. Neither the duration of the battle nor the wiles of the Enemy will permit us to lay aside our armament. Thus the command, "Put on once and for all the whole armor of God!"

The wording *whole armor* refers to all that would be provided by a commander for the safety and protection of his troops, and to enable them to fight an aggressive warfare. It was not a soldier's responsibility to clothe himself. It was the commander's responsibility to provide for all those under his authority. When Paul spoke of the whole armor of God, he was referring to all the equipment God has provided for us so that we who are in His army may be victorious. The battle is the Lord's, and as our commander He has provided what He knows we will need for the battle ahead. If we go down in battle, it will not be because He has failed to provide what we need.

Facing the Adversary

Verse 11 also points out why God has commanded us to put on the whole armor He has provided for us: ". . . that you may be able to stand against the wiles of the devil." God does not lead us into battle to be defeated. He is expecting victory, and He has equipped us that we may be able to stand against the wiles of the devil. The word translated *wiles* here literally means "to stalk." It suggests the image of an animal stalking its prey. This in itself reveals something about the equipment we need, for we are going into a battle where the enemy will not use discernible tactics. We may not know from which direction he will attack. We may not know what means he will use to try to destroy us. But we do know that our adversary will use the craft, guile, subtlety, and deceit of a predatory animal pursuing its prey. Because of these tactics, we need to be fully equipped so that we can stand against his schemes and strategies.

Verse 12 clearly describes our adversary: "We do not wrestle against flesh and blood, but against principalities, against powers, against the rulers of the darkness of this age, against spiritual hosts of wickedness in the heavenly places." Here Paul uses the image of a wrestling match. The Roman wrestler of Paul's day had one goal in mind, and that was to get his two hands around the throat of his opponent and pin him to the ground by strangling him. This was a life-and-death struggle, for if a man's neck was pinned to the ground with a stranglehold, he was entirely at the mercy of his adversary. This verse shows us, then, the seriousness of the conflict in which we are engaged. If we should fall before our adversary, we will not lose our eternal life; but the Enemy is seeking to render us powerless spiritually, to ruin our testimonies, to cause us to fall so hard that we feel we can never get up again and pursue the victorious Christian life. This is not a Sunday school softball game we are playing! We cannot play until we are tired, then sit on the bench and leave the game to others. We are engaged in a life-and-death struggle, and our adversary is trying to destroy us.

The nature of our enemy is found in the statement "we do not wrestle against flesh and blood." *Flesh and blood* is a phrase normally used to describe a human being. If we faced a human adversary, he would have the same strength we have, the same mind, the same tactics, the same basic method of fighting. We would be able to figure out what he would do on the basis of what we would do in a similar situation. But this verse tells us that our adversary is *not* an opponent of flesh and blood; we are wrestling "against principalities, against powers, against the rulers of the darkness of this age, against spiritual hosts of wickedness in the heavenly places." Apart from Christ, we are outmatched!

Ephesians 6:12 shows us that there are different ranks among the spiritual hosts of wickedness comprising all fallen angels. We know from the Bible that angels are beings which were created by God to be His ministering servants, executors of God's will. In God's governmental order, the angels were arranged in different hierarchies, each with differing spheres of authority and responsibility. When Lucifer rebelled against God (see Isaiah 14 and Ezekiel 28), a great host of angels followed him in his rebellion, and Satan became their ruler. Organizing his fallen minions after the pattern of God's organization, Satan became the god of this world. He divided his demons into different classes with various responsibilities and graded authority. If these are listed here in descending order of rule, "principalities" are the leaders among the demons who serve Satan; "powers" refers to those who are under the authority of those leaders; and "rulers" refers to those who are in authority over this world. Thus Christians fight against a highly organized and hostile system.

When Paul says "[we wrestle] . . . against spiritual hosts of wickedness in the heavenly places," he is referring to the character of the principalities, powers, and rulers of Satan's system. We are facing a horde of supernatural fiends who are organized by their evil leader for the purpose of defeating and overthrowing God's children in battle. They are characterized by wickedness. Their nature is evil. Their methods are evil. Their work is evil. Their purpose and design is evil. Yet this evil is not always evident in the material realm so that we can see it, recognize it, and flee from it. First and foremost, it is evil in a spiritual and unseen realm. Paul desired that Christians might get a glimpse of the enormity of the warfare in which we are engaged. The sphere of our warfare is not merely here on this earth; it extends into the heavenlies into which we have been brought with Jesus Christ. Our battle is not in the physical or material realm. Our battle is spiritual and takes place in a spiritual realm.

Standing in Battle

When we grasp Paul's teaching, we can see the reason for his appeal: "Therefore [because you do not wrestle against seen forces, but against unseen forces] take up the whole armor of God, that you may be able to withstand in the evil day" (Ephesians 6:13). Here Paul concludes almost where he began, for in verse 11 he told believers to put on the whole armor of God, once and for all. Now, having shown why the armor is so necessary, he exhorts believers to take up the whole armor of God so that they can withstand the adversary in the evil day. *The evil day* is not the day of judgment when the Christian's service as a soldier of Christ will be examined; it is this day in which we live! The phrase refers to our entire life from the divine viewpoint: we live on this fallen, sin-tarnished world in an evil day. It is an evil day because we are constantly set upon by evil adversaries who seek to destroy us.

Paul also reemphasizes that this life is a battle. He has not held out for us a false hope that the adversary will withdraw or that hostilities will cease, so that we can lay down our armor. He says that this battle will be unrelenting—for as long as we live on this earth. Even though we know the Cross of Christ was God's judgment on Satan, and even though we know from Revelation 20 that Satan will be bound for a thousand years and ultimately banished to eternal punishment, we also know that for us who live today, there is no prospect of being delivered from battle against Satan and his hosts.

We are called to be soldiers as long as we live, and God has made it possible for us to come through that battle victoriously, triumphantly, unscathed. Ephesians 6:13 says, "Take up the whole armor of God, that you may be able to withstand in the evil day, and having done all, to stand." *Standing* in battle is the opposite of *falling* in defeat. The soldier who lost his footing and fell in battle was certain to die under the stroke of the enemy's sword. A soldier who did not stand in battle had no hope of survival, let alone victory. So Paul assures us that when we put on the whole armor of God, we will be able to stand in the battle before us. And to stand means victory!

We need to take special note of several things in these verses. First, it should be clear to each of us that every child of God is a soldier of Jesus Christ. We have been called to battle, and no Christian is exempt from this summons! We have been drafted by the King of kings and Lord of lords to serve in His army. We cannot dodge the draft; we cannot expect a deferment for any reason. We are soldiers of Jesus Christ.

Second, we need to remember the nature of our adversary. We cannot see, touch, or outwit this adversary. Therefore we need protection, wisdom, and strength that is greater than our own. God offers us the strength we need through "the power of His might" (6:10). Our protection is the responsibility of Him who has summoned us into battle; thus He has provided us with the whole armor of God. But it is the soldier's responsibility to put on the armor God has provided. If we are defeated, it is because we have not appropriated by faith the armor He has provided for us, and there are none to blame but ourselves.

A hymn writer asked the question, "Am I a soldier of the cross?" God says we *are* soldiers already. The only question for us to face is, "What kind of soldier am I?" Are we the kind that recognizes the enemy and takes advantage of the whole armor of God so that we can stand against his schemes, strategies, and subtleties? Will we be undefeated in the day of battle?

Notes

1. It has been said of General George S. Patton, Jr., that the only army that could slow down his advance across Europe was his own. The reason Patton gave for his unprecedented rapid advances was that Hitler's Germany had expended all its time, energy, and resources in preparing for *defensive* warfare rather than *offensive* warfare. Could it be that we are setting ourselves up for spiritual defeat when we concentrate on *defensive* rather than *offensive* warfare as soldiers of Christ? As you study the Christian's armor, keep in mind our commission to "go therefore and make disciples of all the nations"—an *offensive* command!

2. Many people possess a certain amount of power in our society (celebrities, politicians, professional athletes); yet we seldom take time to consider the awesome power of Jesus Christ. We may marvel at the unharnessed natural power of an earthquake, volcano, or other natural catastrophe; yet Jesus Christ holds together the entire universe in which those things are tiny details! This the power available to us for engaging in spiritual warfare! The scope of His power is far greater than anything we might ever encounter.

3. Anyone who knows sports knows that sports clothing and equipment—even shoes—are designed with a specific activity in mind. Football players wear helmets and pads to protect them during violent contact; distance runners wear feather-light clothing and shoes that allow them to use their energy for the race; tennis players wear clothing that keeps them as cool as possible and allows freedom of movement; and so on. In the same way, the Christian's armor is more than an illustration. It is essential equipment that God has designed with the specific task of offensive spiritual warfare in mind. If we are serious about the victorious Christian life, we will be serious about our equipment!

4. It has been said that "the soldier of Christ never retires." Though we may work toward enjoying leisure time and eventually retiring from our vocational labor, the Bible teaches that as soldiers and ambassadors for Christ, we are retired only when we go to be with Him.

5. The study of predatory animals can provide us with abundant illustrations of Satan's wiles and strategies. Many a predator, for instance, will follow a herd for days, waiting for just one of its members to show some injury or sign of weakness so it can move in for the kill. Other predators specialize in nabbing the very young from the fringes of a herd. Others trick a herd's sentries into pulling away from the herd to stand alone against what turns out to be a superior enemy. Still others feign weakness or injury themselves to trick the

prey close enough for a fatal attack. All of these and more are the ways Satan preys upon believers—were it not for the protective armor of Ephesians 6!

6. The strategies and tactics Satan employs through his hierarchy of fallen angels certainly aren't limited to the horror movie brand of occultism. The enemy is a liar, a counterfeiter, and a destroyer who can also appear as an angel of light (2 Corinthians 11:14). With the world at his fingertips, he can use any of its trappings to ensnare us. He can sow seeds of mistrust and division within the local Christian fellowship. He can erode our marriages and alienate us from our parents or children. He can slowly pull us down with alcohol or drug dependency; he can destroy our lives quickly through clinical depression and suicide. He can distract us with materialism's trinkets or immorality's appeal to the flesh. He can play to our pride or appeal to our fear of rejection, turning our hearts from the pure truth of God's Word to the false wisdom of human philosophy. His weapons are many, and well-organized. Apart from Christ, we are hopelessly outmatched!

7. If you want confirmation that we live in an evil day, start keeping track of the media's representation of biblical Christianity and its believers. Chances are that for every ten times you see Christians or Christianity mentioned, nine of them will be negative, derogatory, or openly hostile. But remember—this is the outworking of a battle taking place in the *spiritual* realm. Therefore we should seek victory spiritually, while continuing to look for every opportunity to take Christ's love to the lost in this physical world.

8. Someone once described a football game as fifty thousand people desperately in need of exercise watching twenty-two people desperately in need of rest! In some ways, the same description could apply to the church of Jesus Christ today. A very few soldiers of Christ are doing the work and fighting the fight intended for an entire army of His soldiers. Are you in the stands, or are you on the field of play? Are you fulfilling your calling as a soldier in His service?

9. In past centuries, a commander's ability to maintain and rally his troops often was directly tied to his ability to provide for them. "An army travels on its stomach" was more than just an idle saying; only a well-provisioned corps could stay afield long enough to face and defeat the foe. How marvelous it is to know that our Commander has provided everything we need for the battle we face. He has provided our armor, our protection, and our strength, and He deserves our unreserved loyalty.

Questions

1. Read 1 Corinthians 16:8–9. What was Paul's response to the presence of "many adversaries" where he wanted to reach people for Christ? How did he

describe this opportunity? Why do you think he disregarded the opposition he knew was ahead?

2. What act of God demonstrated the magnitude of the power available to each Christian, according to Ephesians 1:19–20? Do you think all Christians experience this power? Why or why not?

3. In light of Ephesians 6:10–11, what should the Christian who is strengthened by the Lord also do? What result can we expect when we do?

4. Read Ephesians 6:12. Why should a Christian be concerned about putting on armor that is spiritual in nature?

5. Which pieces of armor are most important to the believer, in light of verses 11 and 13?

6. What do you think is meant by the phrase *to stand* (6:11, 13)? Spiritually speaking, what do you think would be the opposite of standing? What might this look like in a person's life?

CHAPTER 25

THE GIRDLE OF TRUTH

John 17:13–17; Ephesians 6:14

God has not called us to joust with windmills. We are not even fighting against flesh and blood, against creatures like ourselves. We are fighting a powerful, unseen adversary—Satan. Hosts of fallen angels are organized under his authority to fight his battles. His opposition never ceases. We never know from which direction he will attack, the form he will take, how he will strike, or the devious methods he will use.

If God had not provided adequate armament for His children, He would be like a commander sending soldiers armed with water pistols to fight a foe armed with nuclear weapons. But God has indeed given us an armor that is adequate to "be able to withstand in the evil day, and having done all, to stand" (Ephesians 6:13). But we cannot obey the Bible's instruction to put on the whole armor of God until we understand what the armor of God is, and how we may use it.

A Familiar Figure

The first piece of equipment Paul describes in Ephesians 6:14 is the girdle. He writes, "Stand therefore, having girded your waist with truth . . . ." It seems strange that the apostle should begin with this item, for while the girdle was worn by Roman soldiers, it was not considered a piece of armor, as were the helmet, the breastplate, the shield, and the sword. The girdle, worn externally, was a part of a person's formal dress in Paul's day. It was used to bind a man's long, flowing robe to his body for the sake of modesty as well as ease in moving about. In Matthew 3:4 we read that John the Baptizer wore a coarsely woven garment of camel's hair which was tied about the waist with a leather girdle, like that which the poorer classes often wore. The wealthy wore girdles of silk or linen, embellished with jewels or gold and fastened by a gold buckle. Thus the girdle was an essential part of every person's attire.

For the soldier in Paul's day, the girdle was especially important in preparation for battle. Since long robes could easily trip up a soldier on the battlefield, a soldier would gather up the lower edges of his robe and bind it about his waist with the girdle. Perhaps this is the concept the writer of Hebrews had in mind when he wrote, "Let us lay aside every weight, and the sin which so easily ensnares us, and let us run with endurance the race that is set before us . . ." (12:1). Anything that might obstruct or hinder us should be laid aside. Certainly no soldier in Paul's day would have considered going into battle without a strong girdle to hold aside the robes that might entangle him.

The girdle was also used by a soldier to support his weapons. The swordsman would fasten his girdle in place in order to suspend his sword from it. Likewise, the bowman would use his girdle to support the quiver of arrows he would use in battle. Of course, a silk or linen girdle would be too light to support weapons, so a soldier's girdle was usually a wide leather belt binding his clothing together and possessing sufficient strength to support the weapons he would use in battle.

One other use of a soldier's girdle was as a place to display the decorations and awards he had received from his commander. Thus the girdle became the emblem of accomplishment in battle. In fact, when a military commander led his troops to victory in battle, it was his custom to present special decorative girdles to the captains who had served with distinction under his command. These decorative belts frequently were adorned with gold, silver, or jewels, and represented that soldier's honor and glory. The soldier who went into battle with a plain leather belt hoped that after the battle he would be rewarded with a belt or girdle embellished with the proofs of his valor. So then, when Paul commanded his readers to stand, having girded their waists with truth, he was using an illustration that was familiar and meaningful to them.

Girded With Truth

The most common explanation of what is meant by the girdle of truth is the revelation of truth God has given to humanity, the Word of God. This is the thought in 2 Timothy 1:13–14 where Paul admonished Timothy, "Hold fast the pattern of sound words which you have heard from me, in faith and love which are in Christ Jesus. That good thing which was committed to you, keep by the Holy Spirit who dwells in us." This refers to objective truth, the doctrines God has revealed to humankind. But as good and right as this concept of truth is, it is not the idea behind the belt of truth in Ephesians 6.

In beginning his description of the armor of God, Paul refers to truth in a *subjective* sense. The child of God who is about to go into battle must be clothed, first and foremost, with truthfulness, integrity of character, and sincerity. This will give him courage and confidence as he goes into battle.

The English word *sincere* comes from two Latin words, *sine cerus*, which meant "without wax." Because it was easy for a piece of pottery to get cracked in the firing process, dishonest pottery vendors would cover up such defects by rubbing the cracks with beeswax. The beeswax would fill the crack so that the pottery would appear sound and whole—until the wax wore through or melted away and the vessel leaked. Honest merchants, knowing of this practice, would guarantee their wares were *sine cerus*, without wax. So, to be sincere in the New Testament sense means to have no known but concealed flaws or defects.

Paul referred to this same need for sincerity in the Christian's life when he prayed for the Philippians, "And this I pray, that your love may abound still more and more in knowledge and all discernment, that you may approve the things that are excellent, that you may be sincere and without offense till the day of Christ" (1:9–10). God wants the lives of Christians to be "without wax," that is, without covered-up defects. If we, as Christians, tolerate insincerity in our lives, we will give Satan a beachhead and will fall before the onslaught of the Evil One.

Some years ago I discovered termites around our back patio and called an exterminator. After coming to our home and looking the situation over, he informed us that the termites had found a small crack between the concrete patio and the foundation. They did not need a large opening; that small crack was all they needed to give them entrance to an ideal nesting place. In the same way, Satan does not need a wide-open door to be able to enter a Christian's life. If the smallest crack is open to Satan, he can make his way in. If our lives are not sound, if they have cracks or defects that are concealed with wax, then Satan will be able to make his way in. But a life characterized by sincerity, genuineness, flawlessness, truthfulness, and soundness will prevent Satan from obtaining an entrance.

We cannot overemphasize the value of a good reputation. As an example, a corrupt lobbyist may be tempted to bribe a certain legislator to win his support for a bill being pushed. But because the lobbyist knows the legislator is a man of integrity and cannot be corrupted by a bribe, he will refrain from even approaching the legislator. The reputation of the legislator is well-known: he cannot be bought; he is incorruptible. And his reputation protects him even from being approached by a corrupt lobbyist.

This is the concept Paul had in mind when he wrote about a Christian being girded with truth. Because of this quality the believer is spared from the attacks of the Evil One, because the Enemy knows that his efforts would be futile directed toward someone who is incorruptible. Because the child of God—by the grace of God and the power of the Holy Spirit—always chooses the way of truth and sincerity, the adversary faces an impenetrable front.

Christ the Example

Revelation 1 presents us with a description of the glory of the resurrected Son of God. Verses 12–13 read, "I turned to see the voice that spoke with me. And having turned I saw seven golden lampstands, and in the midst of the seven lampstands One like the Son of Man, clothed with a garment down to the feet and girded about the chest with a golden band." As the Lord Jesus Christ is portrayed in His glory following His death, resurrection, and ascension, He is clothed in a garment which has a whiteness exceeding the shining of the sun. And that garment is bound to His chest by a golden girdle. That girdle manifests His glory, and one of the glories of our Lord is that He is truth.

As Jesus sat with the disciples in the Upper Room He said, "I am the way, the truth, and the life" (John 14:6). He is the truth. Christ's adversaries watched Him through the years of His ministry on earth and yet could find no flaw in Him. Why? Because He was girded about with truth. The Pharisees scrutinized His every word and watched His every move, trying to find something they could use to accuse Him and condemn Him to death. But Jesus could face His adversaries and say, "Which of you convicts Me of sin? And if I tell the truth, why do you not believe Me?" (John 8:46). How was this possible? Our Lord was girded with truth.

When Christ went to the cross, the centurion into whose hands Jesus had been committed for execution watched Him die and said, "Truly this Man was the Son of God!" (Mark 15:39). How could he make such a statement? Because he recognized that Christ was girded with truth. The thief who hung on the cross said, "This Man has done nothing wrong" (Luke 23:41). Why could he say this? Because Jesus Christ was girded with truth. Those who sought to accuse Him found Him impervious to attack. Why? Because He is truth. And when the character of Christ is manifested through the child of God, the child of God is girded with what Jesus Christ is—truth. Thus the child of God becomes invulnerable to the accusations of the Evil One.

There's nothing like a guilty conscience to turn a Christian into a coward. If we are not girded with truth, if we are burdened with guilty consciences, with hidden flaws, with concealed cracks, we will be vulnerable to the attacks and accusations of the Evil One. When trouble comes, we will not be able to recognize the problem for what it really is. When we should be facing the adversary, we will flee. When we should be victorious in battle, we will be defeated.

Paul wrote that the first piece of equipment must be the girdle of truth, which symbolizes integrity, sincerity, and transparency before the Lord and before the world around us. Thus equipped, the child of God can stand against the Evil One.

Notes

1. One of the marks of a military force is its uniform—the very visible fact that all the soldiers in a particular army dress in a "uniform" way. In fact, at times in history (such as the early months of the Civil War) when the uniforms of opposing armies were too similar, close-quarters warfare was a disaster as soldiers were downed by bullets from their own comrades. In a very real sense, the armor of Ephesians 6 is the *uniform* of the soldier of Christ. In fact, if all of His soldiers would wear it, it would be a simple thing to distinguish our comrades in the midst of battle. If you know Christ, you are His soldier. But are you wearing your uniform?

2. If your "belt" is truth, is it of high enough quality that you can "hang" all your other weapons from it? Just think—a rotten belt would cause a soldier to lose all his other weapons along the way and render him ineffective in battle. If there is anything in your life right now that is compromising your integrity and rotting your belt of truth, make it your top priority to go to the Lord in an attitude of confession and repentance, and let Him cleanse and restore you.

3. This matter of personal truth and integrity may seem small to our compromised culture, but it is a major issue with God. In a day when the message seems to be that truth is whatever you want it to be and honesty is for the naive, God expects us to be "without wax"—totally honest according to His standards, not the world's. That includes income tax returns, memos, casual conversations, school exams, business dealings, *everything*.

4. An old Malay proverb states, "A precious stone, though it falls into the mire, does not thereby lose its brilliance." From time to time we may find ourselves in the company of those to whom integrity is an expendable commodity. We may work with dishonest co-workers or be employed by an unscrupulous boss. Even so, we should never forfeit the integrity that God's Word says is an essential piece of our armor. The darker our surroundings, the brighter our light.

5. Is there a burden of guilt on your conscience? If so, the only remedy is to go to God with a willingness to turn away from this wrong and make right any harm it has done. As you do, a good rule of thumb is to make your confession and apologies only as public as the offense. Offer any restitution that might be necessary, then go forward in full assurance of the Lord's forgiveness.

Questions

1. Why do you think truth is the first item mentioned in the Christian's armor? Why do you think it is characterized as a belt or girdle?

2. What is the believer's relationship to truth and truthfulness as revealed in:
    – Romans 9:1
    – Ephesians 4:15
    – 1 John 2:4
    – 3 John 1:3

3. What influences do you think might move a Christian to compromise his or her integrity? How does this relate to the spiritual warfare in which we are engaged?

4. According to 1 Timothy 4:2, what will be one of the chief characteristics of false teachers who deny Jesus Christ? How would you define "speaking lies in hypocrisy"? Can you recognize any examples of this in our society today?

5. Can you think of times when your witness or the message of Christ has been hindered because of a Christian's lack of integrity? What does this tell us about spiritual warfare?

6. Read John 17:17. What is the best way for a Christian to cultivate truth and truthfulness in his or her life?

CHAPTER 26

THE BREASTPLATE OF RIGHTEOUSNESS

2 Corinthians 2:9–11; Ephesians 6:14

In the Roman army of Paul's day, it was a commander's responsibility to see that the soldiers who went into battle under his command were adequately equipped to meet the Enemy. We who have been called as soldiers of the Lord Jesus Christ have a faithful Commander, the Captain of our salvation, who has provided all the armament we need to stand against the Enemy of our souls. The weapons with which we fight are not material, because material weapons would be useless against the unseen hosts of spiritual darkness who war in the spiritual realm.

The next piece of spiritual armor we need to examine, then, is the breastplate of righteousness. It is hard to determine the relative importance of each piece of Roman armor to the soldier of Paul's day, but we can assume the breastplate was among the most important, since it covered the most vulnerable part of a soldier's body. The breastplate frequently was made of overlapping pieces of horn or metal discs, attached to a backing of linen or leather. More frequently, the breastplate was made of metal—woven chain, interlinked rings of metal, or solid metal hinged in two parts so that it could be tied around the torso, front and back, with either a buckle or leather thongs. The purpose of the breastplate was to cover the vulnerable areas of the chest and abdomen. No Roman soldier would have thought of venturing into any kind of battle without a breastplate for his protection, front and back. Paul, therefore, after telling believers that they must have their waists girded with truth, instructs Christians to "put on the breastplate of righteousness" (Ephesians 6:14).

The Biblical Concept of Righteousness

To understand the meaning of the breastplate of righteousness, we must first be clear in our thinking about the scriptural concept of righteousness.

First, we know from Scripture that we are born into the world without any righteousness that renders us acceptable to God. We read in Isaiah 64:6–7, "We are all like an unclean thing, and all our righteousnesses are like filthy rags; we all fade as a leaf, and our iniquities, like the wind, have taken us away. And there is no one who calls on Your name . . . ." In Romans 3:10–12, Paul quotes Psalm 14, which asserts the same truth: "As it is written: 'There is none righteous, no, not one; there is none who understands; there is none who seeks after God. They have all gone out of the way; they have together become unprofitable; there is none who does good, no, not one.' " Paul goes on in Romans 3:13–20 to show how the unrighteousness that characterizes the natural man expresses itself through every member of his body and through every part of his being. In verse 23 he summarizes God's estimate of unsaved man by saying, "All have sinned and fall short of the glory of God."

These are only a few of the many passages that emphasize that the unsaved person has no righteousness acceptable to God. Further, the unsaved person has no righteousness to protect him from the attacks of the Evil One. The natural man, when he is attacked by his unseen adversary, has no weapons whatsoever to protect him. Apart from God's grace, we have no ability to resist the Enemy; we have no equipment with which to defeat Satan.

Second, God gives, or *imputes*, His righteousness to those who accept Jesus Christ as personal Savior. After presenting the unrighteousness of the unsaved in Romans 3, Paul tells how the righteousness of God is given to those who accept Jesus Christ as personal Savior. In Romans 3:22 he refers to "the righteousness of God, which is through faith in Jesus Christ, to all and on all who believe." He then tells how God can impute this righteousness: ". . . being justified freely by His grace through the redemption that is in Christ Jesus, whom God set forth as a propitiation by His blood, through faith, to demonstrate His righteousness, because in His forbearance God had passed over the sins that were previously committed, to demonstrate at the present time His righteousness, that He might be just and the justifier of the one who has faith in Jesus" (Romans 3:24–26).

Again, in Romans 5:17–19 Paul writes, "If by the one man's offense death reigned through the one, much more those who receive abundance of grace and of the gift of righteousness will reign in life through the One, Jesus Christ. Therefore, as through one man's offense judgment came to all men, resulting in condemnation, even so through one Man's righteous act the free gift came to all men, resulting in justification of life. For as by one man's disobedience many were made sinners, so also by one Man's obedience many will be made righteous." When we accept Jesus Christ as personal Savior, God imputes to us Christ's perfection, so that the sinner is clothed with the righteousness of Christ. As a result, anyone who by faith has been born into God's family is as acceptable in God's sight as is the spotless Son of God Himself. We have been given the righteousness of Christ. We have been "accepted in the Beloved" (Ephesians 1:6). We who have accepted Jesus Christ by faith have the same standing before God that Christ Himself has before God.

This righteousness is God's gift to us. It is not something we earn. It is not something we can put off or put on, for the righteousness of Christ is our *eternal* portion given by God once and for all. So when Ephesians 6 exhorts believers to put on the breastplate of righteousness, it cannot be speaking of the imputed righteousness of Christ.

Third, the Spirit of God produces righteousness in the lives of those who have been made righteous by Jesus Christ. We often refer to this as *experiential*, or practical, righteousness. When the Holy Spirit is permitted to reproduce the character of Christ in our lives, He produces in us fruits of righteousness (Philippians 1:11). It is this practical, experiential, personal righteousness that Paul exhorts believers to put on as the breastplate that will protect them against the attacks of the Evil One. Unless we manifest personal righteousness in our daily lives, we face the Enemy without a breastplate. It is not sufficient for us to rejoice that we have been made righteous because of our position in Christ. If the Spirit of God is not reproducing Christ's righteousness in our daily lives, we are incomplete—an essential ingredient is missing.

Paul referred to this personal righteousness in Romans 6:13 when he wrote, "Do not present your members as instruments of unrighteousness to sin, but present yourselves to God as being alive from the dead, and your members as instruments of righteousness to God." Again, in verse 19, Paul wrote, "Just as you presented your members as slaves of uncleanness, and of lawlessness leading to more lawlessness, so now present your members as slaves of righteousness for holiness." And in Romans 8:3–4 Paul said that God sent "His own Son in the likeness of sinful flesh, on account of sin: He condemned sin in the flesh, that the righteous requirement of the law might be fulfilled in us who do not walk according to the flesh but according to the Spirit."

Romans 3, 4, and 5 teach us that God has credited to our account the righteousness of Christ, that we have been clothed in the righteousness of His Son, and that we stand before God as accepted in the Beloved (Jesus Christ). But as we move on, we find that Romans 6, 7, and 8 deal with personal, practical righteousness. We find that we who

have by faith received the righteousness of Christ must now present ourselves to the Holy Spirit as instruments through which He may produce
that which characterizes the life of Christ in us. As this is accomplished
in us, we shall have an impenetrable piece of armor, the breastplate of
righteousness.

The Armor of Personal Righteousness

Obviously, a breastplate was of greatest importance to a soldier
when he was engaged in hand-to-hand combat against the Enemy.
Often, two adversaries, each with a short dagger in the right hand,
would duel with their left hands joined together. In such close proximity,
each would attempt to pierce the breastplate of the other to kill him. The
Christian also stands in hand-to-hand combat with a dangerous, yet
unseen, adversary. The Enemy is searching for any small break in our
breastplates through which he may thrust his dagger. But if our breastplates are complete and sound, we will be able to stand with confidence.

We can well imagine how a soldier may have felt if he had
neglected to care for his breastplate, or if he had gone into battle without
checking the thongs or clasps that held it together. When he suddenly
felt the Enemy take hold of him and saw that dagger approach, he might
have thought with remorse, "If only I had repaired that broken place in
my armor! If only I had been more careful! Now I am vulnerable, and it
may cost me my life." If sins in our lives remain unjudged and uncon-
fessed, they are like a defect in our protective armor. They leave unre-
paired openings through which the Enemy can destroy our lives. Satan's
weapons do not need much of an opening to be able to enter and do
their destructive work. Therefore, if we are to have assurance of being
able to withstand the Enemy in hand-to-hand combat, we must be sure
we have unbroken breastplates of righteousness.

One such break in the breastplate is addressed specifically in Scripture, and is particularly relevant to believers today. That danger is an
unforgiving spirit. In 2 Corinthians 2:9–11, Paul wrote about people he for-
gave ". . . lest Satan should take advantage of us; for we are not ignorant
of his devices." Another area where Satan might gain an advantage over
us is mentioned quite specifically in 1 Timothy 5:14—"I desire that the
younger widows marry, bear children, manage the house, give no opportunity to the adversary to speak reproachfully." Neglecting home responsibilities would give the Enemy a prime opportunity to accuse and slander
Christians.

As we have seen, any departure from the righteousness of Christ gives
Satan an opportunity to establish a beachhead from which he may fan out
his attack and bring about the defeat of a believer. We may exercise great

care about the big sins, refraining from flagrant violations of Scripture, yet become lax about what we consider little things—the little sins, the secret sins. But those secret sins can be as devastating in our lives as the most flagrant violations of holiness and righteousness. And they can give Satan a toehold that can ultimately lead to utter defeat.

Thank God we can stand clothed in the righteousness of Christ. Satan cannot rob us of our glorious position of righteousness before the Father. But we may neglect the armor of personal righteousness. And when the Enemy has taken hold of us and has drawn his dagger to destroy our lives, it is too late to repair a break in the breastplate of righteousness.

Wonderfully, God has provided a method by which we can be kept in good repair, ready for battle. 1 John 1:9 tells us, "If we [God's children] confess our sins [the breaks in our armor], He is faithful and just to forgive us our sins [put back all the missing plates] and to cleanse us from all unrighteousness." Unless we keep our confession of personal sins up to date, we leave ourselves open to the Enemy's attacks. We must maintain and use the equipment God has provided for those who have been made righteous in Jesus Christ.

Notes

1. Why do people react so violently and vehemently against the notion of creationism? Not because it contradicts the raw evidence in nature, but because it requires an all-powerful Creator, which in turn implies that we are accountable for our unrighteousness. Our natural unrighteousness runs so deep that we sense our guilt, yet still flee the God who can cleanse us from it. What an amazing miracle it is, then, when God draws anyone to Himself!

2. The Chinese character for *righteousness* is a combination of two characters— one meaning "lamb" and one meaning "me." When *lamb* is inscribed directly above *me,* it forms the new character *righteousness.* This is a wonderful picture of the way God imputes His righteousness to "me" through His "lamb." Because of the Lamb of God's sacrifice, God has declared you righteous in Him.

3. At various times throughout the history of the church, practicing personal righteousness has become extremely popular and important to God's people. Unfortunately, we are not presently living in one of those periods. Personal righteousness, or piety, can accurately be called a lost art among the majority of Christians. However, it has not lost its popularity with God. He longs for us to enjoy the benefits of personal holiness, which include a clear conscience and clean hands before Him, and a "breastplate" of defense against the Enemy's attacks.

4. When we apply 1 John 1:9 and confess our sins to God, not only does He forgive us, He also is faithful to "cleanse us from all unrighteousness." That means that we can cease worrying about the unknown sins in our lives, the spiritual effects of past wrongs, and the lingering guilt for the sins we confess. It is, in terms of our spiritual armor, a complete repair job!

5. It is said that blackmailers once sent C. H. Spurgeon a letter saying that if he did not leave them an envelope of money at a predetermined time and place, they would give the newspapers embarrassing information to publish about him and ruin his ministry. Spurgeon left an envelope at the designated rendezvous, all right—but it contained the message, "You and your like are requested to publish all you know about me across the heavens." He knew his life was blameless before men, and that his character could not be called into question. Is this the way we conduct our lives?

6. Time spent in God's Word is indeed like standing before a mirror. As we look into its pages daily, God allows us to see places that need His cleansing touch. We should be ready at any time, then, to see that such stains are dealt with through confession and repentance (see James 1:23–25).

Questions

1. What light does 2 Corinthians 2:9–11 shed on our spiritual battle? What is the opposite of being "ignorant of his devices"?

2. Do you think it is significant that the ancient breastplate protected its wearer both front and back? What parallel might we draw from this?

3. Why do you think we have an aversion to being strongly committed to personal holiness today? What benefits does this aversion bring us? What disadvantages does it bring?

4. According to Ephesians 2:10, what is God's desire for us in regard to personal righteousness? Based on this verse, whose responsibility is it to prepare the good works? What is our responsibility?

5. What effect might the absence of personal righteousness have on our ministries to unbelievers, friends, and family? What internal effects might it have in our lives?

6. What is the key to personal righteousness, according to Romans 8:3–4 and Galatians 5:16?

CHAPTER 27

SHOES FOR OUR FEET

Ephesians 6:15

Emphasis on fashion has shifted attention from the utilitarian value of shoes to their decorative value as part of a person's wardrobe—not just for women, but for men and status-conscious teens as well. Originally, though, shoes were designed simply to protect people's feet from stones and thorns. Anyone who crossed the burning sands of a desert needed shoes, as did those who tended herds and had to follow them where they grazed.

In Ephesians 6, Paul showed that he had some concept of the importance of footwear for the soldier as well as the traveler when he referred to the armor God has provided for His soldiers. In Ephesians 6:15, after he has instructed believers to be sure their waists are girded with truthfulness, or sincerity, in the inner person, and that they are wearing the breastplate of personal, practical righteousness, Paul says, " . . . having shod your feet with the preparation of the gospel of peace . . . ."

In Paul's day, Romans as well as Jews normally wore lightweight sandals consisting of a leather sole tied on the feet with leather thongs. Sometimes sandals were ornamented with precious metals, or even jewels. But when a Roman soldier was sent into battle, he laid aside his lightweight sandals and put on a pair of heavy, thick-soled shoes. Further, hobnails were embedded in the soles of these shoes to provide a firm and secure footing in battle.

Footwear for Battle

The soldier of Jesus Christ has been called by God to lay aside that which would merely ornament the feet and to put on the heavy, hobnailed boots that will enable him to stand against the Enemy. As we well know today, an athlete pays particular attention to his footwear. Players in various sports wear shoes specially designed for their sport and adjusted to their individual needs. A tennis player wears one type of shoe, a baseball player wears another, and a football player wears still another design. Because of the different ways an athlete's feet are used in these sports, shoes are designed to give the contestant firm and secure footing.

As Christians engaged in spiritual warfare, we also need a firm and secure footing. Spiritually speaking, our ability to stand before the Enemy will depend on the shoes we have on our feet. It would be poor preparation for battle if we girded our waists with truth, put on the breastplate of personal righteousness, and then did not don proper foot-wear. According to this passage, there is something in the gospel of peace that will enable a believer to stand firmly and securely after put-ting on all the other pieces of armor. Paul emphasizes this when he says that we are to have our feet shod with the *preparation* that the gospel of peace brings.

What exactly does that mean? Since the gospel is the truth that Christ died for our sins and rose again for our justification, we can conclude that the well-equipped soldier will be prepared ahead of time for the conflict by knowing this truth. It would be foolish to be caught fumbling around in a knapsack, looking for shoes to replace light sandals once the battle has begun! We need to put on this footwear before we come to grips with the adversary.

Throughout Ephesians, Paul indirectly refers to the feet, for the word *walk* occurs frequently. In chapter 2 he asked his readers to recall the kind of life they had once lived before they knew Jesus Christ as Sav-ior: "You once walked according to the course of this world, according to the prince of the power of the air, the spirit who now works in the sons of disobedience . . ." (Ephesians 2:2). Their manner of life, as it was expressed through their daily walk, conformed in every respect to the standards, patterns, goals, desires, and ethics of this world, which is under Satan's control.

After reviewing the past walk of the Ephesian believers, Paul exhorted them to a new kind of walk: "This I say, therefore, and testify in the Lord, that you should no longer walk as the rest of the Gentiles walk" (Ephesians 4:17). He had described in detail the kind of walk that characterized the Gentiles. It was a vain, empty walk. Their understand-ing was darkened so they did not know the truth of God. Because of their ignorance, it was a walk in deadness, and they were alienated from the life of God. They gave themselves over to all kinds of immorality, committing all types of uncleanness with greediness.

Having painted this dark picture of what a person's walk was like without knowing the gospel of peace, Paul turned to the positive side and began with this exhortation concerning the new walk: "I, therefore, the prisoner of the Lord, beseech you to have a walk worthy of the calling with which you were called" (Ephesians 4:1). Believers in Christ are called to unity; they are called with a heavenly calling; they are called as the children of God. And their walk is to conform to this high, heavenly, and holy calling.

Of course, Paul recognized that apart from that which the gospel provides believers, his readers could never walk worthy of their calling. So he said, in effect, "If you would fulfill this obligation that rests on you as a child of God, you must prepare for this kind of walk by putting on your feet the shoes of the gospel [that which is provided by the gospel]." Again in Ephesians 5:1–2 he wrote, "Be followers of God as dear children. And walk in love, as Christ also has loved us and given Himself for us, an offering and a sacrifice to God for a sweet-smelling aroma." This tells us that if we want to manifest the love of God and be victorious in our daily walk, we must first put on that which is provided for our feet by the Captain of our salvation so we can walk in love. Paul also said, "You were once darkness, but now you are light in the Lord. Walk as children of light" (5:8). Formerly these believers stumbled because they were in darkness. Since then the gospel had brought light to them, and they now had light on their pathway. But unless their feet were properly equipped, they would not be able to stand against the attacks of the Enemy.

A Sure Foundation

The Bible uses two significant figures to show us that Jesus Christ is the foundation on which we must stand if we want to be victorious and triumphant in our warfare. First, Jesus Christ is referred to as the *rock* or the *stone*. In Matthew 16:18, after Peter's declaration, "You are the Christ, the Son of the living God," Jesus told Him, "You are Peter, and on this rock I will build My church, and the gates of Hades shall not prevail against it." Although there are differing opinions concerning what Jesus meant by "this rock," Paul seems to have identified what was in the Lord's mind when He used this figure, because in 1 Corinthians 10:4 the apostle wrote, "That Rock was Christ."

Christ anticipated that the Holy Spirit would join all believers into one body, the church, on the day of Pentecost. He knew they would be attacked by the Evil One. All of the gates of Hades would seek to overthrow them. But they had been given a Rock upon which to stand, upon which to firmly plant their feet. And when believers' feet are shod with that which is provided by the gospel of peace, and then when their feet are planted on that Rock, they can stand against the attacks of the Evil One.

In Acts 4, Peter used the same figure in relation to Christ. Having preached Jesus to the people, he declared, "Let it be known to you all, and to all the people of Israel, that by the name of Jesus Christ of Nazareth, whom you crucified, whom God raised from the dead, by Him this man stands here before you whole. This is the stone which was rejected by you builders, which has become the chief cornerstone. Nor is there salvation in any other, for there is no other name under heaven given among men by which we must be saved" (verses 10–12). Having heard our Lord say that He would build His church upon the Rock, Peter announced to all those assembled before Him that Jesus Christ is that Rock. And anyone who takes his stand on that Rock has an unshakable and immovable foundation.

The figure of Christ as a rock is also used by Paul when he speaks of the church as a building. In Ephesians 2:20 he says that believers are "built on the foundation of the apostles and prophets, Jesus Christ Himself being the chief cornerstone . . . ." And in writing to the church at Corinth, Paul said that he as a wise master builder had laid the foundation for their faith. Then he added, "But let each one take heed how he builds on it. For no other foundation can anyone lay than that which is laid, which is Jesus Christ" (1 Corinthians 3:10–11). Jesus Christ is the foundation upon which the entire superstructure rests.

It is always interesting to watch preparations for constructing a large office building. The higher the superstructure, the deeper the foundation. If that huge structure is to stand, there must be a solid union between the rock beneath and the superstructure above. That is the thought in Paul's mind when he says that God has laid a foundation for His church. The church will remain because Jesus Christ is our sure foundation. United to Him, believers are invincible only because He is invincible.

Secure Footing

The prophet Isaiah, writing to a rebellious and unrepentant people about God's impending judgment on them, said, "We grope for the wall like the blind, and we grope as if we had no eyes; we stumble at noonday as at twilight; we are as dead men in desolate places. We all growl like bears, and moan sadly like doves; we look for justice, but there is none; for salvation, but it is far from us" (Isaiah 59:10–11).

How did this people come to be a stumbling, groping, blinded people? Verses 12–13 give the answer: "Our transgressions are multiplied before You, and our sins testify against us; for our transgressions are with us, and as for our iniquities, we know them: in transgressing and lying against the Lord, and departing from our God, speaking oppression and revolt, conceiving and uttering from the heart words of falsehood." This pictures Israel as a nation that stumbles in the light of noonday. There is no excuse for this. Why did they stumble in broad daylight? Because of personal sins! If a child of God falls into some sin and then tries to walk in a way that is pleasing to God—walking worthy of God's calling, walking in love and in light—he will find that he can make no progress at all. Why not? Because he has taken off his soldiers' shoes. Isaiah made it very clear that even though God had provided that which would have enabled Israel to walk in righteousness, the nation did not avail itself of God's provision. Therefore Israel stumbled even at noonday.

It is not only by overt acts of sin that we can cast aside that which God has provided for our feet; we can make the same mistake through an attitude of the mind. Psalm 73:2 illustrates this when the psalmist writes, "As for me, my feet had almost stumbled; my steps had nearly slipped." What caused the psalmist to say this? We find the answer in verse 3: "for I was envious of the boastful, when I saw the prosperity of the wicked." A wrong attitude removed the hobnail boots from his feet, so that he slipped and fell into despair.

If we were to choose where we would do battle against the adversary, we would certainly seek a terrain where there would be nothing to cause us to stumble, slip, or fall. But it seems like the Enemy never attacks when we are traveling on smooth ground. It's when we must travel where the going is rough and the footing is unsure that the Evil One attacks. He knows we can be defeated quickly if he can catch us in such surroundings, especially if we are without the footwear provided in the gospel of our salvation. If we could choose the terrain, perhaps we would not feel the importance of preparing our feet beforehand. But because God's soldiers never know when or from what direction the Enemy will attack, we must prepare our feet in advance so that we will be able to stand.

If you are slipping in your walk with Christ, perhaps you have removed the sure-footed shoes of all God has provided in the gospel to enable you to stand. If we walk in the old ways—follow the old patterns, conform to the old habits, live by the old standards and manners of life—we needn't wonder why our feet slip. We must, by God's grace, appropriate what God has provided in the gospel so that we will have secure footing when the adversary attacks.

Notes

1. This description of the gospel as the "gospel of peace" is a beautiful characterization of the good news of Jesus Christ as the only thing that can bring

peace to a person's life—peace between God and sinner. The peace Jesus Christ brings to a person's life is the difference between *peace* as the absence of conflict, and *peace* as divine assurance in the midst of turmoil. How many people do we know who long for this kind of peace?

2. Though we may try to reason with the world concerning moral issues, the understanding of unbelievers is so darkened, anything and everything can eventually be rationalized (as we have seen in our own culture's downward moral spiral). The only cure for this kind of "walk" is the light of the gospel of Jesus Christ. Unless hearts are enlightened and transformed by trusting Christ, conforming to biblical morality will seem like the ultimate in foolishness (see 1 Corinthians 2:14).

3. In some parts of the country, the most scrutinized feature of any home for sale is its foundation. Shifting soil, subsiding mines, unstable clay, and other factors all make for potential disaster if a foundation is not properly laid. On the other hand, if a house's foundation is sure, a buyer can know that the rest of the house will hold up over time. If Jesus Christ Himself is the foundation of our Christian lives, how important is it to pursue, cultivate, seek, develop, and enrich our relationship with Him? Only a solid foundation will ensure our footing when the real battles come.

4. As part of an entire generation of political activists, we can easily begin to think that a nation can be held together by human politics, provided they are constructed properly. The Bible, however, seems to show that Israel could only be held together as a nation by the collective righteousness of its people; and without it the nation became blind and bumbling.

    The state of Hawaii's motto, found on its seal in native Hawaiian, is translated, "The life of the land is preserved in righteousness." Apparently the early missionary work in Hawaii helped its people see that no human governmental structure, no document, no constitution or creed can take the place of the people as a whole recognizing their dire need for God and acceptance of His provision for righteousness.

5. An old Protestant hymn encouraged believers in past generations, "Count your blessings, name them one by one." One of the best defenses against the threat of envying those more prosperous than we are is to count our own blessings, recognizing the great personal wealth God has given us in the relationship we have with Him, and the assurance we have of eternal life. Anything more is blessing in abundance!

6. Part of preparing our feet as soldiers is to acknowledge to our Commander that we are ready and willing to stand, to march, to go, to do whatever He wants us to do.

Questions

1. Why do you think God made a connection between our feet and the gospel of peace? Based on this, what do you think the Christian's marching orders include?

2. Read Ephesians 4:17–19. What things characterize the walk of unbelievers? Why, then, do you think the Christian's walk should include the gospel of peace?

3. Besides revealing that Christ is God's chief cornerstone of His kingdom, what else do we learn from Acts 4:10–12 about who Jesus is?

4. In light of 2 Timothy 4:2, what kind of timing or opportunity will the soldier of Christ look for as he or she takes the gospel of peace to others?

5. What do Isaiah 59:10–13 and Psalm 73:2–3 reveal about the one thing that can erode our sure footing in Christ?

6. Based on this chapter, what does it mean to you to have your feet shod with the preparation of the gospel of peace?

CHAPTER 28

THE SHIELD OF FAITH

1 John 5:1–5

If believers experience any failure or defeat in our Christian lives, it is not because the armor God has provided for us is incomplete in any way. To enable us to stand against the onslaught of the Enemy, the Captain of our salvation has made a full and complete provision. As we read Paul's description of the Christian's armor, we see that a soldier *wears* certain parts of the armor—such as the helmet, the girdle, the breastplate, and the shoes. But as we continue through the description, we see that Paul refers also to movable parts of the equipment Christ provides—specifically, the shield and the sword.

Paul describes the shield in Ephesians 6:16: "Above all, taking the shield of faith with which you will be able to quench all the fiery darts of the wicked one." Several kinds of shields were used by different branches of the Roman military. The gladiator's shield was a small, round shield which he wore strapped to his left arm to parry dagger thrusts, while he used his right arm to counterattack. This small, light shield allowed a soldier great freedom of movement—but it is not the shield Paul had in mind in Ephesians 6.

The more common shield in the Roman military was referred to as the door-shield because of its size. It was a heavy shield approximately thirty inches wide and forty-eight inches high—large enough for a soldier to crouch behind. It was primarily designed to give a soldier protection. A Roman military unit would overlap these shields and advance on the Enemy; then when they came closer, they would stand close enough together that the shields formed a solid wall behind which the archers could fire their arrows, or the infantry could ready itself for attack. Paul had in mind this large, protective door-shield when he told believers to take up "the shield of faith with which you will be able to quench all the fiery darts of the wicked one." When he used this metaphor, he emphasized that we have a full and complete protection. When we stand behind the shield of faith, no part of our persons are unprotected. The Christian soldier, equipped with the door-shield of faith, has full, complete protection provided by God the Father.

Double Protection

The first words of verse 16 have led some to a misunderstanding of what the apostle Paul was teaching. The words *above all* sometimes are interpreted to mean the piece of equipment that is most important. But this was not Paul's thought. These words can be translated "over all." The pieces of armor Paul had described covered the whole person. The Christian soldier is protected from head to toe by the equipment Christ has provided. Therefore, the door-shield cannot be singled out as most important—but it was that piece of equipment that goes in front of, or "over all," the rest, thus providing double protection. When the Christian takes up the door-shield of faith, not even his armor can be touched, let alone the soldier himself. In John 10, Christ spoke of the double security we have in Christ. We are not only in Christ's hand, we are also in the hand of the Father. In the same way, the Christian soldier has double security in Christ.

In verse 16, we see why the Christian needs this protection for his armor. It is to "quench all the fiery darts of the wicked one." What is meant by *fiery darts?* In military terms of the day, this describes missiles that were dipped in pitch, ignited, then thrown or shot at enemy forces. A soldier was powerless to resist such a weapon because of its weight and because it was aflame. Unless a soldier had adequate protection, this fiery dart would hit his armor, splash flaming pitch on it and inside it, and disable or kill him. In the spiritual warfare in which we are engaged, God has provided us with adequate protection against the Enemy's flaming missiles. That protection is the shield of faith behind which we may hide. If Satan's fiery darts come one's way, they will strike the door-shield of faith and not the warrior himself.

Notice that these are the fiery darts of the *wicked one.* This phrase reveals two things. First, it shows the source from which the attack comes. Remember, in verse 12 we read that "we do not wrestle against flesh and blood, but against principalities, against powers, against the rulers of the darkness of this age, against spiritual hosts of wickedness in the heavenly places." Second, this phrase not only reveals the source of the missiles, but the character of the missiles as well. What kind of weapons will they be? Missiles shot or thrown by the adversary possess his very character. They are devilish, diabolical, destructive. Because of the nature of these fiery darts, we need in front of us the door-shield of faith to protect us.

Faith as a Shield

Paul describes this shield as the shield of *faith*. To understand this description, we need to consider two different New Testament uses of the phrase *the faith*. In some places it refers to the whole body of divine revelation, or divine truth. For example, Paul wrote to Timothy, "Now the Spirit expressly says that in latter times some will depart from *the faith*" (1 Timothy 4:1, italics added). One of the characteristics of the current apostasy will be a complete departure from the truth of God's Word. And while Paul's emphasis on holding fast to the divinely revealed truth is certainly important and relevant, this is not the concept he was applying in his letter to the Ephesians.

The second usage of the phrase *the faith* refers to the principle of faith. It is the principle of faith that equips the soldier of God and enables the child of God to be victorious in battle. Faith is an attitude toward God in which we consider Him to be a faithful God who will perform what He has promised. We also believe that He who has begun a good work in us will perform it until the day of Christ Jesus. The shield of faith, then, is not referring to the objective body of God's truth, but to the Christian's trust in God's faithfulness to His promises. And this faith makes the warrior invincible.

Let's look at several passages where this faith principle is affirmed by God's Word. In Colossians 2, for example, Paul wrote to Christians who were being enticed away from the truth. Recognizing that false teachers had come into Colossae and were substituting human philosophy for divine revelation, he wrote, "Now this I say lest anyone should deceive you with persuasive [or flattering] words. For though I am absent in the flesh, yet I am with you in spirit, rejoicing to see your good order and the steadfastness of your faith in Christ" (Colossians 2:4–5). Paul did not say, "I rejoice that you continue to hold sound doctrine in spite of false teaching." Rather, he said, "I rejoice to see your good order and the *steadfastness of your faith* in Christ." Then, in verse 6, he gave them a charge in light of the fact that they are exhibiting a continuing faith in Christ: "As you have therefore received Christ Jesus the Lord, so walk in Him."

We can make two important observations about Paul's words in Colossians 2:6. First, he confirms the principle by which they came to know Christ as Savior: "As you have therefore received Christ Jesus the Lord . . . ." They had come to know Christ by faith; by faith and faith alone they had accepted the gift of God, which is eternal life through Jesus Christ our Lord. They were not saved by rationalization, by good works, by joining a church, by being baptized, or by following human philosophy. They were saved by the faith principle. They accepted God's Word that He would save anyone who comes to Him by faith in Christ. And as a result they were born again.

The second important observation is based on the little word *so.* Just as they had received Jesus Christ by faith, they were to walk daily by faith. This emphasizes that the Christian life is a faith life; the person who is saved by faith does not live the Christian life by a different principle. He does not live the Christian life by following human philosophies, joining a church, or keeping the law. The principle of victory and triumph in the Christian life is the same principle that saved us: the faith principle. If we trust any principle or precept other than the faith principle for our daily lives, we are not using the door-shield of faith by which we can quench the fiery darts of the wicked one. God has only one operating principle—the faith principle. We are saved by faith, we walk by faith, we live by faith, and we face spiritual warfare by faith. The Christian life is a faith life, step by step.

In his first letter, the apostle John made it clear that the world we live in is a glamorous world which makes all kinds of enticing appeals to woo us away from our warfare as good soldiers of Jesus Christ. Therefore he wrote in 1 John 5:4, "Whatever is born of God overcomes the world. And this is the victory that has overcome the world—our faith." Faith is the basis not only of our Christian walk, but also of our victory over the enticements of the world. Of course, Satan will try to use the world to get us to lay down the door-shield of faith. The Roman soldier who had been marching all day while carrying that huge shield must have been tempted many times to lay it aside. But if a Christian soldier surrenders to Satan's persuasion to abandon his shield, he will have no protection for his armor, and consequently no protection from direct attack by the Enemy.

John said there is only one thing that will keep a Christian soldier from yielding to the enticements of the world. That is faith. "Who is he who overcomes the world, but he who believes that Jesus is the Son of God?" (1 John 5:5). We are saved by faith. We who believe that Jesus is the Son of God have been born into the family of God; and that same faith which brought us to salvation must continue to operate as a protective shield before us.

The Triumph of Victory

In 2 Corinthians 2:14 Paul employed a very graphic figure from the Roman military world: "Now thanks be to God who always leads us in triumph in Christ, and through us diffuses the fragrance of His knowledge in every place." The phrase *leads us in triumph in Christ* can be translated literally, "leads us in triumphal procession in Christ." The picture here is that of a conquering military commander returning home after a great victory. It was Roman custom for the commander to be given a great welcome in which he would ride on a white horse at the head of a procession, signifying that he was the victor. Behind him would march the soldiers who had fought at his command in battle; wagons would be loaded with spoils of the conquest to show the great extent of his victory; and the captives taken in battle would follow in the rear. The number of captives would display the greatness of the commander's victory. Based on this, Paul pictures the Lord Jesus Christ as a returning triumphant general. Behind Him will march His soldiers, bearing the spoils of His victory. And when Paul affirms the fact that God leads us in triumph in Christ, he is emphasizing that the battle is over, the victory has been won, and those who march with Him as His soldiers share in His victory.

At the cross, Jesus gained a great victory over Satan. Christ was triumphant through His death and resurrection. Satan is a defeated foe—yet the time for executing God's judgment on him is not yet at hand. Meanwhile, the Lord Jesus Christ is leading in the train of His triumph all those who place their faith in Him. They share His victory. Victory in the Christian life, therefore, depends on the believer's appropriation by faith of the victory Christ has already gained over the Enemy. Only by faith in His triumph can we follow in the train of His triumphal procession.

The Christian life does not depend on our own strength any more than our salvation depends on our ability to save ourselves. Strength in the Christian life is Jesus Christ Himself. By faith we may lay hold of that strength and power. So the Bible tells us that God has given us all the pieces of armor to protect ourselves, but that armor must be protected by the door-shield of faith. As we exercise our faith, we will be invincible in the face of the attacks of the Enemy.

Faith is not natural; it is supernatural. God's desire for us who are soldiers of Christ is that we will learn to live by the faith principle, so that we might be thoroughly equipped for spiritual victory.

Notes

1. Isn't it interesting that the door-shield of the Romans, and many other types of shields throughout history, was most effective when a soldier used his individual shield in unison with many other soldiers' shields? One shield alone did not provide much protection during battle; but many shields together could protect an entire company. In the same way, one believer's faith is certainly adequate for all things; yet when believers come together in the local

assembly, their combined strength can do much to encourage, uplift, and shelter one another in difficult times. We should never lose sight of the benefits of faithful involvement in a local church.

2. Again we see that we are engaged in a frontal attack, face-to-face with the adversary on the battlefield, not huddled behind the battlements of a fort. The Christian life is a spiritually active life, one that eagerly anticipates the testing of one's faith and boldly intercepts the attacks of the Enemy. General Patton often advised, "Never take counsel of your fears." Shrinking from the battle because of sin in our lives or an unwillingness to trust Christ with everything can only lead to spiritual defeat.

3. Sometimes we mistakenly think that our spiritual well-being depends on how great our faith is. We need to remember, however, that faith is simply trust in something we know to be true; and that our faith is only as great as the object of that trust. Those who believe God for great things are not leaning on the greatness of their faith, but on the greatness of the God in whom they have placed their faith. They put their trust in something they know to be true about God. If we want our faith to result in great things, we need to learn more about Him from His Word, that we might know for certain what He can do, and then put our trust in that.

4. Some teachers today want us to believe that salvation in Christ is by grace through faith, but that living the Christian life is entirely up to us; or, worse yet, that we can lose our salvation if we do not perform sinlessly in our Christian lives. Colossians 2:6 puts any such notions to rest. We receive Christ by grace through faith, and we walk in Him the same way.

5. Ever notice how compromise in the Christian life often begins with a small doubt or disagreement about something God has revealed? We might choose to reject a prohibition He has given; we might disagree with His assessment of certain sins; we might doubt that He really has our best in mind; we might choose the world's enticements over the warnings He has given. But whatever the circumstance, when we doubt what He has told us in His word, we are in essence laying aside the shield of faith. We have ceased to trust what He has told us, and we are unprotected from the fiery darts of the Evil One.

6. This same imagery is used in 2 Corinthians 10:5, where Paul talks about "bringing every thought into captivity to the obedience of Christ." The Lord wants our spiritual victories to be not external only, but to permeate our thought lives as well.

Questions

1. Why do you think a shield was so important to an ancient soldier? How was it used? What were its benefits?

2. What did Paul mean by the words *above all?* Why do you think God wants us to have this kind of protection?

3. What might some be of Satan's flaming darts in your life? In others' lives? Do you think *flaming darts* is an accurate description of Satan's attacks? If so, why?

4. What bearing might Romans 10:17 have on our understanding of the shield of faith? Explain.

5. What threat to a believer's faith is addressed in Colossians 2:4–5? Can we see something similar at work today?

6. How does 1 John 5:4 illustrate the practical use of the shield of faith in a Christian's life? How does this relate to 1 John 2:15–16?

CHAPTER 29

THE HELMET OF SALVATION

2 Corinthians 10:1–7

No Roman soldier would think of advancing into battle without a helmet to cover his head. This helmet was usually a cap made of leather to which metal plates had been fastened. Some helmets were made of solid metal cast in the form of a head-covering. But whatever the external form of the helmet, its purpose was the same—to protect a soldier's head from the blows of a broadsword.

An enemy soldier might attack with one of two types of swords. There was a short, dagger-type sword designed to pierce the breastplate and kill the warrior. A soldier did not particularly need a helmet to meet this weapon, because a dagger-thrust could be parried with a shield. But an enemy might wield another type of weapon: the broadsword. This type of sword was three to four feet long and had a long handle a soldier would grip in both hands. He would raise the sword high over his head and bring it down on his opponent's head, killing him instantly by splitting open his skull. Therefore, a Roman soldier expecting attack from an adversary armed with the broadsword would cover his head with a metal or metal-reinforced helmet.

Just as Roman commanders provided their soldiers with head protection, God has provided believers with the helmet of salvation. The helmet of salvation Paul refers to in Ephesians 6:17 is not salvation in the objective sense. Certainly all who have accepted Christ as Savior are safe and secure, with their eternal destiny settled. But believers are still vulnerable to attack in the sense that Satan may tempt us to doubt our salvation. It would seem, then, that the helmet of salvation symbolizes our assurance of the forgiveness of sins, of our safety and security, and of the certainty that we can stand against Satan's onslaught, because he has been judged.

Just as no Roman soldier would think of heading into battle without the helmet his commander had given him for protection against the broadsword, so we should not think of advancing into battle against Satan and his wicked forces without putting on the helmet that is provided in our salvation. We need to lay claim to all God has provided for us in salvation in order to be invincible in the day of attack.

A Sound Mind

Since a helmet is a head covering, we might think of the helmet of salvation as protection for the Christian's thought life. Our thought life determines whether we experience victory or defeat. Solomon, writing in Proverbs 23:7, said that as a man "thinks in his heart, so is he." Before any commander can lead his troops into battle with any expectation of victory, he must build troop morale. This is just as true in the spiritual realm as it is in the physical realm. Unless we are certain—based on the promises of God—that we can defeat the Evil One and emerge victorious and triumphant, we are sure to go in defeat. So when the Bible commands us to take the helmet of salvation, it is commanding us to receive God's promises concerning our position in Christ and victory in Christ. Only as we lay hold of these promises of victory can we expect to stand in this evil day.

Obviously, there is power in positive thinking and defeat in negative thinking. We can exercise God's type of positive thinking about the victory and triumph He has provided for us; we can banish even the very thought of defeat. We are to be strong in the Lord and in the power of His might, and put on the full armor of God with a view to victory against the Evil One. As a man thinks in his heart, so is he. If you are a spiritual coward and afraid to face the adversary, certain that he will overwhelm you, you can fully expect defeat. But defeat is not necessary. If you have the helmet of salvation, that means you are assured from God's Word that victory is certain. If you already know that the Enemy's weapons and ammunition are inferior to the spiritual weapons God has given you, you do not fear him. This is what Paul had in mind when he exhorted believers to put on the helmet of salvation.

In Philippians 4:13 Paul wrote, "I can do all things through Christ who strengthens me." That is an indisputable fact. Notice that no conditions are attached to it. He did not say, "Sometimes I can do all things," or, "I may be able to do all things." He made the positive affirmation, "I can do all things through Christ."

The child of God is expected to believe what God has promised. If God has promised certain victory, then it is unbelief to say that God did not mean what He said. Paul believed He could do all things because of God's promises of strength. He could march fearlessly into the fray, even against an unseen foe, because he already knew the outcome. He had no question about which way the battle would go. It never entered his mind that he could be defeated as long as he relied on the Lord. Of course, he did not feel that he was invincible in himself; but he knew he was invincible because of God's provision for him in the gospel. He knew nothing of a gospel which could save for eternity but was inadequate for daily life. The gospel Paul knew was sufficient not only for the future, but also for daily needs.

If you really believe that you can do all things through Christ, then the very assent of your mind to that fact means that you are putting on the helmet of salvation. When you read that promise in the Word of God and your heart responds with an "amen," your assent to that fact strengthens you for battle. It also means your mind is protected with the helmet of salvation.

In John 16:11, Jesus said that the Holy Spirit will convince the world of judgment, because the prince of this world is judged. If you agree in your mind that God's judgment has already been pronounced on Satan, and that he is a defeated foe, then you are putting on the helmet of salvation. But if you feel that your adversary is invincible, if you are convinced that the enemy who has ambushed you cannot be beaten, then you *are* defeated. That defeat took place in your mind.

James 4:7 tells us, "Resist the devil and he will flee from you." If you doubt that word, then you are well along the path to defeat. But if you count that a true word from God, then you are on your way to victory. The word "resist" means "to stand against," and is the same word used in Ephesians 6:13 where we are told to "withstand in the evil day." James says that if you, as a child of God, firmly stand your ground because your feet are shod with the hobnail boots provided in the gospel, and refuse to be moved before the enemy's attacks, then Satan will turn and run.

We have been led to believe that Satan is anything but a coward. We have been deceived to think that he is absolutely fearless. But Satan is, in fact, a coward. He must come against us with deception, hiding behind a cloak of secrecy. Because of his cowardice, he tries to overwhelm us with fear just like a lion uses his roar to strike terror into his prey. But if a Christian takes a stand against the Evil One, that firm stand will cause him to turn tail and run. That is what James meant when he wrote, "Resist the devil and he will flee from you."

On what grounds can we withstand the Evil One? Remember—we have no strength, no might, no power in ourselves. But when we accept the fact that Satan is a coward, that he will flee from one who is determined to withstand him, we are clothing our minds with the helmet of salvation. This makes us invincible not only to Satan's attacks, it also causes the Enemy to *retreat.* Thus our attitude toward the truth of God's Word is extremely important. Because of this, the Bible has much to say about the mind.

The mind, of course, is the seat of the thought process and plays an active role in exercising faith. In 2 Timothy 1:7, Paul reminded Timothy, "God has not given us a spirit of fear, but of power and of love and of a sound mind." Any expectation of defeat is not from God. That is what Paul meant when he said God has not given us a spirit of fear. We do not advance in battle against the Evil One when we expect to be defeated. A sound mind means we have the ability to apply the Bible's promises to the daily battle we face. Paul was saying to Timothy, "You are going as my representative. You are to teach the Word and ground the saints in the Word of God. In a very real sense, you are going into battle against the Evil One. As you proclaim the Word of God you are dispelling the darkness and bringing people to knowledge which will enable them to defeat and overthrow the Enemy. As you go into this battle, you do not have to fear, because God has given you a sound mind that can appropriate God's promises and respond in faith to that which you know."

In Philippians 4:6 Paul wrote something else concerning the believer's mind: "Be anxious for nothing . . . ," or translated literally, "Don't worry about anything." Does this mean that even when we go into battle against Satan and all his innumerable hosts, we don't have to worry? That is exactly what it means! What is the antidote to worry? "In everything by prayer and supplication, with thanksgiving, let your requests be made known to God" (Philippians 4:6). When our Commander gives the command, "Forward march," should we advance in fear? Not at all. Why not? Because as we march into combat, we can, by prayer and supplication, lay hold of God's promises and commit our way to the Lord. This trust, which expresses itself in prayer, will have the result Paul described in verse 7: ". . . and the peace of God, which surpasses all understanding, will guard [literally, stand sentry duty over] your hearts and minds through Christ Jesus."

As Christian soldiers who have been summoned into battle, we can go with faith, confidence, and trust in God. God stands sentry over our minds so that we are delivered from fear and discouragement, and from even the thought that we may be overthrown in battle. When we enter the battle prayerfully, trusting in the promises of God and resting on certainty of victory, we will find that even those intrusive thoughts of defeat will be kept out as the peace of God, which passes all understanding, stands guard over our hearts and minds.

Thought Life

Paul was deeply concerned about the Christian's thought life in relation to the spiritual warfare we face. In 2 Corinthians 10:5 he wrote about ". . . casting down arguments and every high thing that exalts itself against the knowledge of God, bringing every thought into captivity to the obedience of Christ." If we want victory, we must cast down arguments and everything that exalts itself against the knowledge of God. These arguments and high things exalted against God include thoughts we might entertain about the possibility of defeat. Using the picture of the military, if a soldier marches into battle and with every step tells himself he is one step nearer to death or defeat, he will certainly go down in defeat. As we march into battle, we must bring such thoughts of defeat, such arguments against ourselves, into captivity to the obedience of Christ. Why? Because He has assured us of victory. As a result, we can march into battle with the certainty that we will walk in the train of Christ's triumph.

We cannot underestimate the importance of our thought lives as good soldiers of Jesus Christ. The abilities of the mind defy description. The mind can be here one moment, then the next moment be hundreds of miles away. It can be occupied with one thing at one moment, and then be completely occupied with something else the next moment. The mind can be focused on the Lord Jesus Christ one moment, and then the next moment be diverted to that which is entirely displeasing to God.

Unless we bring every thought into subjection to the Lord Jesus Christ, we will be defeated. In effect, taking up the helmet of salvation means, "Do not forget that your mind must be protected with everything salvation supplies. If you do not have the helmet of salvation, if your mind is not brought into subjection to the Lord Jesus, then it can be the avenue of approach by which Satan will bring defeat to you." We must continually sit in judgment over our thought lives, lest we open the door to defeat by not believing God's promises, or by letting our minds dwell on things that are abominable to God. "As a man thinks in his heart, so is he."

When you are not consciously directing your attention toward God, where does your mind wander? What are the first thoughts that flash through your mind when you wake up in the morning, or when you are too sleepy to focus your attention? What occupies your thoughts in those last moments before you drop off to sleep at night. Do you commit your mind to the Lord's keeping? May God enable us to lay hold of His promise of victory in the gospel so that our every thought may be obedient to Christ. In this way the peace of God will garrison our hearts and minds, and we will be confident of victory in the Lord Jesus Christ.

Notes

1. The real tragedy of the mistaken belief that we can lose our salvation is that believers held back by this fear never have the chance to move on toward Christian maturity. They are as immobile and ineffective as a soldier who must stop every few steps and make sure he is still wearing a helmet! The wonderful fact of the matter is that God has provided us with a permanent, irrevocable salvation; and now we can move forward confidently into the spiritual battles ahead of us.

2. There is a great contrast between God's brand of positive thinking and that pandered by today's positive-thinking gurus. In the secular world, positive thinking is the process of trying to make something true by believing it beforehand. In God's economy, thinking positively is affirming in our minds something that is *already* true. We should not get the two confused.

3. Following the decisive two-day offensive in the Persian Gulf War, General Norman Schwarzkopf said of the once-formidable Iraqi army, "In 48 hours they went from being the fourth-largest army in the world to being the second-largest army in Iraq." No matter how powerful and ready it once seemed, the Iraqi army was a defeated foe with no power to resist Coalition forces. At the point of salvation, Satan went from being the largest army in our lives to being an utterly defeated foe with no power to resist the strength and victory of Jesus Christ. What a shame it would be, then, to submit ourselves again to the Enemy's control. Instead, we can walk in the victory Christ has already won!

4. If the devil had no fear of Christ's power in our lives, he would not have to use deception, trickery, and subtle temptation to try to trip us up.

5. The word *worry* reportedly is derived from the Old German word *wurgen*, which meant "to choke." Apparently the word came to mean "to choke the mind"—which is exactly what anxiety does to us. But God's Word promises that by letting our requests be made known to God through prayer and supplication, with thanksgiving, we can escape this insidious mental strangulation.

6. Discouragement is one of the Enemy's most powerful weapons, particularly because it is one malady that prevents us from seeing or applying God's remedy. J. Francis Peak once said, "The major cause of discouragement is a temporary loss of perspective. Restore proper perspective, and you take new heart." God's Word can give us the perspective we need to realize His victory over discouragement, if we will remember to flee there when discouragement overtakes us.

7. For many years The Navigators, a marvelous Christian organization, has strongly encouraged Scripture memorization as a weapon to wield in the battle for our thought lives. What better way to bring a wandering mind in check than to return to a well-known verse of Scripture? "Your word I have hidden in my heart," says Psalm 119:11, "that I might not sin against You."

Questions

1. What does Proverbs 23:7 reveal about the effect a person's thought life will have on his actions? Why is this important for the soldier of Christ?

2. Why does the helmet of salvation allow us to enter confidently into spiritual conflict? What do you think Paul means by his statement in Philippians 4:13?

3. What effect might John 16:11 have on our outlook as Christ's soldiers? Does this mean we will not encounter spiritual conflict? If not, what does it mean?

4. In light of James 4:7, what should be our outlook on confrontations with Satan's schemes and strategies? How does this relate to Ephesians 6:13?

5. What do 2 Timothy 1:7 and Philippians 4:6 caution against? When might these things become issues for a Christian? When in the past have they been issues for you?

6. Relate 2 Corinthians 10:3–5 to what you have learned so far about spiritual warfare and the Christian's armor. How do you think this passage might be lived out in your daily life?

CHAPTER 30

THE SWORD OF THE SPIRIT

2 Peter 1:15–21

A hymn writer once asked the question, "Am I a soldier of the cross?" In light of Scripture, there can be only one answer to the question. For the child of God, the answer must be "Yes!" for we have been called to spiritual warfare. Paul, writing to a young minister who had been entrusted with the responsibility of guiding a flock, told him to "endure hardship as a good soldier of Jesus Christ" (2 Timothy 2:3). The Word of God knows nothing of retired officers or enlisted men whose duty is concluded. The Christian has been called to a continuous, unrelenting battle.

When the children of Israel crossed the Jordan after their wilderness experience and entered the land of promise, the land of milk and honey, they also entered a new kind of life—a life of rest. But that life did not exclude continuous warfare, for there were many adversaries in the land. In the New Testament, Paul addressed the believer's relationship to Satan in the same way. He did not present the idea that Satan will cease to war against the person who has trusted Christ as Savior. Nor did he present the Christian life as a tranquil, placid kind of existence. Rather, Paul's instructions anticipated a life of continuous conflict. And the more we resolve to be faithful to the Lord Jesus Christ, the greater the conflict will become. While our future prospect is that of being transported out of this earth into a new sphere in the heavenlies, as long as we live on this earth we will be in the midst of conflict.

The Word of Authority

In previous chapters we examined the components of defensive equipment God has given the child of God. Now, however, we come to the only piece of equipment the Captain of our salvation has given us for *offense*. Paul writes, "Take the . . . sword of the Spirit, which is the word of God" (Ephesians 6:17). The girdle, the breastplate, the shoes, the shield of faith, and the helmet of salvation are all defensive. Not one of these five, in themselves, can defeat the enemy. They were all for the soldier's protection. Even more significantly, of all the pieces of armor Paul describes in Ephesians 6, the sword is the only one Paul explains. For all the other pieces of equipment, we had to go to other passages of Scripture to understand what he had in mind. But Paul considers the sword so important that he pauses to explain this piece so there can be no question what it represents.

The words *of God* describe the source from which this weapon comes. It is not of human origin; it was not forged on human anvils of earthly steel. Rather, this is a weapon of divine origin, a weapon adequate for conflict with the kind of adversary we face. Because our enemy is not flesh and blood, human weapons will not qualify.

As we consider "the sword of the Spirit, which is the word of God," remember that it is not our evaluation of God's Word that gives it value; nor is it our interpretation or presentation of Scripture that makes it authoritative. What Scripture is intrinsically, in and of itself, gives it authority. Therefore, without depending on anything outside of itself, the Word of God is a powerful offensive weapon that can successfully rout the wicked enemy we are fighting.

Peter, coming to the close of his earthly life, was concerned about the spiritual maturity and development of the believers he was leaving behind. For this reason he commanded the elders to tend, or feed, the flock of God. This ministry of feeding the sheep should be accomplished not through the words of men, but through the Word of God. This is what he had in mind when, anticipating his departure, he said, "I will be careful to ensure that you always have a reminder of these things after my decease" (2 Peter 1:15). He had presented the gospel to them. He had delivered the truths he had received by divine revelation. As long as he was with them, he could repeat what he had received from God. But he also knew that he would not be with them much longer, so he was concerned about the ministry of the Word of God continuing after he was gone so that they could continue to grow spiritually.

Peter confirms this in verse 16: "We did not follow cunningly devised fables when we made known to you the power and coming of our Lord Jesus Christ, but were eyewitnesses of His majesty." Peter was reminding them that Jesus Christ will return to this earth to rule as King. As one of the three who had personally witnessed the transfiguration of Christ on the mount, he had seen the advance revelation of the glory that will be Christ's at His second coming. So he was passing on to them what he had seen with his own eyes and heard with his ears, an event that could also be verified by two other witnesses.

After telling them what he had seen and heard, Peter goes on to make an amazing statement: "We also have the prophetic word made more sure" (2 Peter 1:19). The word *confirmed* may be translated "more certain." More certain than what? More certain than the event Peter, James, and John had seen with their own eyes and heard with their own ears. What could be more certain than that? Peter tells us in verses 20–21: "No prophecy of Scripture is of any private interpretation, for prophecy never came by the will of man, but holy men of God spoke as they were moved by the Holy Spirit." A common but incorrect understanding of the phrase, *no prophecy . . . is of any private interpretation* is that one does not have the right to study and interpret the Word of God for oneself, or that every person must look to the church for a correct interpretation of Scripture. But what Peter wrote may be rendered literally, "No prophecy of Scripture comes out of private disclosure." Peter is dealing here with the *source* from which the Scriptures came. They are not of human origin.

As he explains, we can believe the Word of God because Scripture did not originate with men, but holy men of God spoke as they were moved by the Holy Spirit. The word *moved* is a word that was used to describe a ship that was borne along as the wind filled its sails and propelled it through the water. In other words, holy men of God spoke as they were borne along by the Holy Spirit, in the same way the wind bears along a sailing ship. Peter is telling us that the Bible is trustworthy and authoritative, and that it should be believed even above that which men say they have personally seen and heard and experienced. Why? Because the Word of God came as the Holy Spirit carried along holy men as the instruments through whom Scripture was given.

So when Paul wrote in Ephesians 6:17 that we are to take the sword of the Spirit, which is the Word of God, the phrase *of God* encompasses all the truth that Peter spelled out so clearly in 2 Peter 1. The Word of God is completely sufficient because of its source.

Another familiar passage concerning God's Word is 2 Timothy 3:16, which anticipates the rise of false teachers. Earlier in the chapter, Paul wrote, "Know this, that in the last days perilous times will come" (2 Timothy 3:1). One of the characteristics of the last days, according to verse 5, is that people will have a form of godliness, but will deny the power thereof. In the verses that follow, Paul shows the results of renouncing divine truth, then he speaks of the moral corruption and perversion that will characterize people.

Timothy was being sent out as a minister of the gospel to a world characterized by doubts, denials, deceptions, perversions of divine truth, and rejection of God's Word. What would be sufficient for Timothy's ministry? Paul points him straight to the Word of God: "[You must] continue in the things which you have learned and been assured of, knowing from whom you have learned them, and that from childhood you have known the Holy Scriptures, which are able to make you wise for salvation through faith which is in Christ Jesus" (2 Timothy 3:14–15). The Word of God is the only effective instrument in days like those Paul outlined in verses 3–9.

Why is Scripture sufficient in such dark days? Verse 16 tells us: "All Scripture is given by inspiration of God." This statement translated literally is, "All Scripture is God-breathed." The Bible we have in our hands is the result of the out-breathing of God. God used human instruments to bring the Scriptures to us, but the Scriptures are authoritative only because they are God-breathed.

"All Scripture is given by inspiration of God, and is profitable for doctrine, for reproof, for correction, for instruction in righteousness, that the man of God may be complete, thoroughly equipped for every good work" (2 Timothy 3:16–17). Because the Scriptures are God-breathed, they are profitable for doctrine; that is, for teaching divine truth. Moreover, the Bible is profitable for reproving the godless, and for correcting those whose ways have been perverted by false teachers. And the Word of God is useful for instructing in righteousness those who want to walk in a way that pleases God. So when Paul tells us that God has put a sword in our hands, we can know that this sword is sufficient to defeat the enemy because it has come from God through the process of divine revelation. When we face the adversary, we can move confidently against him with only one weapon, because that weapon is powerful enough to defeat him.

Christ Used the Word

Christ's defeat of Satan's temptations in Matthew 4 furnishes us with a great example of how to use the sword of the Spirit against our spiritual foe, because our adversary is the same enemy that tempted Christ. After John the Baptist introduced Jesus to the nation of Israel as their God-given Messiah who had come to redeem and reign, Jesus was led by the Spirit out into the wilderness. There He entered into conflict with Satan and proved His moral right to be both Redeemer and King. After Christ had fasted for forty days, Satan came to tempt Him saying, "If You are the Son of God, command that these stones become bread" (Matthew 4:3).

Notice Christ's defense against Satan's attack. Jesus said, "It is written . . . ." He met the attack of the prince of the power of the air by drawing the sword of the Spirit, which is the Word of God, and quoting Deuteronomy 8:3—"But He answered and said, 'It is written, "Man shall not live by bread alone, but by every word that proceeds from the mouth of God." ' " Literally, Christ said, "It stands written." What stood written was unalterable and unchangeable.

Interestingly, in each of His three temptations Christ quoted Deuteronomy. While the book of Leviticus governed Israel's worship, the book of Deuteronomy controlled the people's daily walk. When Satan came to divert the Lord Jesus Christ from the path of perfect obedience to the Father's will, He quoted the book that governed the believer's walk, using it as a sword to turn aside the enemy's attack. After Christ quoted Scripture in response to the devil's first temptation, that testing was immediately dropped. There was no argument, no rebuttal. Satan knew he must attack along another avenue.

In verse 5 we find that "the devil took Him up into the holy city, set Him on the pinnacle of the temple, and said to Him, 'If You are the Son of God, throw Yourself down. For it is written . . . .' " Notice that Satan adopted Christ's tactics! He said, in effect, "If you use the Word of God against me, I'll use the Word of God against you." So Satan said, "It is written, 'He shall give His angels charge concerning you,' and, 'In their hands they shall bear you up, lest you dash your foot against a stone.' " But again Jesus turned to Deuteronomy and quoted a verse that was particularly applicable: Deuteronomy 6:16. Jesus said, "It is written again, 'You shall not tempt the LORD your God' " (Matthew 4:7). Once again Satan dropped the temptation without an argument. The Word of God is irrefutable.

Satan then made a third attack. We read in verses 8–9, "Again, the devil took Him up on an exceedingly high mountain, and showed Him all the kingdoms of the world and their glory. And he said to Him, 'All these things I will give You if You will fall down and worship me.' " Again Jesus referred to the book of Deuteronomy: "Away with you, Satan! For it is written, 'You shall worship the LORD your God, and Him only you shall serve' " (Matthew 4:10). And the devil left Him. He didn't argue the case; he didn't beg; he didn't plead. He left! Why? Because of the effectiveness of the sword of the Spirit, which is the Word of God.

It was not diplomacy, argument, debate, tact, flattery, nor the offering of a truce that caused Satan to depart. It was Christ's use of the sword of the Spirit. It did not have to be explained, defended, or demonstrated. Satan knew its power, and when he saw the sword drawn, he immediately dropped the issue and turned to something else. And when Jesus persisted in meeting every attack with a carefully aimed thrust from the Word of God, Satan abandoned the attack altogether and left.

The Christian's Use of the Word

Perhaps Paul had Christ's experience in mind when he pictured the believer clothed in the whole armor of God and using the sword of the Spirit. The enemy has no defense against the sword of God's Word. Satan has no armor to protect him against the sword-thrust of the authoritative, infallible, inspired Word of God. And when you do battle against Satan with the sword of the Spirit in your hand, he is defenseless. You stand fully clothed, fully equipped, and strengthened by God—and Satan stands helpless and defenseless.

Among several New Testament terms translated "word" is one which refers to the Word of God in its entirety. We do not hesitate to say that our Bible, in its entirety, is the Word of God. But when Paul referred to the sword of the Spirit, he did not use the term which refers to the Word in its totality; instead he used a significant word which refers to the Scriptures as composed of individual sayings. In other words, he referred to the Word of God as it is applied in specific instances. It is the Scriptures we have personally appropriated and experienced.

By using this particular term, Paul is teaching us a very important concept. Only that portion of the Word of God which we know and which has particular relevance to the temptation at hand may be considered the sword that will defeat the enemy. When Satan tempted Christ, Jesus used a specific verse that dealt with that specific problem, and He quoted that verse as the answer to the temptation.

This means that we do not possess the sword of the Spirit simply because we own a leather-bound, gilt-edged copy of the Holy Bible. We possess the sword of the Spirit only when that which is *in* the Bible has been transferred to the mind and heart, so that when Satan comes we can apply what we have learned and defeat him in that particular battle. The pastor's sermons aren't swords for us. Our sword is not what we can find in a concordance or what is written in the margins of our Bibles. The sword of the Spirit is the Word of God which we *know* and can *use* against Satan.

Today, we are not encouraged to learn the Bible for ourselves. We are not challenged to memorize the Scriptures, nor to know specific verses for specific circumstances. We are told that sermons that teach the Bible are "dry," and so we are fed platitudes and clichés in its place because they are more "culturally relevant" and "practical." But they are not the sword of the Spirit, and they will not frighten the enemy.

Often we feel we are too old or too busy to learn the Word of God for ourselves. But this just isn't true. We can learn! But it takes time and effort. Which is better? To prepare for an attack you know will come sooner or later, or to fall to an attack because you failed to prepare? We must study God's Word, know God's Word, understand God's Word, and memorize God's Word, so that we may be able to stand.

As a Christian soldier, you can have victory because you know the Word of God, you have possessed it for yourself, and you know how to use it when the enemy comes to tempt you.

Notes

1. One of many traits that set apart General Patton from his military peers was his insistence that all military personnel be battle-ready and consider themselves on call. More than once during his campaign leading up to V-E Day the general reassigned office staff to the front lines, moved inactive artillery crews to infantry, and placed his commanding officers alongside foot soldiers so they could have an informed command over the battle. The Christian life is no different—we should all seek to be battle-ready and on call, no matter what our vocation. We are all enlisted as good soldiers of Jesus Christ.

2. For a time during the brief spiritual awakening of the late 60s and early 70s, high school and college students developed the habit of referring to the Bible as "my Sword," "your Sword," and so on. More than a cliché, it was a verbal reminder of the Bible's indispensable importance in the Christian life. Without it, we have no offensive weapon in our warfare.

3. While a few arguments against "dry doctrine" may be valid, can it be that a certain mental or spiritual laziness has made it popular to disparage in-depth Bible teaching and a thorough knowledge of God's Word? We may be quick to talk about how we want our Bible teaching made relevant or easily applicable, but the Word itself clearly indicates that the Bible has its own inherent, intrinsic value. Knowing God's Word is *always* of value, both when specific applications are spelled out for the hearers, and when they are not.

4. While some Christians crave some kind of miraculous, highly visible, indisputable sign of God's power in their lives, 2 Peter 1:19–21 tells us that the most sure, indisputable, powerful, authoritative manifestation of God we will ever encounter is the Bible. Do you consider the Word of God more significant, more important in your life than the Transfiguration of Christ was in Peter's life? Do you devote as much attention to it as you would to a personal visit from Jesus Christ? That is the place we should give it—at the very least!

5. What an accurate description 2 Timothy 3:1 gives us of the culture around us! Isn't it amazing that homosexuals would claim to be authorities on love, or

that pro-abortion environmentalists would lecture us about caring for living things? These are indeed perilous times!

6. The word *reproof* in 2 Timothy 3:16–17 is a word that was used of shedding light on an injury. We might draw a parallel today to a doctor's examination using x-rays. The next word, *correction,* is the same word that was used to describe setting a broken bone. What this means to us is that as we study the Bible, God will use it not only to reveal spiritual injuries, but to heal them as well.

7. Notice that even the devil can quote Scripture! Quoting the Bible out of context to persuade someone to violate another portion of Scripture is one of Satan's favorite ruses. Just because someone supports his teaching with Scripture does not mean he is right. We need to evaluate what we hear in light of its context and compared to the full counsel of Scripture.

8. How powerful is Scripture? Jesus used the Word of God and nothing else to turn aside Satan's best frontal attack. We can do the same.

9. Do you have a personal Bible study plan? Are you part of a group study at church, or a home Bible study, or even a radio class that carefully studies the Word of God? If not, make it a priority—your *top priority*—to begin studying the Word of God daily, that you might be able to wield the sword of the Spirit that has been given to you.

Questions

1. Compare Ephesians 6:17 with Hebrews 4:12. What additional characteristics of God's Word do we learn from Hebrews 4?

2. What does 2 Peter 1:19–21 teach us concerning the origin of God's Word? What does this mean concerning its authority and accuracy?

3. According to 2 Timothy 3:16–17, what portions of Scripture are most profitable? Why? What portion of the Bible did Jesus use to defeat Satan's strategy of temptation? What portions of the Bible should we concentrate on learning for ourselves?

4. In light of the situation described in 2 Timothy 4:1–2, what was Paul's solution for Christians living in such a time (see 2 Timothy 4:13, 15–16)? Do you think this will work even in our day? Does this seem to be what most Christians in our culture are doing? If not, why not?

5. What might a Christian substitute for the "sword of the Spirit" in his or her life, thinking it will provide the same benefits?

6. Based on this chapter, what do you think should be the role of Bible study in a believer's life? What role does it play in your life?

CHAPTER 31

COMING TO MATURITY

Hebrews 5:1–14

The writer of Hebrews presents the Lord Jesus Christ as preeminent in the program through which God has revealed Himself to humankind. In the prologue to this letter, found in the first three verses, the writer shows us that Jesus Christ is superior—as a revealer of God—to every other form and kind of revelation God has given. Jesus Christ is superior to the angels, who were instruments of revelation in the Old Testament. He is superior to Moses, through whom the greatest of the Old Testament revelations of God were made. Jesus Christ is superior to Joshua, who led the children of Israel into rest in the Promised Land, for Christ leads us into a better rest. Christ is also superior to Aaron as a priest, for His ministry rests on a better covenant, and Christ ministers in a superior priestly order. To illustrate this, the writer of Hebrews takes his readers back into the books of Genesis and Psalms to Melchizedek, recognizing that in order for his readers to follow his explanation, they must be able to transfer truth. Specifically, they must be able to understand what is true concerning the relationship of Melchizedek to Aaron; transfer that truth to the relationship between Aaron and Christ; then deduce the superiority of Christ over Aaron because of the superiority of Melchizedek over Aaron. In short, Christ is superior to Aaron because He is of a priestly order superior to Aaron's.

But before he develops this argument in detail, the writer of Hebrews pauses to give an extended exhortation (5:11–6:12), because he recognizes that the truth he is presenting is *for those who have approached maturity in Christ.* Apart from spiritual maturity they will not be able to make the logical connection and see how Christ is superior to Aaron. Therefore we would do well to examine this contrast between immaturity and maturity, between babyhood and adulthood in the things of Christ. In particular, we want to look at Hebrews 5:11–14.

In these four verses we come face-to-face with important contrasts between the person who is a baby (verse 13) and the person who is full grown (verse 14); between the one who needs milk (verse 12), and the person who can subsist on strong meat. These contrasts point out the contrast between childhood and adulthood in the Christian life, or between immaturity and maturity in spiritual things.

Milk and Meat in Development

Before we look further, we need to understand what the writer had in mind when he spoke of milk and meat. The difference between milk and meat does not refer to the *area* of truth being considered. For example, some people might refer to truths concerning salvation as milk-type doctrine, but would refer to truths concerning Christian practice, or prophecy, or Christ's return as meat-type doctrine. They would say that if you are interested only in the simple things of salvation, you are existing on milk; but if you are interested in the deeper life, or in prophecy, or in the second coming, then you have gone beyond milk to meat.

However, in the mind of the writer of Hebrews, the distinction between milk and meat refers not to the *area* of biblical truth, but rather to the *depth* to which the child of God can go in any area of biblical truth. Therefore we must adjust our thinking to realize that there are certain doctrines that belong to Christian babyhood, and doctrines reserved for those who are mature. Salvation may be understood only to the level of milk, or it may be studied and understood to the level of meat. Prophecy may be understood only to the level of milk, or it may be understood to the level of meat. The difference is not in the *topic*, but in the depth to which that topic is studied and understood.

In our physical lives, we all face a process of maturing. A newborn baby is just that—a newborn baby. He cannot be anything beyond that at that early stage of development. Normally, a newborn baby will progress from infancy to childhood, to adolescence, to adulthood. This process follows a predictable pattern of development. An infant is marked by his lack of knowledge. Because of this lack of knowledge, early in life he begins to ask "why?" He also is characterized by dependence on his parents for food, shelter, clothing, guidance, protection, everything he needs. He is characterized, too, by a lack of judgment, because maturity to make sound judgments comes only with the passage of time. In physical growth, it is impossible for a child to be mature apart from the passage of time. But spiritual maturity may follow a slower or more accelerated time frame. Physically a child may be bound by time in the process of maturity, but spiritually this is not the case—although, as we shall see, time is a factor.

Spiritual Infancy

In considering the issue of spiritual maturity, we need to look at the writer's three characterizations of spiritual infancy. In verses 10–11 he writes concerning "Melchi-zedek, of whom we have much to say, and hard to explain, since you have become dull of hearing." The last phrase in verse 11 presents the first characterization of spiritual babyhood—*dull of hearing*. We need to remind ourselves of 1 Corinthians 2, where Paul wrote that the natural man cannot receive any divine truth. Why is it impossible for him to understand and appropriate anything of divine revelation? Because he possesses no capacity to receive spiritual things.

God, however, has made known to believers spiritual things which the natural eye, ear, and mind cannot appropriate or understand, and we can receive those things as the Spirit of God teaches us the deep things of God. When we receive Christ and are born again, we are given a new capacity—a capacity to *receive* the revelation God has made of Himself, to *understand* that revelation, and to *assimilate* its content and make it our own.

How many times have we heard someone say as the Word of God was taught, "Oh, I see it now"? That Christian was showing evidence of the Holy Spirit's work of illuminating divine truth for believers. First Corinthians 2:15 tells us that the spiritual person, that is, the one in whose life the Holy Spirit is unhindered as a teacher, has the capacity to understand all things. The spiritual person discerns, or understands, all things, because he or she has the mind of Christ. Therefore, in Hebrews 5:11 the apostle says that one of the first characterizations of spiritual immaturity is an inability to receive the deep things of God. This inability cannot be blamed on a lack of clarity in proclamation, nor on an illogical presentation by the teacher.

For a newborn child of God, this inability to hear and understand the deeper truths of God's Word is natural, normal, and to be expected. There are some things a newborn baby simply cannot understand, because he needs to grow in ability to hear and to understand. But in 1 Corinthians 3 Paul said he was speaking to the Corinthian believers as to "babes in Christ." Here spiritual immaturity was reprehensible, because the Corinthians' failure to grow was due to their carnality. Carnality can produce in the Christian life some of the same characteristics as a newborn babe. If you have been saved and find it difficult to understand the Word of God and to accept its truths, then you may well be in a state of spiritual babyhood. And if you have known Christ for some years, but the Word of God is tedious to you and you have no appetite for it, then you should question whether you are carnal.

We find the second characteristic of babyhood in Hebrews 5:12: "Though by this time you ought to be teachers, you need someone to teach you again the first principles of the oracles of God." The first sign that they were babies in Christ was their lack of knowledge. The second is their utter dependence on someone else to teach them spiritual truths. The Spirit of God has been given to every child of God. The indwelling Spirit has come to assume, among other roles, the ministry of teacher (John 14:26). The Holy Spirit in the Christian meets the need for an understanding of divine revelation and appropriating divine truth. But if the child of God does not depend on the teaching ministry of the Holy Spirit and cannot, apart from dependence on some other teacher, discover the truths of Scripture, then that is an evidence of immaturity in Christ.

It would be perfectly normal for a newborn child of God to depend on someone to nurture him in the truths of Scripture, just as it is natural for a newborn baby to depend on another for nourishment. That is why the New Testament gives many instructions concerning those who are pastors or teachers of God's Word. The Word of God anticipates that need. But if someone has been in God's family for a long time and still must depend wholly on someone else, and cannot through independent study of the Bible find spiritual nourishment, that person is manifesting signs of spiritual infancy.

The third characteristic of spiritual babyhood is found in verse 13: "Everyone who partakes only of milk is unskilled in the word of righteousness, for he is a babe." Everyone who can take only the milk level of divine truth is a baby. And what does the writer mean by the word *unskilled?* Such people lack judgment, or the skill to apply Scripture to various situations in life. They are unskilled in using the Scriptures to guide their conduct. If you must continually go to someone else and ask if it is right for a believer to do or not to do a particular thing, and if you are unable to take the principles of the Word of God and determine for yourself what is right and wrong for the child of God, you are showing—by your lack of skill or judgment—that you are a spiritual baby.

It is important to notice that the original readers of Hebrews were not babies because they were newborn believers. They had been Christians for some time; therefore their case is inexcusable. They bore the responsibility for their spiritual condition. The writer said in verse 12, "Though by this time you ought to be teachers, you need someone to teach you again." This might be translated, "Considering the time that has elapsed, you ought to be teachers of the Word; but instead you need someone to teach you again the first principles of divine revelation."

These Christians had been saved for a sufficient length of time, and had heard enough of the Word of God, that they should have been teaching others instead of being taught. They should have been able to stand independently instead of depending on someone else. Merely sitting under the ministry of the Word will not bring us maturity; we must appropriate the truth we are hearing. We should never get the idea that just because we have been under sound teaching for a long period of time we can be classified as mature believers!

This passage also shows that those who are in spiritual infancy are held responsible because their lives are marked by regression, by moving *backward*. The Hebrews needed someone to teach them *again* the first principles of the oracles of God. They were told, "You have come to need milk and not solid food." In other words, they had been born into God's family; they had begun to grow to maturity; they had understood and applied divine truth. But what had happened? They had retrogressed. They turned back from their path of spiritual growth and, hoping to remove the stigma of the cross in the eyes of unbelieving Jews, went back to temple worship and Jewish ritual. This is what the writer classified as spiritual regression.

Spiritual Maturity

In these same verses (Hebrews 5:12–14), the writer gives three characteristics of maturity, answering the three deficiencies that characterize spiritual babies.

First he says, "Though by this time you ought to be teachers" (verse 12). He is coupling knowledge with maturity. He is saying, "By now you should have appropriated and assimilated sufficient truth so that you can impart that truth to others." The first sign of maturity, then, is knowledge. This knowledge is not measured by the number of sermons we have heard, the amount of notes we have taken, the number of tapes to which we have listened—but by the amount of God's truth we possess. And we do not really know something until we can state it to someone else. To lack such knowledge of God's truth is to be stalled in immaturity.

The second characterization of a mature believer is given in verse 14: "Solid food belongs to those who are of full age, that is, those who by reason of use have their senses exercised to discern both good and evil." This tells us that the mature Christian is the one who *can put into use* the truth he or she has learned. The mature believer, instead of being dependent on others like a child is dependent on his parents, is independent when it comes to the things of God. He knows how to use the Word and is skillful in its application. When a decision confronts him, he is able to go to the Word of God and discern the will of God as he applies God's truth to the situation in front of him. The mature Christian is not only able to teach the Word, but to use the Word properly and skillfully to settle his own problems and difficulties, and to discover the will of God for himself. This ability answers the dependence which marks those who are stuck in spiritual infancy.

The third characterization of the mature Christian is found in the last part of verse 14: ". . . who by reason of use have their senses exercised to discern both good and evil." The mature Christian is able to judge what is right and what is wrong in his Christian experience. He does not have to run to someone else and ask, "Do you think it's right for me to do this?" He knows the Word of God and can apply the Word to each situation. He knows what is right and what is wrong for a believer, and can judge good and evil based on the perfect standard of God's Word. This ability to discern is in direct contrast to the lack of judgment that marks those who are spiritual babes.

Let's contrast, then, the spiritual baby and the mature Christian. First, the spiritual infant is characterized by a lack of knowledge, while the mature Christian is characterized by a knowledge that is so full and complete that others can be taught from it. Second, the baby is marked by an utter dependence on someone else for spiritual discernment, while the mature believer is marked by spiritual independence. Of course, the mature Christian is not independent of the teaching ministry of the Holy Spirit or the clear instruction of God's Word. But the mature Christian does not have to depend on someone else's understanding of the Word in the same way a baby depends on its parents. Third, the spiritual baby is characterized by a lack of judgment, while the mature believer is marked by sound judgment that is unquestionably consistent with the Word of God.

Here the Scriptures have presented, in a very clear and simple way, three tests by which we can determine into which category of spiritual development we fit—maturity or immaturity. Is your life characterized by knowledge or lack of knowledge? Independence or dependence? An ability to use the Word of God or an inability to apply its principles and precepts to your daily conduct?

As we evaluate our lives in light of these questions, we can determine whether we fit into the category of spiritual babies, or qualify as those who are maturing in our spiritual experience.

Notes

1. One thing we need to understand about the process of maturing in Christ is that we do not need to get something that we don't already have (such as a gift, an experience, or whatever). Just like a baby who is born with all the

arms, legs, organs, and everything else he or she will have as a mature person, so we are born spiritually as complete in our spiritual makeup as we will ever be. Maturity is the process of nourishing, growing, developing in Christ.

2. An aggressive businessman, bemoaning the lack of mature prospective employees for a position, was told that perhaps he could find a twenty-year-old with the experience and maturity of a forty-year-old. To this the executive replied, "For a twenty-year-old to gain the experience and maturity of a forty-year-old takes roughly twenty years." We should not lose sight of the role time plays in the process of maturity. While some Christian grow more rapidly than others, and we do not want to be content to stagnate in our spiritual growth, we also need to expect the process of maturity to take time in our lives. There is no such thing as instant maturity.

3. As the Holy Spirit illuminates God's Word, we can expect the Lord to touch areas of our lives that previously went unnoticed or unconvicted. Attitudes and actions that we might tolerate or ignore in immaturity become unacceptable as we mature in Christ.

4. The process of teaching less mature believers what we know about the Jesus Christ and the Christian life is the logical next step to being grounded in our faith. While there is indeed a responsibility to teach correctly, it is also a tremendous privilege and enhancement to our own walk with Christ. If you have never taken the opportunity to teach spiritual truth to others, consider volunteering to teach young believers (children, youth, or adults) in your own local fellowship. It may require some training and a certain time commitment, but the spiritual dividends will more than make up for it.

5. What would we see if everyone was dressed according to the spiritual, rather than physical, maturity? Grown adults in toddlers' clothes? Teenagers in diapers? The possibilities are pretty ludicrous—but God views us in terms a lot like that. Once we know Him, He is intensely concerned that we grow to maturity. Are we as concerned as He is?

6. This indictment against the Hebrew believers implies a grave responsibility for Christian leaders—that they continually help the people of God move on to maturity. Just as it is a mistake for an immature follower to sit under good teaching and yet never apply it toward maturity, things are no better when a Christian leader neglects to give the good teaching in the first place.

7. Once a year or so, commercial airline pilots must report to their companies' headquarters to be tested in sophisticated flight simulators. Each is put through numerous small and large emergencies and is expected to maneuver the simulator's controls in such a way that it would not be lost if it were the real thing. For the pilots, however, it is as close to the real thing as they want to get—because if they fail, they're fired. The point is that a pilot's knowledge

is no good to the company unless he or she can quickly and properly apply it when it's needed. If not, it costs dearly. We should look on our study of God's Word in much the same way. Our salvation doesn't depend on it, but our maturity and steadfastness in this life may rest on our ability to use what we know.

8. Is it possible that we have lost sight of this process of spiritual maturity, believing that "a Christian is a Christian is a Christian"? Coming to know Christ is indeed the most serious issue in life, and it is wonderful to fellowship on equal footing with others who know Him and love Him. At the same time, God calls us to take seriously the process of growth, maturity, and development in Him. There is much, much more beyond the point of knowing Him as Savior, and He longs for us to know and enjoy that abundance!

Questions

1. Why do you think the argument the writer of Hebrews presented was intended only for those how have approached maturity in Christ? Does this mean that God somehow discriminates against those who are immature in Him? What does it mean?

2. Read Hebrews 5:12–14. What is the difference between milk and solid food in spiritual things? How do these relate to spiritual maturity?

3. What does it mean to be "dull of hearing" (Hebrews 5:11)? What is the result of this dullness?

4. What logical process is implied in Hebrews 5:12? Where did the Hebrew believers fail in this process? With what result?

5. In light of Hebrews 5:13–14, contrast the immature believer's relationship to the Word of God with the mature believer's. In which category would you classify yourself? Why?

6. Based on this chapter, what things are necessary in order for a believer to move toward spiritual maturity? Do you feel you are involved in this process?

CHAPTER 32

STEPS TO MATURITY

Hebrews 6:1–2

After presenting a contrast between the mature Christian and the immature Christian (Hebrews 5:11–14), the writer of Hebrews goes on to give instructions that will lead a person out of babyhood into spiritual adulthood (Hebrews 6:1–12). Notice first of all that in writing to these believers the apostle is placing upon them a responsibility to progress in the Christian life. While no one comes to maturity apart from the grace of God and the operation of the Holy Spirit, responsibility for growth is placed squarely on our shoulders as believers. As we have discovered in previous chapters, unless we present ourselves to God as a living sacrifice, unless we present our members as instruments of His righteousness and holiness, we will not progress toward maturity.

In Hebrews 6, the writer emphasizes the human side of going on to maturity. God places on each one of us a responsibility to grow out of infancy to maturity. Because of the results of the Fall and the effects of sin, it is sometimes true in the physical realm that some people never grow into adulthood. But in the spiritual realm, there are no birth defects, no congenital deformities, nothing to prevent us from going on to spiritual maturity. Everyone born into God's family is born with the potential to progress out of infancy into maturity in Christ. The writer of Hebrews knew that, and to those who were in danger of returning to the old things to escape persecution, he gave an exhortation reminding them that God had placed on them a responsibility to go on to maturity.

Progression is Essential

Hebrews 6:1 reads, "Leaving the discussion of the elementary principles of Christ, let us go on to perfection." When the human author of Hebrews used the word translated *perfection,* he was not talking about sinless perfection in the sense of an inability to sin. The word used for *perfection* literally means "maturity," "completion," or "adulthood." In the verses that follow, the apostle gives several clues that will enable the child of God to progress out of infancy to adulthood.

The first principle is related to knowledge. He wrote, "Therefore . . . let us go on to perfection." How? By "leaving the discussion of the elementary principles of Christ." What does that mean? Literally it means, leaving the elementary teaching concerning the doctrines upon which your life has been based." He is telling them to leave the milk and move on. The "elementary principles" were the doctrines of Judaism that helped lead them to faith in Christ, principles they already knew because they were trained in the Old Testament. But if they continued only in those things, they would never move on to maturity.

The first elementary principle the writer mentions is "repentance from dead works." Because his readers had accepted Christ, they had repudiated animal sacrifices as meaningless before God. But they had to go beyond this milk level of truth if they were to go on to maturity.

"Faith toward God" also is in the realm of elementary truth. We recognize that a person is related to God by faith; but if we stop after we have grasped that simple principle, we will never move on to a diet of the meat of God's Word.

These believers were also to leave the "doctrine of baptisms"—the ceremonial washings that rendered something acceptable to God—and of "laying on of hands," which refers to the Jewish ordinances of identification. Other milk-level understanding included the resurrection of the dead and eternal judgment, as taught in the Old Testament.

We might sum up this way: "If you, in your Christian experience, dwell only on those elementary teachings you have heard from childhood out of the Old Testament, you will never progress out of babyhood." They had come to the place where they should have left those principles behind as they moved on to the meat of the Word.

Knowledge of the Truth

In the previous chapter we examined the contrast between milk and meat. We saw that we cannot designate some doctrines as milk doctrines and others as meat doctrines. The difference between milk and meat is not in the *area* of truth, but in the *depth* we can go in any area of divine truth. Every area of doctrine, therefore, has its milk as well as its meat.

So when the writer of Hebrews says that believers must go on and leave the elementary principles of the doctrines of Christ, he is indicating that maturity is inseparably united to knowledge of divine truth. It is impossible for a Christian to mature who does not know the truth of the Scriptures. Apart from a personal knowledge and understanding of the

Word, a Christian will remain in spiritual infancy, no matter how long it has been since the point of salvation.

In Romans 10:17 Paul emphasized the importance of knowledge of God's Word when he wrote, "Faith comes by hearing, and hearing by the word of God." We cannot believe something of which we are ignorant. We have to have some objective fact to believe. The Bible has given us facts to accept, and when we believe we accept the facts of the Word of God, because God has revealed them as divine (not human) truth. Thus faith is inseparably united to knowledge.

In 2 Timothy 4:1–2 Paul wrote to a young pastor, "I charge you therefore before God and the Lord Jesus Christ, who will judge the living and the dead at His appearing and His kingdom: Preach the word!" Why did he charge Timothy to preach the Word? Because the Word of God would bring believers out of immaturity into maturity in Christ. Therefore Paul added, "Be ready in season and out of season. Convince [with the Word], rebuke [with the Word], exhort [with the Word], with all long-suffering and teaching. For the time will come when they will not endure sound doctrine, but according to their own desires, because they have itching ears, they will heap up for themselves teachers." Paul warns Timothy that when he begins to set the table with the meat of the Word, some will come and ask, "Where is the milk?" They won't want the meat of the Word. Nevertheless, Timothy is to go on teaching the Word, exhorting with the Word, rebuking with the Word, using the Word to move believers on to maturity.

Apart from being steeped in the Word of God, no one can move on to maturity in the Christian life. But when a Christian so saturates himself in the Bible that in any situation a pertinent verse of Scripture immediately comes to mind, then there is evidence of the process of maturity. Of course, it is good to place ourselves under the qualified teaching of God's Word in a church or Bible class, as an aid to the maturing process. But that is not the key to maturity. The key is to study the Bible for yourself, digest it for yourself, assimilate it for yourself, apply it for yourself. Then it becomes your own. Many of the best sermon-listeners and sermon-tasters you've ever known are still spiritual babies. That's because it is not until we get into the Scriptures for ourselves that we get into the meat that produces spiritual development. And if you would move on to maturity in your Christian life, you must follow some plan of systematic Bible study.

Good Works

In Hebrews 6:9–10 the writer gave a second clue to spiritual progress: "Beloved, we are confident of better things concerning you, yes, things that accompany salvation, though we speak in this manner. For God is not unjust to forget your work and labor of love which you have shown toward His name, in that you have ministered to the saints, and do minister." The good works done in the name of the Lord Jesus Christ provided evidence that these people were saved people. The good works we do are not only evidence of our salvation, but are a means of moving us toward maturity. If we would go on to spiritual adulthood, the Word we have taken in must be worked out in practical living. First John 3:17 illustrates this when the apostle John poses the question, "Whoever has this world's goods, and sees his brother in need, and shuts up his heart from him, how does the love of God abide in him?" John says that if we see a brother in material need and have the means to help him, but don't help him, then the love of God is not perfected—has not come to maturity—in us. The Word of God received by the child of God must be translated into action. There must be an outworking of Word as it is taken in. Therefore, when a child of God who has been well taught in the Word of God sees a need and responds to it, he is manifesting growth and developing in maturity. Response to need in the family of God indicates one's degree of maturity.

Maturity is also related to our dependence or independence. If a mother has to say to a child, "Will you please clean up that mess?" the child probably is immature. But if without any prompting the child begins to clean up the mess, that is a sign of development. Some Christians reveal that they are babies because they cannot use the Word of God by themselves. They have to be prompted in every action. But others can use the Word without any outside prompting, which indicates their progress toward maturity in Christ. One means, then, of moving on to maturity in Christ is applying the Word of God by responding to a need.

Patience

In verses 11–12 we find another clue to spiritual maturity: "We desire that each one of you show the same diligence to the full assurance of hope until the end, that you do not become sluggish [or lazy], but imitate those who through faith and patience inherit the promises." What these verses imply is that there can be no maturity apart from the passage of some time. Remember, the writer referred to the passage of time when he said that "by now" they should have been teachers. In moving on to maturity, we need patience. For example, in raising our children we have no right to expect them to act beyond their years. What we expect of a seventeen-year-old will be quite different from what we expect of a nine-year-old, because each is in a different stage of development. Thus Hebrews reminds us of the need for patience in our spiritual growth.

We must not be indifferent or lazy concerning our growth, but we must be followers of those who through faith and patience inherit the promises. The promise we desire to see fulfilled in our lives is maturity, conformity to Christ. We will not be made like Him overnight. This life, this growth, this process demands constant cultivation day after day, week after week, year after year. There is no end to the process of maturing in spiritual things. The Christian who has been a believer for fifty years still has an unpossessed land ahead, just as the one who as been a Christian for five years, or five months, or five weeks. We can never sit back in complacency and self-satisfaction and say, "I have arrived. I am mature." We must beware of becoming spiritually lazy. We need patience and diligence as we aim for constant growth and development in our lives.

The Danger of Failure

This chapter of Hebrews contains one passage that, perhaps more than any other passage in the New Testament, has perplexed believers. The author writes, "It is impossible for those who were once enlightened, and have tasted the heavenly gift, and have become partakers of the Holy Spirit, and have tasted the good word of God and the powers of the age to come, if they fall away, to renew them again to repentance, since they crucify again for themselves the Son of God, and put Him to an open shame" (Hebrews 6:4–6). Is the writer teaching that if a person has been saved and then commits a sin, he loses his salvation and can never be saved again? God forbid! That denies all of divine revelation! Rather, these verses—which contain the most sober warning to Christians found anywhere in the Word of God—have to do with the danger of not progressing from spiritual infancy on to Christian maturity.

The writer is showing us, from the divine viewpoint, how serious it is for someone not to heed the exhortation, "Let us go on to perfection." How serious it is for Christians to continue as milk-fed babies when they should be moving on to adulthood! God wants not only to save us, but also to bring us to the position of adult sons and daughters in His family. It is a very serious thing not to fulfill His purposes for us, and this is why the writer of Hebrews sternly warns those who have been saved but who have not progressed to maturity, or who are moving backward.

To summarize his argument, he says that it is impossible to erase the record of failure and immaturity by losing our salvation and being saved all over again. If we could lose our salvation, being saved a second time would erase all previous failure. But we can't do that. Suppose I live my

Christian life for twenty-five years as a spiritual baby—in slothfulness, indifference, carelessness—on a milk diet. At the end of that time I realize that my record is one of prolonged infancy and failure, and I want to erase that record. How would I do it? If I could be lost and saved all over again, all that record of failure would be blotted out. That would be convenient, wouldn't it? But the writer of Hebrews says that is impossible.

A person, by falling away, cannot erase his record of failure. His record must stand, and he must face it at the judgment seat of Christ. We must exercise care over our spiritual diet, over our spiritual growth, for it is impossible—by any means—to remove the record of failure. God has made us responsible for growth, and at the judgment seat of Christ we will be examined as believers in regard to our growth.

The thought in the author's mind could perhaps best be illustrated by thinking of a skier at the top of a ski jump. He is under no compulsion to plant his poles and propel himself down the slope which would hurl him into space, hopefully to land safely below. But after pushing off from the platform, there is no way to reverse his decision and return to the safety of the platform. He is irreversibly headed to the bottom. So, if one willfully leaves the path of progress toward maturity and fails to "go on to maturity," he inevitably will suffer the consequences of his decision—he will be consigned to a state of immaturity. This is a serious warning indeed concerning our failure to progress to maturity.

The last words Peter wrote to those who would read his letters were the words, "Grow in the grace and knowledge of our Lord and Savior Jesus Christ" (2 Peter 3:18). Grow in grace! That is your responsibility, child of God. God has provided the means—but you will never grow unless you diligently appropriate and apply what He has given you. Are you growing? Are you any stronger today than you were yesterday? Do you know more of Him today than you knew yesterday? If not, you need to heed these words: "Let us go on to maturity."

Notes

1. Instructors throughout the history of our military academies have consistently noticed a difference in the attention level of cadets, based on the world situation. During times of peace and political stability, it is difficult to keep students' attention focused on the subject matter. During times of war and unrest, however, students focus intently on the course content and excel in their course work. Why? Because when war is raging, military cadets are acutely aware that their lives may soon depend on how well they listened in class. Their development as officers, then, is a matter of survival, not just status. Because we are engaged in a perpetual spiritual conflict, the survival of our Christian walk really depends on how seriously we take the process of maturity.

2. Obviously, nobody's perfect. But when the Bible uses the word *perfect*, it means "complete," something that has been brought to fruition or full progress. Understanding that, we can see that Christian maturity is something that we can realistically endeavor to reach in our lives. That does not mean we will become sinlessly perfect, or not have to engage in spiritual warfare. But it does mean that the course of our lives will be decidedly set in the direction of ongoing spiritual growth.

3. This analogy is simple. Physical maturity is dependent on our intake of physical food; spiritual maturity is dependent on our intake of spiritual food. That's as simple as it gets!

4. In 2 Timothy 4:3–4 we read a warning concerning an activity that is going on right before our eyes—theology shopping! In our country, religious plurality without a strong, evangelizing, discipling church has produced a society in which many people believe there is no such thing as absolute truth. "What's right for you is right for you!" is the battle cry. Our responsibility? It's in verse 5.

5. Believe it or not, only a generation or so ago Christians used to encourage one another by quoting passages of Scripture that might apply to a particular situation. Now, however, many Christians don't even know where in the Bible to find encouraging verses, let alone what they say. This is tragic! But it is not irreversible. Begin to make the Word of God your own, by memorizing it, that you might encourage others, and enhance your own spiritual maturity.

6. At the top of God's list of good works is ministering to the saints. We should look *first* within our own local fellowship and the body of Christ and meet the needs of fellow Christians. When we care for our own in the body, we are showing a labor of love toward His name.

7. If there is a synonym for *spiritual laziness,* it would have to be "complacency." Do we become spiritually lax as we prosper materially? As we accumulate more money, do we show less concern for those in the body who have none? As our local churches grow in numbers, do we lose our zeal for evangelism? Complacency can take many forms, and we need to wary of its presence in our lives.

8. Perhaps the notion of not being able to regain years lost in disobedience troubles us. Perhaps we resent the idea that we will be accountable to Jesus Christ for what we did with the great salvation He has given us. In any case, if we are looking at things left undone, we may never get done those things He has left us to do. Nate Saint, one of five missionaries who were killed by Auca Indians in Ecuador, once said that his life did not change until he came to grips with the idea that "obedience is not a momentary option. It is a die-cast decision made beforehand." Choose obedience, for a lifetime, starting today.

Questions

1. What does *perfection* mean in Hebrews 6:1? What is the foundation we should not need to lay again?

2. How would you define spiritual maturity? Can you support your definition from Hebrews 5:12–16:2?

3. What does each passage below reveal concerning spiritual maturity?
   – Romans 10:17
   – Ephesians 2:10
   – 2 Timothy 4:1–2

4. What evidence of spiritual maturity is described in Hebrews 6:9–10?

5. Based on Hebrews 6:11–12, what does the process of spiritual maturity require in terms of time and commitment?

6. Are you content with your progress toward maturity in Christ today? If not, what might you plan to do about it?

NOTE TO THE READER

The publisher invites you to share your response to the message of this book by writing Discovery House Publishers, P.O. Box 3566, Grand Rapids, MI 49501, U.S.A. or by calling 1-800-283-8333. For information about other Discovery House publications, contact us at the same address and phone number.

Other Discovery House books
by J. DWIGHT PENTECOST

Prophecy for Today—God's Purpose and Plan for Our Future

A Faith That Endures—The Book of Hebrews Applied to the Real Issues of Life